*"Restaurant patrons looking for
quality dining have Zagat to guide
their cuisine needs.
For the recruitment industry,
the name is Weddle ...
Peter Weddle that is."*

—American Staffing Association

What People are Saying about WEDDLE's Books and Services:

As a Resource for Everyone:

"... a wealth of useful, updated information."

—*Library Journal*

"refreshingly unassuming and hype-free text.... It's all excellent stuff...."

—CNN

"This book is a great resource.... It's like a travel guide to job boards."

—Recruiter
BrassRing Systems

"I've known Pete Weddle for years. He is an immensely likeable guy. He is also extremely knowledgeable. He's been the master for years of the whole field called 'The Web', and the job-boards in particular .... And let me add: Pete Weddle is also very smart. He's asked the right questions of those boards. Highly recommended!"

—Richard Nelson Bolles
author of *What Color is Your Parachute?*

"WEDDLE's is the gorilla of knowledge and Web-sites when it comes to getting a job, managing human resources and recruiting on the Internet."

—President
Stone Enterprises, Ltd

As a Resource for Recruiters & HR Professionals:

"WEDDLE's is a very useful tool that recruiters and HR professionals will find helpful."

—*Fortune Magazine*

"Peter is just outstanding."

—President
Frank Palma Associates

"The WEDDLE's Seminar has been held in cities around the country to rave reviews; in fact, more than 95% have said they found the seminars to be both very informative and very helpful."

—CareerJournal.com
from *The Wall Street Journal*

"Peter Weddle's Wednesday post-conference session, "Internet Recruiting Strategy Update" was rated highest at our Staffing Industry Management Institute, as well as at last year's Staffing Industry Executive Forum. Typical was this comment, *'Gave me up-to-date, now information that I could use immediately.'*"

—Staffing Industry Report
Global Staffing Industry Report

"WOW!! I had the opportunity to listen to Peter Weddle speak last week at a conference and 'WOW!!' does NOT do justice to how I felt after listening to him!"

—Recruiter
American Multiline Corporation

"I've just attended [Peter Weddle's] session and it was really great. Peter is giving new information I've never heard before and has some really helpful insights. Please pass my compliments on to Peter...."

—Marketing Manager
DBM

"... a 'real' source of practical advice in our business."

—President
JobsHawaii.com

"Good information for those who want to be the best of the best."

—President
The RADS Group

As a Resource for Job Seekers & Career Activists:

"The *WEDDLE's Job Seeker's Guide to Employment Web Sites* supplies clear, completely current information about each site's services, features and fees—helping users instantly determine which site best meets their needs. If you are looking for an objective guide to employment websites, ExecuNet recommends *WEDDLE's Guide*."

—ExecuNet
The Center for Executive Careers

"It's been a couple of decades since I have had a need for a resume, and found your book insightful and most helpful. Thank you for taking the time to write it."

—Job Seeker, Canada

"Hi, I just went to your Web-site and was blown away by all the neat material. It is presented so well and is very compelling—I could hardly resist ordering . . . !!!"

—Career Counselor, JobWhiz

"I found your book in the public library. Recently, I purchased my own copy from Amazon. com. It is a terrific book for breaking down the complexity of preparing resumes for the computer age. Thank you for writing this book."

—Job Seeker

"Here's one of the best Web-sites to visit and refer to regarding job-hunting. Look into it first . . . It'll provide you with a great competitive edge in the job market."

—Job Seeker, Washington, D.C.

"Just wanted you to know that ALL the participants rated today's program and presenter as excellent! You were informative, funny, and you put things into context so they could be easily understood. It was a terrific program!"

—WEBS Career & Educational Counseling Service
Westchester County (NY) Library System

Also by Peter Weddle

WIZNotes: Finding a Job on the Web

WIZNotes: Writing a Great Resume

Computer-Based Instruction in Military Environments
(with Robert J. Seidel)

Electronic Resumes for the New Job Market

Generalship: HR Leadership in a Time of War

Internet Resumes: Take the Net to Your Next Job

Postcards From Space
Being the Best in Online Recruitment & HR Management
(2001, 2003)

'Tis of Thee
A Son's Search for the Meaning of Patriotism

WEDDLE's Recruiter's Guide to Employment Web Sites
(annually, 1999–2007)

WEDDLE's Job Seeker's Guide to Employment Web Sites
(annually, 2000–2007)

WEDDLE's Directory of Employment-Related Internet Sites
(annually, 2002–2007)

WEDDLE's Recruiter's Guide to Association Web Sites

Career Fitness: How to Keep Employers from Kicking Sand in Your Face

WEDDLE's Directory

of Employment-Related Internet Sites

2007/8

for
- Recruiters & HR Professionals
- Job Seekers & Career Activists

Peter Weddle

ISBN: 1-928734-40-5

Special discounts on bulk quantities of WEDDLE's books are available for libraries, corporations, professional associations and other organizations. For details, please contact WEDDLE's at 203.964.1888.

WEDDLE's
www.weddles.com
2052 Shippan Avenue
Stamford, CT 06902
Where People Matter Most

CONTENTS

for
Recruiters & Job Seekers
both of whom deserve the best resources available

Welcome Back!

Welcome to the 2007/8 edition of *WEDDLE's Directory of Employment-Related Internet Sites*. This is the sixth consecutive edition of the Directory to be published. To those who have been with us since the beginning, we say "Welcome Back!" and to those who are using our book for the first time, we hope that it serves you well.

Think of WEDDLE's Directory as the address book of job boards, resume databases, career portals and other employment-related resources on the Internet. These sites have been organized by the career fields, industries and/or geographic locations in which they specialize or provide the majority of their services. The Directory, then, is a one-of-a-kind reference to information and services for your success.

As our "long-time" readers know, we update and publish the Directory every other year because the online employment services industry is dynamic and always changing.

- We collect new sites, eliminate discontinued sites and revise site addresses that have changed. Typically, these revisions involve hundreds of online destinations.

- In addition, we provide a continuous stream of updates throughout the year so that you are aware of site changes as soon as they occur. You can access this information **free of charge** at the WEDDLE's Web-site, www.weddles.com.

This year's edition lists over 9,000 sites, including many niche or specialty sites that are appearing in the Directory for the first time. In addition, each year we research the job market to identify new areas of employment that may be of interest to our readers and are served by three or more job boards. Based on that investigation, we have added six new site classifications to the 2007/8 Directory. They are:

- Blogs (for both job seekers and recruiters)
- Cosmetology
- Employee Referral
- Exchanges (that connect employers and contractors)
- Networking
- Search Engines (that specialize in employment)

With all of these changes and improvements, we think the 2007/8 edition of WEDDLE's Directory represents the single, most comprehensive and up-to-date roster of online employment resources available anywhere. That makes it an especially powerful reference for recruiting great talent *and* for finding a new or better job.

In fact, whether you're a:

- Recruiter or Human Resource professional,
- Job Seeker or Career Activist,
- or both,

the WEDDLE's Directory will put you on the Information Superhighway to career success. We hope you'll use it often and benefit greatly from that use.

All the Best,
Peter Weddle
Stamford, CT

About This Directory

The WEDDLE's Directory presents the Internet address (also called the Universal Resource Locator or URL) of Internet sites that provide employment-related services to recruiters and/or job seekers. To be included in the Directory, the site must post or fill jobs, post or distribute resumes, or provide recruitment support, career counseling and/or job search assistance over the Internet.

The Directory is designed to be used just as you would a traditional telephone directory. Sites are listed alphabetically by their name in one or more of three categories of classifications:

- **Occupational field** (e.g., finance and accounting, engineering, sales and marketing)

- **Industry** (e.g., construction, banking, healthcare, insurance)

- **Specialty** (e.g., diversity, bilingual/multilingual professionals, military personnel transitioning into the private sector)

In addition, international sites and regional sites in the United States are organized by their specific geographic focus. For a complete list of the classifications used in this Directory, please see the **Site Classifications & Index** on Page 25.

HOW CAN THIS DIRECTORY HELP YOU?

There are over 40,000 employment-related sites currently operating on the Internet. Whether you're a recruiter, a job seeker or a person proactively managing your own career, you need to know your options in order to make the best use of these powerful resources. This Directory can help you do that. It will make sure that you don't overlook a site that can assist you and quickly identify those sites best able to address your specific situation or objective as well as their location on the Internet.

For example:

- If you're a recruiter who is looking for candidates to fill a senior level finance position located in California, you could check the listings under Finance (where you would find over 135 sites), Executive/Management (where you would find over 55 sites) and Regional-California (where you would find more than 65 sites).

- On the other hand, if you're a senior level financial executive who is living in California and interested in finding a new or better job, you could check the same listings and take advantage of the same sites to find that recruiter's opening and others posted online.

There's no guesswork, no slogging through thousands of unrelated listings on a search engine and no wandering around the Internet trying to find what you need by hit or miss. The Directory enables you to identify just the sites you need quickly and put their resources to work for you effectively. That's the way you maximize your ROI ... your return on the Internet.

A WORD ABOUT WEB-SITE ADDRESSES

A Web-site address or Universal Resource Locator (URL) typically includes two basic elements: <u>The root address</u> (e.g., the-name-of-the-site.com) and <u>extensions</u> which identify specific areas of the site. For example: (e.g., the-name-of-the-site.com/JobPostings.html or the-name-of-the-site.com/resumes).

When you select a Web-site to visit and enter its URL into your computer, remember the following two rules:

- **In most cases, address extensions are case sensitive.** In other words, if the address that is listed in the Directory indicates that the extension includes one or more capital letters, make sure that you include them exactly as shown in the address.

- **In many cases, extensions change.** The best Web-site operators are continuously updating and improving their sites, and when they do, they often change the extensions to reflect their modifications. How can you still use the address if the extensions listed in the Directory don't seem to work? Use a technique called "peeling." It involves nothing more than sequentially eliminating each of the extensions between the forward slashes in a site's address. Begin with the last extension in the address and eliminate one extension at a time until the Web-site opens. Then, look for links on the open page to find that area of the site you are trying to reach.

    For example, the Directory might list the following address for a site you want to visit: www.the-name-of-the-site.com/adposts/jobs/newposts.html. If you enter that address into your computer and the site doesn't open (or you get an error message), then peel back the last extension (newposts.html) and try again. If the site still doesn't open, peel back the next extension (jobs) and try again. Continue this process, until the site opens and then look for a link to the area on the site of interest to you. When you click on that link, note the new address that appears on your computer tool bar. Record that address on the Notes page of your Directory so that it will be readily available the next time you want to visit the site.

KEEPING OUR INFORMATION UP-TO-DATE

WEDDLE's makes every effort to keep the information it publishes current and up-to-date. The Internet, however, is always changing, and WEDDLE's is always seeking updates and corrections to its listings. If you find a discrepancy, please notify us at 203.964.1888 or on the Internet at corporate@weddles.com. We appreciate your assistance and pay careful attention to what you tell us.

Whenever we become aware of a change or discrepancy, we contact the appropriate site, obtain the correct information and then publish it on our Web-site for you and others to see. So, **log onto www.weddles.com regularly** and click on the link entitled Free Book Updates on our toolbar. It's the best way to stay on top of the ever-changing universe of helpful employment resources on the Internet.

What is WEDDLE's?

WEDDLE's is a research, publishing, consulting and training firm specializing in HR leadership, employment, job search and career self-management.

Since 1996, WEDDLE's has conducted groundbreaking surveys of:

- recruiters and job seekers behavior and preferences on the Internet, *and*
- the features, resources and fees of Web-sites providing employment-related services.

Our research and findings have been cited in such publications as *The Wall Street Journal*, *The New York Times*, and in *Money*, *Fortune*, and *Inc.* magazines.

WEDDLE's also publishes books, guides and directories that focus on organizations' acquisition and leadership of human capital and on individuals' achievement of their employment and career goals.

For recruiters and HR professionals, its publications include:

- *WEDDLE's Guide to Employment Web Sites on the Internet*
- *WEDDLE's Directory of Employment-Related Internet Sites*
- *WEDDLE's Guide to Association Web Sites*
- *Postcards From Space: Being the Best in Online Recruitment & HR Management*
- *The Keys to Successful Recruiting and Staffing*
- *Generalship: HR Leadership in a Time of War*
- *WEDDLE's bi-weekly e-Newsletter for Recruiters & HR Professionals* [FREE]

For job seekers and career activists, its publications include:

- *WEDDLE's Guide to Employment Web Sites on the Internet*
- *WEDDLE's Directory of Employment-Related Internet Sites*
- *WEDDLE's Guide to Association Web Sites*
- *WizNotes: Fast Guides to Job Boards and Career Portals* with tailored guides for:
    - Engineers,
      Sales & Marketing professionals,
      Finance & Accounting professionals,
      Human Resource professionals,
      Scientists,
      Women professionals
      Managers & Executives, and
      Recent College Graduates
- *WizNotes: Finding a Great Job on the Web*
- *WizNotes: Writing a Great Resume*
- *Career Fitness: How to Keep Employers from Kicking Sand in Your Face*
- *WEDDLE's bi-weekly e-Newsletter for Job Seekers & Career Activists* [FREE]

WEDDLE's also provides consultation to organizations in the areas of:

- HR leadership,
- Human capital formation,
- Recruitment strategy development,
- Employment brand articulation and positioning,
- Recruitment process reengineering and optimization, *and*
- Web-site design, development and implementation.

WEDDLE's delivers private seminars and workshops on the following subjects:

- Best Practices in Internet recruiting
    - for in-house corporate recruiters and managers
      for staffing firm recruiters and managers

- Optimizing the candidate experience
- Human Resource leadership.

WHO IS PETER WEDDLE?

Peter Weddle is a former recruiter and business CEO turned author and speaker. He writes a bi-weekly column for the Interactive Edition of *The Wall Street Journal* and two newsletters that are distributed worldwide. Weddle has also authored or edited over twenty books and written numerous articles for leading magazines and journals. He has been cited in *The New York Times, The Washington Post, The Boston Globe, U.S. News & World Report, The Wall Street Journal, USA Today* and numerous other publications and has spoken to trade and professional associations and corporate meetings all over the world.

2006 User's Choice Awards

RECRUITERS & JOB SEEKERS PICK
THE TOP SITES ON THE WEB

Who has the best perspective on which employment sites are most help-ful? We think the answer to that question is obvious . . . it's YOU, the recruiters and job seekers who have used the sites. You, better than any-one else, know which sites work best.

WEDDLE's User's Choice Awards give you a way to make your preferences known. It's your chance to:

- recognize the Web-sites that provide the best level of service and value to their visitors, *and*
- help others make best use of the employment resources online.

WEDDLE's User's Choice Awards are the only awards for employ-ment sites where YOU pick the winners. Public balloting is conducted all year long at the WEDDLE's Web-site, and the 30 sites with the most votes at the end of the year are declared the Award winners. The sites selected for the 2006 User's Choice Awards are presented on the next page.

For more information about the Awards and to cast your vote for the 2007 winners, please visit the WEDDLE's site at www.weddles.com and click on the Online Poll button on our Home Page.

WEDDLE's 2006
User's Choice Awards

The Elite of the Online Employment Services Industry

America's Job Bank

Best Jobs USA

CareerBank.com

CareerBuilder.com

CareerJournal.com

ComputerJobs.com

Computerwork.com

craigslist

DICE

eFinancialCareers.com

EmploymentGuide.com

ExecuNet

HEALTHeCAREERS

jobsinthemoney

JobsinLogistics.com

JobsinME.com

LatPro.com

MarketingJobs.com

Monster.com

Net-Temps

SHRM/HRJobs

6FigureJobs

TalentZoo.com

TopUSAJobs.com

TrueCareers

USAJOBS

Vault

VetJobs.com

Workopolis

Yahoo! HotJobs.com

Site Classifications & Index

This section contains an alphabetical listing of all of the classifications under which Web-sites are listed in the Directory. To find a specific classification's location in the Directory, check its page number listed in the Index below. Sites are listed alphabetically in a classification by their name (which may not be their URL or Internet address).

NOTES
Favorite Sites / Useful Resources

WEDDLE's
2007/8 Directory of Internet Addresses
for Employment-Related Sites

All addresses in this Directory were obtained from public sources.
Some addresses may have changed since publication of the Directory.

◤ **Indicates 2006 WEDDLE's User's Choice Award Winner**

-A-

Administrative/Clerical/Secretarial (See also Classifieds)

Administrative Resource Network	www.adresnet.com/jobs.html
AdminJob.ca [Canada]	www.adminjob.ca
GxPJobs.com [United Kingdom]	www.gxpjobs.com
iHireMedicalSecretaries.com	www.ihiremedicalsecretaries.com
iHireSecretarial.com	www.ihiresecretarial.com
International Association of Administrative Professionals Job Board	http://jobs.iaap-hq.org
MyOwnVA.com [United Kingdom]	www.myownva.com
National Association of Executive Secretaries and Administrative Assistants	www.naesaa.com/verifjb.asp
ReceptionistJobStore.com	www.receptionistjobstore.com
SecretaryJobStore	www.secretaryjobstore.com
secsinthecity [United Kingdom]	www.secsinthecity.co.uk
VirtualAssistants.com	www.virtualassistants.com

Advertising/Public Relations

NationJob Network-Advertising & Media Jobs Page	www.nationjob.com/media
Adweek	www.adweek.com
The American Advertising Federation	www.aaf.org/jobs/index.html
The Association for Interactive Marketing Career Center	www.interactivehq.org/ industry/careers.asp
Association of National Advertisers Job Opportunities	www.ana.net/hr/hr.htm
Communicators & Marketers Jobline	http://cmjobline.org
CopyEditor.com	www.copyeditor.com
Direct Marketing Association	www.the-dma.org/jobbank
MarketingHire.com	www.marketinghire.com
MassMediaJobs.com	www.massmediajobs.com

Notes

Favorite sites, useful resources

Advertising/Public Relations (continued)

MediaRecruiter.com	www.mediarecruiter.com
PaidContent.org	www.paidcontent.org/jobs
Promotion Marketing Association Job Bank	www.pmalink.org/resources/careers.asp
⋈ TalentZoo.com	www.talentzoo.com
Television Bureau of Advertising	www.tvb.org/jobcenter/index.html
Women Executives in Public Relations	www.wepr.org
Work in PR	www.workinpr.com

Agriculture

Ag Jobs USA	www.agjobsusa.com
Agricultural Employment in British Columbia	www.island.net/~awpb/emop/startag.html
American Agricultural Economic Association Employment Service	www.aaea.org/classifieds
American Society of Agricultural Engineering	www.asae.org/membership/career.html
American Society of Agricultural and Biological Engineers	www.asabe.org
American Society of Agronomy	www.asa-cssa-sssa.org/career
American Society of Animal Science	www.asas.org
American Society of Horticultural Science HortOpportunities	www.ashs.org/careers.html
California Agricultural Technical Institute ATI-Net	www.atinet.org/jobs.asp
Dairy Network Career Center	www.dairynetwork.com
Farms.com	www.farms.com/calssifieds/index.cfm
Texas A&M Poultry Science Department	http://gallus.tamu.edu/careerops.htm
Weed Science Society of America WeedJobs: Positions in Weed Science	www.wssa.net/weedjobs

Archeology/Anthropology

American Anthropology Association	www.aaanet.org/careers.htm
Society for American Archeology Careers, Opportunities & Jobs	www.saa.org/careers/index.html
Southwest Archeology	www.swanet.org/jobs.html

Architecture

AEC Job Bank	www.aecjobbank.com
American Institute of Architects Online	www.aia.org/careers_default
ArchitectJobs.com	www.architectjobs.com

Notes

Favorite sites, useful resources

Architecture (continued)

Environmental Construction Engineering
  Architectural Jobs Online   www.eceajobs.com
ReferWork-Jobs.com   www.referwork-jobs.com
Society of Naval Architects and Marine Engineers   www.sname.org

Arts

ArtJob Online   www.artjob.org
ArtsJobsOnline.com [United Kingdom]   www.artsjobsonline.com
Art Libraries Society of North America JobNet   http://arlisna.org/jobs.html
ArtNetwork   http://artmarketing.com
The Arts Deadline List   http://artdeadlineslist.com
Freelancers/TalentX   www.talentx.com
New York Foundation for the Arts   www.nyfa.org/opportunities.asp
                                                       ?type=Job&id=94&fid=6&sid=17

Association-Professional & Trade/Affinity Group

Academic Physician & Scientist   www.acphysci.com/aps.htm
AcademyHealth   www.academyhealth.org
Academy of Family Physicians   www.fpjobsonline.org
Academy of Managed Care Pharmacy   www.amcp.org
Academy of Medical-Surgical Nurses   www.medsurgnurse.org
The Advanced Computing Systems Association   www.usenix.org
Allegheny County Medical Society   www/acms.org
Alliance of Merger and Acquisition Advisors   www.advisor-alliance.com
American Academy of Dermatology   www.aad.org
American Academy of Otolaryngology-
  Head & Neck Surgery   www.entnet.org/careers
American Academy of Ambulatory Care Nursing   www.aaacn.org
American Academy of Cardiovascular
  and Pulmonary Rehabilitation   www.aacvpr.org
American Academy of Nurse Practitioners   www.aanp.org
American Academy of Pharmaceutical Physicians   www.aapp.org
American Academy of Physician Assistants   www.aapa.org
American Academy of Professional Coders   www.aapc.com
American Accounting Association   http://aaahq.org/placements/
  Web Placement Service   default.cfm
The American Advertising Federation   www.aaf.org/jobs/index.html
American Agricultural Economic
  Association Employment Service   www.aaea.org/classifieds
American Anthropology Association   www.aaanet.org/careers.htm
American Association of   www.asbcnet.org/SERVICES/
  Brewing Chemists   career.htm
American Association for Budget and
  Program Analysis   www.aabpa.org/employ.html

Notes

Favorite sites, useful resources

Association-Professional & Trade/Affinity Group (continued)

American Associatin of Cardiovascular and
  Pulmonary Rehabilitation — www.aacvpr.org
American Association of Cereal Chemists — www.aaccnet.org/membership/
  careerplacement.asp

American Association for Clinical Chemistry — www.aacc.org
American Association of
  Critical Care Nurses — www.aacn.org
American Association of
  Finance & Accounting — www.aafa.com/career.htm
American Association of Gynecologic
  Laparoscopists — www.aagl.com
American Association of Law Libraries
  Job Placement Hotline — www.aallnet.org/hotline
American Association of Medical Assistants — www.aama-ntl.org
American Association for Medical
  Transcription — www.aamt.org
American Association of Neurological Surgeons — www.aans.org
American Association of Neuromuscular &
  Electrodiagnostic Medicine — www.aanem.org
American Association of Occupational
  Health Nurses — www.aaohn.org
American Association of Oral & Maxillofacial
  Surgeons — www.aaoms.org
American Association of Pharmaceutical
  Sales Professionals — www.pharmaceuticalsales.org
American Association of Pharmaceutical
  Scientists — www.aaps.org
American Association of Respiratory Care — www.aarc.org
American Astronomical Society — www.aas.org/JobRegister/
  Job Register — index.html
American Bankers Association — http://aba.careerbank.com
American Bankruptcy Institute Career Center — www.abiworld.org/abi
  careercenter

American Chemical Society
  cen-chemjobs.org — www.cen-chemjobs.com
American College of Allergy, Asthma & Immunology — www.acaai.org
American College of Cardiology — www.acc.org
American College of Chest Physicians — www.chestnet.org
American College of Clinical Pharmacology — www.accp1.org
American College of Clinical Pharmacy — www.accp.com
American College of Emergency Physicians — www.acep.org
American College of Foot and Ankle Surgeons — www.acfas.org
American College of Healthcare
  Executives Employment Service — www.ache.org
American College of Nurse Midwives — www.acnw.org

Notes

Favorite sites, useful resources

Association-Professional & Trade/Affinity Group (continued)

American College of Obstetricians and
  Gynecologists   www.acog.org
American College of Occupational and
  Environmental Medicine   www.acoem.org
American College of Physicians   www.acponline.org/careers
American College of Physician Executives   www.acpe.org
American College of Preventive Medicine   www.acpm.org
American College of Rheumatology   www.rheumatology.org
American College of Surgeons   www.facs.org
American Counseling Association   www.counseling.org
American Dental Hygienists' Association   www.adha.org/careerinfo/
                                                       index.html
American Design Drafting Association   www.adda.org
American Dietetic Association   www.eatright.org
American Educational Research   http://aera.net/jobposts/
  Association Job Openings   default.asp
American Evaluation Associaton   www.eval.org/JobBank/
                                                       jobbank.htm
American Forest & Paper Association   www.afandpa.org/careercenter
American Foundation for the Blind   www.afb.org/CareerConnect/
  AFB Career Connect   users/careers.asp
American Gastroenterological Association   www.gicareersearch.com
American Geriatrics Society   www.americangeriatrics.org
American Healthcare Radiology Administrators   www.ahraonline.org
American Hotel and Lodging Association   www.ahla.com/careers
American Industrial Hygiene Association   www.aiha.org/Employment
                                                       Service/html/employmentservice
                                                       home.htm
American Institute of Architects Online   www.aia.org/careers_default
American Institute of Biological Sciences   www.aibs.org
American Institute of Certified Public Accountants   www.cpa2biz.com/
  Career Center   Career/default.htm
American Institute of Chemical Engineers
  Career Services   www.aiche.org/careers
The American Institute of Chemists   www.theaic.org
American Institute of Graphic Arts   www.aiga.org
American Institute of Physics Career Services   www.aip.org/careersvc
American Library Association Library
  Education and Employment Menu Page   www.ala.org/education
American Marketing Association   www.marketingpower.com/live/
  Career Center   content.php?Item_ID=966
American Medical Association
  Journal of the AMA (JAMA)
  Physician Recruitment Ads   www.ama-assn.org
American Medical Technologists   www.amtl.com

Notes

Favorite sites, useful resources

Association-Professional & Trade/Affinity Group (continued)

American Meteorological Society
  Employment Announcements — www.ametsoc.org
American Nurses Association — www.nursingworld.org
American Occupational Therapy Association — www.aota.org
American Pharaceutical Association — www.aphanet.org
American Psychiatric Association — www.psych.org
American Psychiatric Nurses Association — www.apna.org
American Physical Society — www.aps.org/jobs
American Physical Therapy Association — www.apta.org
American Psychological Association Online
  PsycCareers — www.psyccareers.com
American Psychological Society
  Observer Job Listings — www.psychologicalscience.org/jobs
American Registry of Diagnostic Medical
  Sonographers — www.ardms.org
American Registry of Radiologic Technologists — www.arrt.org
American Society of
  Agricultural Engineering — www.asae.org/membership/career.html
American Society of Agricultural and
  Biological Engineers — www.asabe.org
American Society of Agronomy — www.asa-cssa-sssa.org/career
American Society of Animal Science — www.fass.org/job.asp
American Society for Cell Biology — www.ascb.org
American Society for Clinical Laboratory Science — www.ascls.org
American Society for Clinical Pathology — www.ascp.org
American Society of Clinical Pharmacology
  and Therapeutics — www.ascpt.org
American Society of Gene Therapy — www.asgt.org
American Society of General Surgeons — www.theasgs.org
American Society of Horticultural Science
  HortOpportunities — www.ashs.org/careers.html
American Society of Interior Designers
  Job Bank — www.asid.org/career_center/job_opp/job.asp
American Society of Journalists & Authors — www.freelancewritersearch.com
American Society for Law Enforcement Training — www.aslet.org
American Society of Mechanical Engineers
  Career Center — www.asme.org/jobs
American Society for Microbiology — www.asm.org
American Society of PeriAnesthesia Nurses — www.aspan.org
American Society of Pharmacognosy — www.phcog.org
American Society of Plant Biologists — http://www.aspb.org
American Society of Professional Estimators — www.aspenational.com
American Society of Radiologic Technologists — www.asrt.org
American Society for
  Training & Development Job Bank — http://jobs.astd.org

Notes

Favorite sites, useful resources

Association-Professional & Trade/Affinity Group (continued)

American Society of Travel Agents — www.astanet.com

American Society of Women Accountants Employment Opportunities — www.aswa.org/i4a/pages/index.cfm?pageid=3281

American Speech-Language Hearing Association Online Career Center — www.asha.org/about/career

American Statistical Association Statistics Career Center — www.amstat.org/careers

American Veterinary Medical Association Career Center — http://jobs.avma.org

American Water Works Association Career Center (Water Jobs) — www.awwa.org

Arizona Hospital and Healthcare Association AZHealthJobs — www.azhha.org

Art Libraries Society of North America JobNet — http://arlisna.org/jobs.html

Association for Applied Human Pharmacology [Germany] — www.agah-web.de

Association of Career Professionals International — www.iacmp.org

Association of Certified Fraud Examiners Career Center — www.cfenet.com services/career.asp

Association of Clinical Reseach Professionals Career Center — www.acrpnet.org

Association for Computing Machinery Career Resource Center — http://acpinternational.org

Association for Educational Communications and Technology Job Center — www.aect.org

Association for Environmental and Outdoor Education — www.aeoe.org

Association of ex-Lotus Employees — www.axle.org

Association of Finance Professionals Career Services — www.afponline.org/careerservices

Association of Graduate Careers Advisory Service [United Kingdom] — www.agcas.org.uk

The Association for Institutional Research — www.airweb.org/page.asp?page=2

The Association for Interactive Marketing Career Center — www.interactivehq.org/industry/careers.asp

Association of Internet Professionals National Job Board — www.association.org

AssociationJobBoards.com — www.associationjobboards.com

Association of Latino Professionals in Finance & Accounting Job Postings — www.alpfa.org

Association of Legal Information Systems Managers Job Listings — www.alism.org/jobs.htm

Association of Management Consulting Firms — www.amcf.org

Notes

Favorite sites, useful resources

Association-Professional & Trade/Affinity Group (continued)

Association of National Advertisers
Job Opportunities — www.ana.net/hr/hr.htm

Association of Perioperative — www.aorn.org/
Registered Nurses Online Career Center — Careers/default.htm

Association of Staff Physician Recruiters — www.aspr.org

Association for Strategic Planning — www.strategyplus.org

Association of Teachers of Technical Writing — www.attw.org

Association of University Teachers
[United Kingdom] — www.AUT4Jobs.com

Association for Women in Computing — www.awc-hq.org

Association of Women's Health, Obstetric &
Neonatal Nurses — www.awhonn.org

Bank Administration Institute — www.bai.org

Bank Marketing Association — www.bmanet.org

Bay Area Bioscience Center — www.bayareabioscience.org

Biomedical Engineering Society — www.bmes.org

Biotechnology Association of Alabama — www.bioalabama.org

Biotechnology Association of Maine — www.mainebiotech.org

Biotechnology Council of New Jersey — www.newjerseybiotech.org

Black Data Processing Association Online — www.bdpa.org

Biotechnology Association of Alabama — www.bioalabama.com

Board of Pharmaceutical Specialties — www.bpsweb.org

Business Marketing Association — www.marketing.org

Business Test Publishers Association
[United Kingdom] — www.assessmentjobs.com

California Academy of Family Physicians — www.fpjobsonline.org

California Agricultural Technical Institute
ATI-Net AgJobs — www.atinet.org/jobs.asp

California Dental Hygienists' Association
Employment Opportunities — www.cdha.org/employment/
index.html

California Mortgage Brokers Association
Career Center — www.cambweb.org

California Separation Science Society — www.casss,org

Canadian Society of Biochemistry and
Mollecular and Cellular Biologists
Experimental Medicine Job Listing — www.medcor.mcgill.ca/
EXPMED/DOCS/index.html

Capital Markets Credit Analysts Society
Resume Service — www.cmcas.org/
resumeservice.asp

Chicago Medical Society — www.cmsdocs.org

College of American Pathologists — www.cap.org

College and University Personnel Association
JobLine — www.cupahr.org/jobline

Colorado Academy of Family Physicians — www.fpjobsonline.org

Colorado Health and Hospital Association — www.cha.com

Notes

Favorite sites, useful resources

Association-Professional & Trade/Affinity Group (continued)

Computing Research Association
Job Announcements — www.cra.org/main/cra.jobs.html
Controlled Release Society — www.controlledrelease.org
Council for Advancement & Support
of Education Jobs Online — www.case.org/jobs
Dermatology Nurses' Association — www.dnanurse.org
Design Management Institute Job Bank — www.dmi.org/dmi/html/
jobbank/jobbank_d.jsp

Digital Printing and Imaging Association
Employment Exchange (with the Screenprinting — www.sgia.org/
& Graphic Imaging Association International) — employ/employ.html
Direct Marketing Association — www.the-dma.org/jobbank
Drilling Research Institute Classifieds — www.drillers.com/classifieds.cfm
Drug Information Association
Employment Opportunities — www.diahome.org/docs/Jobs/
Jobs_index.cfm
Editorial Freelancers Association — www.the-efa.org
Emergency Medicine Residents Association — www.emra.org
Employers Resource Association — www.hrxperts.org
Financial Executives Institute Career Center — www.fei.org/careers
Financial Management Association
International Placement Services — www.fma.org/2003placement
Financial Managers Society Career Center — www.fmsinc.org/cms/?pid=1025
Financial Women International Careers — www.fwi.org/careers/careers.htm
Florida Academy of Family Physicians — www.fpjobsonline.org
Global Association of Risk Professionals — www.garp.com/
Career Center — careercenter/index.asp
Georgia Academy of Family Physicians — www.fpjobsonline.org
Georgia Association of Personnel Services — www.jobconnection.com
Georgia Pharmacy Association — www.gpha.org
Graphic Artists Guild JobLine — www.gag.org/jobline/index.html
Harris County Medical Society — www.hcms.org
Healthcare Businesswomen's Association — www.hbanet.org
Healthcare Information and Management Systems — www.himss.org
Hispanic American Police Command Officers
Association — www.hapcoa.org
History of Science Society — www.hssonline.org
HIV Medicine Association — www.hivma.org
HTML Writers Guild HWG-Jobs — www.hwg.org/lists/hwg-jobs
Human Resource Association
of the National Capital Area Job Bank Listing — http://hra-nca.org/job_list.asp
Human Resource Independent Consultants (HRIC) — www.hric.org/
On-Line Job Leads — hric/hrcaopp1.html
Human Resource Management
Association of Mid Michigan Job Postings — http://hrmamm.com/jobs.asp
Illinois Academy of Family Physicians — www.fpjobsonline.org

Notes

Favorite sites, useful resources

Association-Professional & Trade/Affinity Group (continued)

Illinois Recruiters Association	www.illinoisrecruiters.org
Infectious Diseases Society of America	www.idsa.org
Institute of Electrical & Electronics Engineers Job Site	www.ieee.org/jobs
Institute of Clinical Research [United Kingdom]	www.instituteofclinical research.org
Institute of Food Science & Technology	www.ifst.org
Institute of Internal Auditors Online Audit Career Center	www.theiia.org/careercenter/ index.cfm
Institute of Management Accountants Career Center	www.imanet.org/ima/ sec.asp? TRACKID=&CID=12&DID=12
Institute of Management and Administration's Supersite	www.ioma.com
Institute of Real Estate Management Jobs Bulletin	www.irem.org
Institute for Supply Management Career Center	www.ism.ws/ CareerCenter/index.cfm
The Instrumentation, Systems and Automation Society Online ISA Jobs	www.isa.org/isa_es
International Association of Administrative Professionals Job Board	http://jobs.iaap-hq.org
International Association of Business Communicators Career Centre	www.iabc.com
International Association of Conference Centers Online (North America)	www.iaccnorthamerica.org/ resources/index.cfm? fuseaction=JobBoard
International Association for Commercial and Contract Management	www.iaccm.com
International Association for Human Resource Information Management Job Central	http://ihr.hrdpt.com
International Code Council	www.iccsafe.org
International Customer Service Association Job Board	http://secure2.neology.com/ICSA/ jobs/employer/welcome.cfm
International Foundation of Employee Benefit Plans Job Postings	www.ifebp.org/jobs/default.asp
Independent Human Resource Consultants Association	www.ihrca.com/ Contract_Regular.asp
International Society for Molecular Plant-Microbe Interactions	www.ismpinet.org/career
International Society for Performance Improvement Job Bank	www.ispi.org
International Society for Pharmaceutical Engineering	www.ispe.org
Iowa Biotechnology Association	www.iowabiotech.org

Notes

Favorite sites, useful resources

Association-Professional & Trade/Affinity Group (continued)

JAMACareerNet [Journal & Archives Journals of the American Medical Association] — http://jamacareernet.ama-assn.org

Latinos in Information Sciences and Technology Association — www.a-lista.org

Marine Executive Association — www.marineea.org

Maryland Association of CPAs Job Connect — www.macpa.org/services/jobconnt/index.htm

Massachusetts Biotechnology Council — www.massbio.org

Massachusetts Environmental Education Society — www.massmees.org

Massachusetts Healthcare Human Resources Association — www.mhhra.org

MdBio, Inc. (Maryland Bioscience) — www.mdbio.org

Media Communications Association International Job Hotline — www.mca-i.org

Media Human Resource Association — www.shrm.org/mhra/index.asp

Medical-Dental-Hospital Business Associateion — www.mdhbaorg

Medical Group Management Association — www.mgma.com

Medical Marketing Association — www.mmanet.org

Metroplex Association of Personnel Consultants — www.recruitingfirms.com

MichBIO — www.michbio.org

Michigan Pharmacists Association — www.mipharm.com

The Minerals, Metals, Materials Society JOM — www.tms.org/pubs/journals/JOM/classifieds.html

Missouri Academy of Family Physicians — www.fpjobsonline.org

Missouri Pharmacy Association — www.morx.com

Music Library Association Job Placement — www.music.indiana.edu/som/placement/index.html

National Alliance of State Broadcasters Associations CareerPage — www.careerpage.org

National Association of Black Accountants, Inc. Career Center — www.nabainc.jobcontrolcenter.com

National Association of Boards of Pharmacy — www.nabp.net

National Association for College Admission Counseling Career Opportunities — www.nacac.com/classifieds.cfm

National Association of Colleges & Employers (NACE) — www.nacelink.com

National Association for Female Executives — www.nafe.com

National Association of Hispanic Nurses Houston Chapter — www.nahnhouston.org

National Association of Hispanic Publications Online Career Center — www.nahp.org

National Association of Orthopaedic Nurses — www.orthonurse.org

National Association of Pharmaceutical Sales Representatives — www.napsronline.org

Notes

Favorite sites, useful resources

Association-Professional & Trade/Affinity Group (continued)

National Association for Printing Leadership	www.napl.org
National Association of Printing Ink Manufacturers	www.napim.org
National Association of Sales Professionals Career Center	www.nasp.com
National Association of School Psychologists	www.naspcareercenter.org
National Association of Securities Professionals Current Openings	www.nasphq.com/career.html
National Association of Securities Professionals (Atlanta) Current Openings	www.naspatlanta.com/ career.html
National Association of Securities Professionals (New York) Underground Railroad	www.nasp-ny.org
National Association of Social Workers Joblink	www.socialworkers.org/ joblinks/default.asp
National Black Police Association	www.blackpolice.org
National Community Pharmacists Association Independent Pharmacy Matching Service	www.ncpanet.org
National Contract Management Association	www.ncmajobcontrolcenter.com
National Defense Industrial Association	www.defensejobs.com
National Environmental Health Association	www.neha.org
National Federation of Paralegal Associations Career Center	www.paralegals.org/ displaycommon.cfm?an=20
National Field Selling Association	www.nfsa.com
National Fire Prevention Association Online Career Center	www.nfpa.org/catalog/ home/CareerCenter/index.asp
National Funeral Directors Association	www.nfda.org
National Insurance Recruiters Association Online Job Database	www.nirassn.com/positions.cfm
National Latino Peace Officers Association	www.nlpoa.org
National League for Nursing	www.nln.org
National Network of Commercial Real Estate Women Job Bank	www.nncrew.org/job_bank/ job_bank_introduction_frm.html
National Organization of Black Law Enforcement Executives	www.noblenational.org
National Organization for Professional Advancement of Black Chemists and Chemical Engineers University of Michigan Chapter	www.engin.umich.edu/ soc/nobcche
National Parking Association	http://careers.npapark.org
National Rural Recruitment & Retention Network	www.3rnet.net
National Society of Black Engineers	www.nsbe.org
National Society of Collegiate Scholars Career Connection	www.nscs.org/ CareerConnections/index.cfm
National Society of Hispanic MBAs Career Center	www.nshmba.org

Notes

Favorite sites, useful resources

Association-Professional & Trade/Affinity Group (continued)

National Society of Professional Engineers Employment	www.nspe.org/ em-home.asp
National Venture Capital Association	www.nvca.org
National Weather Association Job Corner	www.nwas.org/jobs.html
National Women's Studies Association	www.nwsa.org
National Writer's Union Job Hotline	www.nwu.org/hotline/index.html
Nationwide Process Servers Association	www.processservers association.com
New Jersey Metro Employment Management Association	www.njmetroema.org
New Jersey Human Resource Planning Group	www.njhrpg.org
The New York Biotechnology Association	www.nyba.org
New York New Media Association	www.nynma.org
New York Society of Association Executives Career Center	www.nysaenet.org
New York Society of Security Analysts Career Resources	www.nyssa.org/jobs
New York State Academy of Family Physicians	www.fpjobsonline.org
Newspaper Association of America Newspaper CareerBank	www.naa.org/careerbank
North American Association for Environmental Education	www.ee-link.net
North American Spine Society	www.spine.org
Northeast Human Resource Association	www.nehra.org
Oklahoma State Medical Association	www.osmaonline.org
Orelans Parish Medical Society	www.opms.org
Oregon Bioscience Association	www.oregon-bioscience.com
Pennsylvania Academy of Family Physicians	www.fpjobsonline.org
Petroleum Services Association of Canada Employment	www.psac.ca
Professionals in Human Resource Association Career Center	www.pihra.org/capirasn/ careers.nsf/home?open
Project Management Institute Career Headquarters	www.pmi.org/CareerHQ
Promotion Marketing Association Job Bank	www.pmalink.org/resources/ careers.asp
Radiological Society of North America	www.rsna.org
Radiology Business Management Association	www.rbma.org
Real Estate Lenders Association	www.rela.org
Risk & Insurance Management Society Careers	www.rims.org/Template.cfm? Section=JobBank1&Template=/ Jobbank/SearchJobForm.cfm
Sales & Marketing Executives International Career Center	www.smei.org/ careers/index.shtml

Notes

Favorite sites, useful resources

Association-Professional & Trade/Affinity Group (continued)

Screenprinting & Graphic Imaging Association International — www.sgia.org/employ/employ.html

Securities Industry Association Career Resource Center — www.sia.com/career

Sheet Metal and Air Conditioning Contractor's Association — www.smacna.org

Society for American Archeology Careers, Opportunities & Jobs — www.saa.org/careers/index.html

Society of Automotive Engineers Job Board — www.sae.org/careers/recrutad.htm

Society of Competitive Intelligence Professionals Job Marketplace — www.scip.org/jobs/index.asp

Society of Diagnostic Medical Sonographers — www.sdms.org

Society of Gastroenterology Nurses & Associates — www.sgna.org

Society of Hispanic Professional Engineers Career Services — www.shpe.org

Society of Hospital Medicine Career Center — www.hospitalmedicine.org

≋ Society for Human Resource Management HRJobs — www.shrm.org/jobs

Society for Industrial & Organizational Psychology JobNet — www.siop.org/JobNet

Society of Mexican American Engineers and Scientists — www.maes-natl.org

Society of Naval Architects and Marine Engineers — www.sname.org

Society of Nuclear Medicine — www.snm.org

Society of Petrologists & Well Log Analysts Job Opportunities — www.spwla.org

Society of Risk Analysis Opportunities — www.sra.org/opptys.php

Society of Satellite Professionals International Career Center — www.sspi.broadbandcareers.com/Default.asp

Society of Women Engineers Career Services — www.societyofwomenengineers.org/specialservices/careerservices.aspx

SPIE Web-International Society for Optical Engineering — www.spieworks.com

Strategic Account Management Association Career Resources — www.strategicaccounts.com/public/career/index.asp

Student Conservation Association — www.thesca.org

Teachers of English to Speakers of Other Languages Job Finder — www.tesol.org

Technical Association of the Pulp & Paper Industry Jobline — www.tappi.org/index.asp?ip=-1&ch=14&rc=-1

Telecommunication Industry Association Online — www.tiaonline.org

Texas Academy of Family Physicians — www.fpjobsonline.org

Texas Healthcare & Bioscience Institute — www.thbi.org

Notes

Favorite sites, useful resources

Association-Professional & Trade/Affinity Group (continued)

Texas Medical Association — www.texmed.org
Utah Life Sciences Association — www.utahlifescience.com
Virginia Biotechnology Association — www.vabio.org
Washington Biotechnology & Biomedical
  Association — www.wabio.com
Weed Science Society of America
  WeedJobs: Positions in Weed Science — www.wssa.net/weedjobs
Wisconsin Academy of Family Physicians — www.fpjobsonline.org
Wisconsin Biotechnology Association — www.wisconsinbiotech.org
Wisconsin Medical Society — www.wisconsinmedical
  society.org
Women in Technology — www.worldWIT.org
Women in Technology International (WITI) 4Hire — www.witi4hire.com
Women Executives in Public Relations — www.wepr.org

Astronomy

American Astronomical Society
  Job Register — www.aas.org/JobRegister
Board of Physics & Astronomy — www.nas.edu/bpa
Higher Careers.com — www.highercareers.com
The Chronicle of Higher Education
  Academe This Week — http://chronicle.merit.edu/jobs
SpaceCareers.com — www.spacecareers.com
SpaceJobs.com — www.spacejobs.com

Automotive

Autocareers — www.autocareers.com
Auto Head Hunter — www.autoheadhunter.net
AutoJobs.com — www.autodealerjobs.com
AutomotiveCareerCenter.com — www.automotivecareer
  center.com
Auto Techs USA — www.autotechsusa.com
Auto Town — www.autotown.com
Auto Jobs — www.autodealerjobs.com
Auto Tech USA — www.autotechusa.com
Automotive Aftermarket Jobs — www.customtrucks.net
AutomotiveTechs.com — www.automotivetechs.com
Car Careers — www.carcareers.com
CarDealerJobs.com — www.cardealerjobs.com
CareerRPM.com — www.careerrpm.com
InAutomotive.com [United Kingdom] — www.inautomotive.com
Motor Careers — www.motorcareers.com
NeedTechs.com — www.needtechs.com

Notes

Favorite sites, useful resources

Automotive (continued)

Racing Jobs	www.racingjobs.com
ShowroomToday.com	www.showroomtoday.com

Aviation

Aeroindustryjobs	www.aeroindustryjobs.com
Aerospace Jobs	http://hometown.aol.com/ aerojobs
AeroSpaceNews.com	www.aerospacenews.com
AVCrew.com	www.avcrew.com
Aviation Employment	www.aviationemployment.com
Aviation Employment NOW	www.aenworld.com
Aviation Employment Placement Service	www.aeps.com
AviationJobSearch.com	www.aviationjobsearch.com
Aviation World Services	www.aviationworldservices.com
AVJobs.com	www.avjobs.com
Careers in Aviation	www.aec.net
Federal Aviation Administration	http://ftp.tc.faa.gov/avi_edu/coop/ Resumes
Find A Pilot	www.findapilot.com
FliteJobs.com	www.flitejobs.com
Just Helicopters	www.justhelicopters.com
Landings	www.landings.com
The Mechanic	www.the-mechanic.com/jobs.html
NationJob Network-Aviation	www.nationjob.com/aviation
Pilot Jobs	www.pilot-jobs.com
Space Careers	www.spacelinks.com/ spacecareers

-B-

Banking

Alliance of Merger and Acquisition Advisors	www.advisor-alliance.com
American Banker Online Career Zone	www.americanbanker.com/ Careerzone.html
American Bankers Association	http://aba.careerbank.com
American Bankruptcy Institute Career Center	www.abiworld.org/abi careercenter
Bank Administration Institute	www.bai.org
Bank Jobs	www.bankjobs.com
Bank Marketing Association	www.bmanet.org
BankingBoard.com	www.bankingboard.com
Banking Job Site	www.bankingjobsite.com

Notes

Favorite sites, useful resources

Banking (continued)

Banking Job Store — www.bankingjobstore.com
⛏ CareerBank.com — www.careerbank.com
CreditCardJobs.net — www.creditcardjobs.net
CreditUnionJobs.com — www.creditunionjobs.com
Financial Job Network — www.fjn.com
FINANCIALjobs.com — www.financialjobs.com
Financial Women International Careers — www.fwi.org/careers/careers.htm
The Finance Beat — http://business.searchbeat.com/finance.htm

Florida Bankers Association — www.fba.careersite.com
GTNews [United Kingdom] — www.gtnews.com
iHireBanking.com — www.ihirebanking.com
The Investment Management and Trust Exchange — www.jobdirect.com
Jobs4Banking.com — www.jobs4banking.com
JobsinCredit.com [United Kingdom] — www.jobsincredit.com
Loan Closer Jobs — www.loancloserjobs.com
LoanOfficerJobs.com — www.loanofficerjobs.com
Loan Originator Jobs — www.loanoriginatorjobs.com
LoanProcessorJobs.com — www.loanprocessorjobs.com
LoanServicingJobs.com — www.loanservicingjobs.com
Mortgage Job Store — www.mortgagejobstore.com
Real Estate Finance Jobs — www.realestatefinancejobs.com
Real Estate Lenders Association — www.rela.org
Society of Risk Analysis Opportunities — www.sra.org/opportunities.php
TitleBoard.com — www.titleboard.com

Bilingual/Multilingual Professionals

Asia-Net — www.asia-net.com
BilingualCareer.com — www.bilingualcareer.com
Bilingual-Jobs — www.bilingual-jobs.com
CHALLENGEUSA — www.challengeusa.com
Eflweb — www.eflweb.com
Euroleaders — www.euroleaders.com
Hispanic Chamber of Commerce JobCentro — www.jobcentro.com/jobcentro/index.asp
iHispano — www.ihispano.com
⛏ LatPro — www.latpro.com
National Society of Hispanic MBAs Career Center — www.nshmba.org
SaludosWeb — www.saludos.com
Society of Hispanic Professional Engineers Career Services — www.shpe.org
Spanish JobSite — www.gojobsite.es
TopLanguageJobs.co.uk [United Kingdom] — www.toplanguagejobs.co.uk
Zhaopin.com — www.zhaopin.com

Notes

Favorite sites, useful resources

Biology/Biotechnology

American Institute of Biological Sciences	www.aibs.org
American Society of Agricultural and Biological Engineers	www.asabe.org
American Society for Cell Biology	www.ascb.org
American Society of Gene Therapy	www.asgt.org
American Society for Gravitational and Space Biology	www.indstate.edu/asgsb/index.html
American Society of Limnology and Oceanography	http://aslo.org
American Society for Microbiology	www.asm.org
American Society of Plant Biologists	http://www.aspb.org
Bay Area Bioscience Center	www.bayareabioscience.org
BC Biotechnology Alliance [Canada]	www.bcbiotech.ca
Bermuda Biological Station for Research, Inc.	www.bbsr.edu
Biocareer.com	www.biocareer.com
BioCareers.co.za [South Africa]	www.biocareers.co.za
BioExchange.com	www.bioexchange.com
Biofind	www.biofind.com/jobs
BioFlorida	www.bioflorida.com
BioJobNet.com	www.biojobnet.com
Biomedical Engineering Society	www.bmes.org
Bio Research Online	www.bioresearchonline.com
BioSource Technical Service	www.biosource-tech.com
BioSpace Career Center	www.biospace.com/b2/job_index.cfm
BioTech	http://biotech.icmb.utexas.edu/
BioTech Job Site	www.biotechjobsite.com
Biotechnology Association of Alabama	www.bioalabama.com
Biotechnology Association of Maine	www.mainebiotech.org
Biotechnology Calendar, Inc.	www.biotech-calendar.com
Biotechnology Council of New Jersey	www.newjerseybiotech.org
Biotechnology Industry Organization	www.bio.com
BioView	www.bioview.com
Canadian Society of Biochemistry and Mollecular and Cellular Biologists Experimental Medicine Job Listing	www.medcor.mcgill.ca/EXPMED/DOCS/index.html
CanMed [Canada]	www.canmed.com
Cell Press Online	www.cellpress.com
Cen-ChemJobs.org	www.cen-chemjobs.org
ChemPharma.org	www.chempharma.org
Connecticut's BioScience Cluster	www.curenet.org
Drug Information Association Employment Opportunities	www.diahome.org/docs/Jobs/Jobs_index.cfm
GxPJobs.com [United Kingdom]	www.gxpjobs.com
HireBio.com	www.hirebio.com

Notes

Favorite sites, useful resources

Biology/Biotechnology (continued)

HireHealth.com	www.hirehealth.com
Iowa Biotechnology Association	www.iowabiotech.org
Jobbiology.com	www.jobbiology.com
Jobclinical.com	www.jobclinical.com
Jobgenome.com	www.jobgenome.com
Jobscientist.com	www.jobscientist.com
The London Biology Network [United Kingdom]	www.biolondon.co.uk
Massachusetts Biotechnology Council	www.massbio.org
MdBio, Inc. (Maryland Bioscience)	www.mdbio.org
Medzilla	www.medzilla.com
MichBIO	www.michbio.org
Nature	www.nature.com
The New York Biotechnology Association	www.nyba.org
North Carolina Biotechnology Center	www.ncbiotech.org
North Carolina Genomics & Bioinformatics Consortium	www.ncgbc.org
Oregon Bioscience Association	www.oregon-bioscience.com
PharmacyWeek	www.pharmacyweek.com
PharmaOpportunities	www.pharmaopportunites.com
PharmaVillage.com [United Kingdom]	www.pharmavillage.com
RPhrecruiter.com	www.rphrecruiter.com
Rx Career Center	www.rxcareercenter.com
Rx Immigration	www.rximmigration.com
Science Careers	www.sciencecareers.org
Sciencejobs.com	www.sciencejobs.com
SCIENCE Online	www.scienceonline.org
Scijobs.com	www.scijobs.com
SciWeb Biotechnology Career Center	www.biocareer.com/index.cfm
Texas Healthcare & Bioscience Institute	www.thbi.org
Utah Life Sciences Association	www.utahlifescience.com
Virginia Biotechnology Association	www.vabio.org
Washington Biotechnology & Biomedical Association	www.wabio.com
Wisconsin Biotechnology Association	www.wisconsinbiotech.org

Blogs-Job Search/Careers

Adventures of a Work-at-Home Mom	http://journals.aol.com/bltshw/ MelodysMommy
Baily WorkPlay	http://baileyworkplay.com
BlogEmploi [France]	www.blogemploi.com
BoldCareer.com	www.boldcareer.com
BostonWorks The Job Blog	http://bostonworks.boston.com/ blog
Career Advice & Resources Blog	www.resumelines.com/blog
Career Assessment Goddess	http://blog.careergoddess.com

Notes

Favorite sites, useful resources

Blogs-Job Search/Careers (continued)

Career Chaos — www.coachmeg.typepad.com/career_chaos/

CareerHub — http://careerhub.typepad.com/main

Career and Job Hunting Blog — www.quintcareers.com/career_blog

CollegeRecruiter.com Insights By Candidates Blog — www.collegerecruiter.com/insightblog

Dave Opton's Blog at ExecuNet — www.execunet.com

DearAnyone.com — www.dearanyone.com/work

DefenseJobsBlog.com — www.defensejobsblog.com

Dr. Bamster's Blog — http://drbamstersblog.squarespace.com

Dream Big — http://letsdreambig.blogspot.com

ElectricalJobs — http://erecruitingsolutions.typepad.com/electricaljobs/

Employment Digest — www.seniorsuccess.net

Find A New Job — http://findnewjob.blogspot.com

From the Inside Out — http://iyjnjen.blogspot.com

Get That Job — http://getthatjob.blogspot.com

GetTheJob's Job Seeker Blog — www.getthejob.com

Guerrilla Job Hunting — http://guerrillajobhunting.typepad.com/guerrilla_job_hunting

Heather's Blog at Microsoft — http://blogs.msdn.com/heatherleigh

HireBlog — http://hireblog.blogspot.com

IWorkWithFools.com — www.iworkwithfools.com

Job Search Opportunity Tips & Advice — http://job-search-opportunity.blogspot.com/

Jobs Blog/Technical Careers at Microsoft — http://blogs.msdn.com/jobsblog

Jobs, Job Seekers, Employers & Recruiters — http://employment.typepad.com

Knock 'em Dead Blog — http://blog.knockemdead.com

Life@Work — http://dbcs.typepad.com

The Monster Blog — http://monster.typepad.com/monsterblog

My Blog By Jan Melnik — http://myblog.janmelnik.com

The Occupational Adverture — http://curtrosengren.typepad.com/occupationaladventure

Retail Anonymous — http://retailanonymous.blogspot.com

Secrets of the Job Hunt — http://secretsofthejobhunt.blogspot.com/

SecurityClearanceJobsBlog.com — www.securityclearancejobsblog.com

TechLawAdvisor.com Job Postings — www.techlawadvisor.com/jobs

Notes

Favorite sites, useful resources

Blogs-Job Search/Careers (continued)

TechnicalSalesJobsBlog.com — www.technicalsalesjobsblog.com

The Virtual Handshake — http://thevirtualhandshake.com/blog

WildJobSafari — www.wildjobsafari.blogspot.com

WorkBloom — http://workbloom.com/default.aspx

Workers Work — www.workerswork.com

Wurk — www.wurk.net

Yaps4u.net — www.yaps4u.net

Blogs-Recruiters

Advanced Online Recruiting Techniques — http://recruiting-online.spaces.msn.com/PersonalSpace.aspx

Amitai Givertz's Recruitomatic Blog — http://recruitomatic.wordpress.com

The Asia Pacific Headhunter — http://searchniche.blogs.com

Blog Indeed — http://blog.indeed.com

Cheezhead.com — www.cheezhead.com

CyberSleuthing Blog (Shally Steckerl) — www.ere.net/blogs/CyberSleuthing

Digability by Jim Stroud — http://digability.blogspot.com

Hiring Technical People — www.jrothman.com/weblog/htpblogger.htm

Jobster — http://jobster.blogs.com

MarketingHeadhunter.com — www.marketingheadhunter.com

Miles From the Curb — http://patrickburke1980.typepad.com

Mini Microsoft — http://minimsft.blogspot.com

MN Headhunter — www.mnheadhunter.com

PassingNotes.com — www.passingnotes.com

Recruiter Illuminati — http://portal.recruiting.com/RecruiterIlluminati

Recruiting.com — www.recruiting.com

RecruitingAnimal.com — www.recruitinganimal.com

Resourcing Strategies — http://resourcingstrategies.com

Seth Godin's Blog — http://sethgodin.typepad.com

SimplyHired Blog — http://blog.simplyhired.com

Talentism — http://jjhunter.typepad.com

TechCrunch — www.techcrunch.com

Building Construction/Management (See also Construction)

AllHousingJobs.co.uk [United Kingdom] — www.allhousingjobs.co.uk

Building Industry Exchange — www.building.org

Notes

Favorite sites, useful resources

Building Construction/Management (continued)

Builder Online   www.builder.net
EstimatorJobs.com   www.estimatorjobs.com
HelmetstoHardhats.com   www.helmetstohardhats.com
HVACagent.com   www.hvacagent.com
iHireBuildingTrades.com   www.ihirebuildingtrades.com
International Code Council   www.iccsafe.org
MaintenanceEmployment.com   www.maintenance
                                                employment.com
NewHomeSalesJobs.com   www.newhomesalesjobs.com
ProjectManagerJobs.com   www.projectmanagerjobs.com
SuperintendentJobs.com   www.superintendentjobs.com
QCEmployMe.com   www.qcemployme.com
Sheet Metal and Air Conditioning
  Contractor's Association   www.smacna.org
UtilityJobSearch.com [United Kingdom]   www.utilityjobsearch.com

Business

Alliance of Merger and Acquisition Advisors   www.advisor-alliance.com
American Bankruptcy Institute Career Center   www.abiworld.org/abi
                                                careercenter
American Society for Quality   http://career-services.asq.org
APICS   www.apics.org
Association for Strategic Planning   www.strategyplus.org
Barron's Online   www.barrons.com
Big Charts   www.bigcharts.com
Billboard   www.billboard.com
Biz Journals   www.bizjournals.com
Bloomberg.com   http://about.bloomberg.com/
                                                careers/opportunities.html
BPOJobSite.com [India]   www.bpojobsite.com
Business Finance   www.businessfinancemag.com
BusinessJobsNow.com   www.businessjobsnow.com
Business Marketing Association   www.marketing.org
Capital Hill Blue   http://chblue.com
⚑ CareerJournal.com   www.careerjournal.com
CareerMarketplace.com   www.careermarketplace.com
Careers In Business   www.careers-in-business.com
CNBC/Career Center   www.cnbc.com
Cnnfn   www.cnnfn.com
CondeNet   www.condenet.com
Corporate Finance Net   www.corpfinet.com
Corporate Watch   www.corpwatch.org
CreditCardJobs.net   www.creditcardjobs.net
Crain's Chicago   www.crainschicagobusiness.com

Notes

Favorite sites, useful resources

Business (continued)

Customer Service Management	www.csm-us.com
Customer Service University	www.customerservice university.com
Degree Hunter	www.degreehunter.com
Dow Jones Business Directory	http://businessdirectory. dowjones.com
e-Marketer	www.e-marketer.com
Entrepreneur	www.entrepreneurmag.com
Fortune	www.fortune.com
Global Careers	www.globalcareers.com
Harvard Biz Review	www.hbsp.Harvard.edu
Hollywood Reporter	www.hollywoodreporter.com
HomeOfficeJob.com	www.homeoffice.com
Hoover's Online	www.hoovers.com
iHireSecurity.com	www.ihiresecurity.com
Inc.	www.inc.com
Industry Week	www.industryweek.com
International Association of Business Communicators	www.iabc.com
International Association for Commercial and Contract Management	www.iaccm.com
International Customer Service Association Job Board	http://secure2.neology.com/ICSA/ jobs/employer/welcome.cfm
Internet News	www.internetnews.com
Jane's Defence	www.janes.com
JobsinRisk.com [United Kingdom]	www.jobsinrisk.com
Journal of Commerce	www.joc.com
Kiplinger	www.kiplinger.com
MBA Careers	www.mbacareers.com
MBA-Exchange.com	www.mba-exchange.com
MBA Free Agents	www.mbafreeagents.com
MBAGlobalNet	www.mbaglobalnet.com
MBAJobs.net	www.mbajobs.net/
MBAmatch.com [United Kingdom]	www.mbamatch.com
MBA Style Magazine	http://members.aol.com/ mbastyle/web/index.html
MBATalentWire.com	www.mbatalentwire.com
MedBizPeople.com	www.medbizpeople.com
MeetingJobs.com	www.meetingjobs.com
Multiunitjobs.com	www.multiunitjobs.com
National Association of Executive Secretaries and Administrative Assistants	www.naesaa.com/verifjb.asp
National Society of Hispanic MBAs Career Center	www.nshmba.org
New York Black MBA	www.nyblackmba.org/

Notes

Favorite sites, useful resources

Business (continued)

P-Jobs   www.pjobs.org
Pro2Net   www.pro2net.com
Product Development & Management Association   www.pdma.org
ReceptionistJobStore.com   www.receptionistjobstore.com
Red Herring   www.redherring.com
Securities Industry Association
  Career Resource Center   www.sia.com/career
Smart Money   www.smartmoney.com
Society of Competitive Intelligence
  Professionals Job Marketplace   www.scip.org/jobs/index.asp
Strategy+Business   www.strategy-business.com
The Street   www.thestreet.com
TANG   www.stern.nyu.edu/~tang
Top Startups   www.topstartups.com
Upside Today   www.upside.com
VAR Business   www.channelweb.com/
                                                    sections/careers/jobboard.asp
⚑ Vault.com   www.vault.com
WetFeet.com   www.wetfeet.com

-C-

Call Center

CallCenterCareers.com   www.callcentercareers.com
CallCenterJob.ca [Canada]   www.callcenterjob.ca
CallCenterJobs.com   www.callcenterjobs.com
CallCenterProfi.de [Germany]   www.callcenterprofi.de
Teleplaza   www.teleplaza.com/jp.html

Career Counseling/Job Search Services

America's Career InfoNet   www.acinet.org
American Evaluation Associaton   www.kistcon.com/jobbank
American Job Search Trainers   www.ajst.org
Association of Career Professionals International www.iacmp.org
Association of Graduate Careers
  Advisory Service [United Kingdom]   www.agcas.org.uk
BlueSteps.com   www.bluesteps.com
BrainBench   www.brainbench.com
Canadian Association of Career Educators
  & Employers   www.cacee.com
CanadianCareers.com   www.canadiancareers.com
CareerDNA   www.careerdna.com

Notes

Favorite sites, useful resources

Career Counseling/Job Search Services (continued)

CareerFlex.com	www.careerflex.com
CareerHarmony.com	www.careerharmony.com
Career Management International	www.cmi-lmi.com
CareerVoyages.gov	www.careervoyages.gov
ComputerPsychologist.com	www.computerpsychologist.com
Computing Technology Industry Association	
Career Compass	http://tcc.comptia.org
Cool Choices	www.coolchoices.com
CVTips.com [United Kingdom]	www.cvtips.com
DDI	http://ddiworld.com
eLance	www.elance.com
Eliyon	www.eliyon.com
The Engineering Specific Career Advisory	
Problem-Solving Environment	www.ecn.purdue.edu/escape
ePredix	www.epredix.com
Executive Agent	www.executiveagent.com
ExecutiveResumes.com	www.executiveresumes.com
ExecutiveTalent.net	www.executivetalent.net
Exxceed	www.exxceed.com
FreeLancingProjects.com	www.freelancingprojects.com
GetHeadHunted [United Kingdom]	www.getheadhunted.co.uk
Get Me A Job	www.getmeajob.com
GotResumes.com	www.gotresumes.com
Gray Hair Management LLC	www.grayhairmanagement.com
Guru.com	www.guru.com
Hoovers Online	www.hoovers.com
JibberJobber.com	www.jibberjobber.com
JobConnect.org	www.jobconnect.org
Jobfiler.com	www.jobfiler.com
Job Hunter's Bible	www.jobhuntersbible.com
JobSearchNews.com	www.jobsearchnews.com
JobseekersAdvice.com [United Kingdom]	www.jobseekersadvice.com
JobStar	www.jobstar.org
JustCareersUSA.com	www.justcareersusa.com
The Limited	www.thelimited.com
The Momentum Journey	www.themomentumjourney.org
National Association of Colleges & Employers	www.jobweb.com
NavAgility LLC	www.navagility.com
Kaplan Career Services	www.kaplan.com
LiveCareer.com	www.livecareer.com
National Association for College	
Admission Counseling Career Opportunities	www.nacac.com/classifieds.cfm
National Association of Colleges &	
Employers (NACE)	www.nacelink.com
National Board for Certified Counselors	www.nbcc.org

Notes

Favorite sites, useful resources

Career Counseling/Job Search Services (continued)

National Career Development Association — www.ncda.org
ThePhoenixLink.com — www.thephoenixlink.com
Ready Minds — www.readyminds.com
RealContacts.com [New Zealand] — www.realcontacts.com
Real-Home-Employment — www.real-home-employment.com
RentaCoder.com — www.rentacoder.com
ResumeBlaster — www.resumeblaster.com
ResumeXPRESS — www.resumexpress.com
Resume Monkey — www.resumemonkey.com
Resume Network — www.resume-network.com
The Resume Place, Inc. — www.resume-place.com
ResumeRabbit.com — www.resumerabbit.com
Resumes on the Web — www.resweb.com
Resume Workz — www.resumeworkz.com
The Riley Guide — www.rileyguide.com
Salary.com — www.salary.com
Skill Scape — www.skillscape.com
SoloGig — www.sologig.com
▨ Vault.com — www.vault.com
WEDDLE's Newsletters, Guides
  & Directories — **www.weddles.com**
Wetfeet.com — www.wetfeet.com
WorkMinistry.com — www.workministry.com

Chemistry

American Chemical Society Chemistry.org — www.acs.org
American Chemical Society Rubber Division — www.rubber.org
American Association of — www.asbcnet.org/SERVICES/
  Brewing Chemists —   career.htm
American Association of Cereal Chemists — www.aaccnet.org/membership/
    careerplacement.asp

American Association for Clinical Chemistry — www.aacc.org
American Chemical Society cen-chemjobs.org — www.cen-chemjobs.org
American Institute of Chemical Engineers
  Career Services — www.aiche.org/careers
The American Institute of Chemists — www.theaic.org
Chem Jobs — www.chemjobs.net
ChemPeople.com [United Kingdom] — www.chempeople.com
ChemPharma.org — www.chempharma.org
Chem Web — www.chemweb.com
Chememploy — www.chemploy.com
Chemist Jobs — www.chemistjobs.com
Chemistry & Industry — www.chemind.org/CI/
    jobs/index.jsp

Notes

Favorite sites, useful resources

Chemistry (continued)

Chemistry & Industry Magazine http://pharma.mond.org
iHireChemists.com www.ihirechemists.com
Intratech www.intratech1.com
Jobscience Network www.jobscience.com
Poly Sort www.polysort.com
Organic Chemistry Jobs Worldwide www.organicworldwide.net/
  [Belgium] jobs/jobs.html
Science Careers www.sciencecareers.org
Sciencejobs.com www.sciencejobs.com
Scijobs.org www.scijobs.org
PlasticsJobsForum.com www.plasticsjobsforum.com

Child & Elder Care

AuPair In Europe www.planetaupair.com/
  aupaireng.htm
CareGuide www.careguide.net
4Nannies.com www.4nannies.com
SitterByZip www.sitterbyzip.com/

Classifieds-Newspaper

National
The Wall Street Journal www.wsj.com
USA Today www.usatoday.com

Alabama
Birmingham News www.bhnews.com
Huntsville Times www.htimes.com

Alabama (continued)
Mobile Register Online www.mobileregister.com
Montgomery Advertiser www.montgomeryadvertiser.com
The Tuscaloosa News www.tuscaloosanews.com

Alaska
Anchorage Daily News www.adn.com/classified/
  employment
Fairbanks Daily News http://fairbanks.abracat.com
Frontiersman www.frontiersman.com/class
Juneau Empire www.juneauempire.com
Nome Nugget www.nomenugget.com

Notes

Favorite sites, useful resources

Classifieds-Newspaper (continued)

Arizona
Arizona Daily Sun (Flagstaff)   www.azdailysun.com
The Daily Courier (Prescott)   www.prescottaz.com
East Valley Tribune (Mesa)   www.arizonatribune.com
Phoenix News Times   www.phoenixnewstimes.com
Today's News-Herald (Lake Havasu City)   www.havasunews.com

Arkansas
Arkansas Democrat (Little Rock)   www.ardemgaz.com
Benton Courier   www.bentoncourier.com
Jonesboro Sun   www.jonesborosun.com
Ozark Spectator   www.ozarkspectator.com
The Sentinel-Record (Hot Springs)   www.hotsr.com

California
BayAreaClassifieds.com   www.bayareaclassifieds.com
Inland Valley Daily Bulletin   www.dailybulletin.com
Los Angeles Daily News   www.dailynews.com
Los Angeles Times   www.latimes.com
Mercury News (San Jose)   www.bayarea.com
Orange County Register   www.ocregister.com
Pasadena Star-News   www.pasadenastarnews.com
Press Telegram of Long Beach   www.presstelegram.com
Redlands Daily Facts   www.redlandsdailyfacts.com
Sacramento Bee   www.sacbee.com
San Bernadino Sun   www.sbsun.com
San Francisco Chronicle   www.sfgate.com
San Gabirel Valley Tribune   www.sgvtribune.com
Whittier Daily News   www.whittierdailynews.com

Colorado
Aspen Daily News   www.aspendailynews.com
Colorado Springs Independent   www.csindy.com
The Daily Sentinel (Grand Junction)   www.gjsentinel.com
Denver Post   www.denverpost.com
Durango Herald   www.durangoherald.com

Connecticut
The Advocate (Stamford)   www.stamfordadvocate.com
Danbury News-Times   www.newstimes.com
TheDay.com (New London)   www.theday.com
Hartford Courant   www.ctnow.com
New Haven Register   www.newhavenregister.com
Waterbury Republican American   wws.rep-am.com

Notes

Favorite sites, useful resources

Classifieds-Newspaper (continued)

Delaware
Dover Post www.doverpost.com
The News Journal (Wilmington) www.delawareonline.com

District of Columbia
The Washington Post www.washingtonpost.com
Washington Times www.washtimes.com

Florida
Florida Times Union (Jacksonville) www.jacksonville.com
Miami Herald www.miami.com
Orlando Sentinel www.orlandosentinel.com
Pensacola News Journal www.pensacolanewstimes.com
St. Petersburg Times www.sptimes.com

Georgia
The Albany Herald www.albanyherald.net/
  classbrowse.htm
Atlanta Journal and Constitution www.ajcjobs.com
Augusta Chronicle www.augustachronicle.com
Macon Telegraph www.macon.com
Savannah Morning News www.savannahnow.com

Hawaii
Hawaii Tribune-Herald (Hilo) www.hilohawaiitribune.com
Honolulu Advertiser www.honoluluadvertiser.com
Honolulu Star-Bulletin www.starbulletin.com
Maui News www.mauinews.com
West Hawaii Today (Kailua) www.westhawaiitoday.com

Idaho
Cedar Rapids Gazette www.gazetteonline.com
The Daily Nonpareil (Council Bluffs) www.nonpareilonline.com
Des Moines Register www.dmregister.com
Quad City Times (Davenport) www.qctimes.com
Sioux City Journal www.trib.com/scjournal

Illinois
Chicago Tribune www.chicagotribune.com
The Daily Register (Canton) www.cantondailyledger.com
Herald & Review (Decatur) www.herald-review.com
The News-Gazette (Champaigne) www.news-gazette.com
Register-News (Mount Vernon) www.register-news.com
The State Journal Register (Springfield) www.sj-r.com

Notes

Favorite sites, useful resources

Classifieds-Newspaper (continued)

Indiana
The Herald-Times (Bloomington)   www.heraldtimejonline.com
Indianapolis Star News   www.indystar.com
The News-Sentinel (Fort Wayne)   www.fortwayne.com
Post-Tribune (Gary)   www.post-trib.com
South Bend Tribune   www.sbinfo.com

Kansas
Daily Union (Junction City)   www.dailyu.com
Kansas City Kansan   www.kansascitykansan.com
Salina Journal   www.saljournal.com
The Topeka Capital Journal   www.cjonline.com
Wichita Eagle   www.kansas.com

Kentucky
The Courier-Journal (Louisville)   www.courier-journal.com
The Daily News (Bowling Green)   www.bgdailynews.com
Grayson County News-Gazette (Leitchfield) www.gcnewsgazette.com
Lexington Herald Leader   www.kentucky.com
Sentinel News (Shelbyville)   www.shelbyconnect.com

Louisiana
The Advocate (Baton Rouge)   www.advocate.com
The Jackson Independent (Jonesboro) www.jackson-ind.com
The Times (Shreveport)   www.shreveporttimes.com
The Times-Picayune (New Orleans)   www.nola.com

Maine
Bangor Daily News   www.bangornews.com
Kennebec Journal (Augusta)   www.kjonline.com
Lewiston Sun Journal   www.sunjournal.com
Portland Press Herald   www.portland.com
The Times Record (Brunswick)   www.timesrecord.com

Maryland
Baltimore Sun   www.sunspot.net
The Capital (Annapolis)   www.hometownannapolis.com
The Herald-Mail (Hagerstown)   www.herald-mail.com
Maryland Times-Press (Ocean City)   www.marylandtimespress.com
The Star Democrat (Easton)   www.stardem.com

Massachusetts
The Boston Globe   www.boston.com
The Eagle-Tribune (Lawrence)   www.eagletribune.com
The Sun (Lowell)   www.lowellsun.com

Notes

Favorite sites, useful resources

Classifieds-Newspaper (continued)

Massachusetts (continued)
The Salem News — www.salemnews.com
Union-News & Sunday Republican (Springfield) — www.masslive.com

Michigan
Ann Arbor News — www.annarbornews.com
Detriot Free Press — www.freep.com
Flint Journal — www.flintjournal.com
Grand Rapids Press — www.gr-press.com
Lansing State Journal — www.lansingstatejournal.com

Minnesota
Duluth News-Tribune — www.duluthsuperior.com
Elk River Star News — www.erstarnews.com
The Journal (New Ulm) — www.oweb.com/newulm
Minneapolis Star Tribune — www.startribune.com
Saint Paul Pioneer Press — www.twincities.com

Mississippi
The Clarion Ledger (Jackson) — www.clarionledger.com
Meridian Star — www.meridianstar.com
The Natchez Democrat — www.natchezdemocrat.com
The Sun Herald (Biloxi) — www.sunherald.com
The Vicksburg Post — www.vicksburgpost.com

Missouri
The Examiner (Independence) — www.examiner.net
Hannibal Courier-Post — www.hannibal.net
Jefferson City News Tribune — www.newstribune.com
Joplin Globe — www.joplinglobe.com
Springfield News-Leader — www.springfieldnews-leader.com

Montana
Billings Gazette — www.billingsgazette.com
Bozeman Daily Chronicle — www.gomontana.com
Helena Independent Record — www.helenair.com
Missoulian — www.missoulian.com
The Montana Standard (Butte) — www.mtstandard.com

Nebraska
Columbus Telegram — www.columbustelegram.com
Lincoln Journal Star — www.journalstar.com
North Platte Telegraph — www.nptelegraph.com
Omaha World-Herald — www.omaha.com
Scotts Bluff Star-Herald — www.starherald.com

Notes

Favorite sites, useful resources

Classifieds-Newspaper (continued)

Nevada
Elko Daily Free Press	www.elkodaily.com
Las Vegas Review-Journal	www.lvrj.com
Las Vegas Sun	www.lasvegassun.com
Nevada Appeal (Carson City)	www.nevadaappeal.com
Reno Gazette Journal	www.rgj.com

New Hampshire
Concord Monitor	www.concordmonitor.com
Keene Sentinel	www.keenesentinel.com
Portsmouth Herald	www.seacoastonline.com
The Telegraph (Nashua)	www.nashuatelegraph.com
The Union Leader (Manchester)	www.theunionleader.com

New Jersey
Asbury Park Press	www.app.com
Courier-Post (Cherry Hill)	www.courierpostonline.com
The Montclair Times	www.montclairtimes.com
The Star Ledger (Newark)	www.nj.com
The Trentonian	www.trentonian.com

New Mexico
Albuquerque Journal	www.abqjournal.com
The Gallup Independent	www.gallupindependent.com
Los Alamos Monitor	www.lamonitor.com
Santa Fe New Mexican	www.sfnewmexican.com
The Silver City Daily Press	www.thedailypress.com

New York
Albany Democrat Herald	www.dhonline.com
Ithaca Times	www.ithacatimes.com
New York Post	www.nypost.com
The New York Times	www.nytimes.com
Syracuse New Times	www.newtimes.com

North Carolina
Charlotte Observer	www.charlotte.com
Greensboro News-Record	www.news-record.com
News & Observer (Raleigh)	www.newsobserver.com
Wilmington Star	www.wilmingtonstar.com
Winston-Salem Journal	www.journalnow.com

North Dakota
Bismarck Tribune	www.bismarcktribune.com
Grand Forks Herald	www.grandforks.com

Notes

Favorite sites, useful resources

Classifieds-Newspaper (continued)

North Dakota (continued)
The Jamestown Sun   www.jamestownsun.com
Minot Daily News   www.minotdailynews.com

Ohio
Cincinnati Enquirer   www.enquirer.com
The Cleveland Nation   www.clnation.com
Columbus Dispatch   www.dispatch.com
Dayton Daily News   www.daytondailynews.com
Springfield News Sun   www.springfieldnewssun.com

Oklahoma
Altus Times   www.altustimes.com
Lawton Constitution   www.lawton-constitution.com
The Oklahoman (Oklahoma City)   www.newsok.com
Ponca City News   www.poncacitynews.com
Tulsa World   www.tulsaworld.com

Oregon
East Oregonian (Pendleton)   www.eonow.com
The Oregonian (Portland)   www.oregonian.com
The Register-Guard (Eugene)   www.registerguard.com
Springfield News   www.hometownnews.com
Statesman Journal (Salem)   www.statesmanjournal.copm

Pennsylvania
Erie Daily Times-News   www.goerie.com
The Philadelphia Inquirer   www.philly.com
Pittsburg Post-Gazette   www.post-gazette.com
Scranton Times Tribune   www.scrantontimes.com
The Times Leader (Wilkes Barre)   www.timesleader.com

Rhode Island
The Narragansett Times (Wakefield)   www.narragansetttimes.com
The Pawtucket Times   www.pawtuckettimes.com
Providence Journal Bulletin   www.projo.com
Sakonnet Times (Portsmouth)   www.eastbayri.com

South Carolina
Camden Chronicle Independent   www.chronicle-independent.com
Free Times (Columbia)   www.free-times.com
The Greenville News   www.greenvilleonline.com
The Post and Courier (Charleston)   www.charleston.net
The Sun Times (Myrtle Beach)   www.myrtlebeachonline.com

Notes

Favorite sites, useful resources

Classifieds-Newspaper (continued)

South Dakota
Argus Leader (Sioux Falls)   www.argusleader.com
Brookings Daily Register   www.brookingsregister.com
The Capital Journal (Pierre)   www.capjournal.com
The Freeman Courier   www.freemansd.com
Huron Plainsman   www.plainsman.com

Tennessee
Chattanooga Times Free Press   www.timesfreepress.com
Daily Post-Athenian   www.dpa.xtn.net
Knoxville News Sentinel   www.knoxnews.com
Memphis Flyer   www.memphisflyer
The Tennessean (Nashville)   www.onnashville.com

Texas
Austin American-Statesman   www.austin360.com
Dallas Morning News   www.dallasnews.com
El Paso Times   www.elpasotimes.com
Houston Chronicle   www.chron.com
San Antonio Express News   www.mysanantonio.com

Utah
The Daily Herald (Provo)   www.harktheherald.com
Herald Journal (Logan)   www.hjnews.com
Salt Lake Tribune   www.sltrib.com
Standard-Examiner (Ogden)   www.standard.net

Vermont
Addison County Independent (Middlebury)   www.addisonindependent.com
Burlington Free Press   www.burlingtonfreepress.com
Deerfield Valley News (West Dover)   www.dvalnews.com
Stowe Reporter   www.stowereporter.com
Valley News (White River Junction)   www.vnews.com

Virginia
The Daily Progress (Charlottesville)   www.dailyprogress.com
Danville Register Bee   www.registerbee.com
The News-Advance (Lynchburg)   www.newsadvance.com
Richmond Times-Dispatch   www.timesdispatch.com
Virginian-Pilot (Norfolk)   www.pilotonline.com

Washington
The Columbian (Vancouver)   www.columbian.com
The News Tribune (Tacoma)   www.tribnet.com
The Olympian (Olympia)   www.theolympian.com

Notes

Favorite sites, useful resources

Classifieds-Newspaper (continued)

Washington (continued)
Seattle Post-Intelligencer	www.seattlepi.nwsource.com
The Spokesman-Review (Spokane)	www.spokane.net

West Virginia
Charlestown Daily Mail	www.dailymail.com
Clarksburg Exponent Telegram	www.cpubco.com
The Dominion Post (Morgantown)	www.dominionpost.com
Times West Virginian (Fairmont)	www.timeswv.com
Wheeling News-Register	www.news-register.com

Wisconsin
Green Bay Press Gazette	www.greenbaypressgazette.com
The Journal Times (Racine)	www.journaltimes.com
La Crosse Tribune	www.lacrossetribune.com
Milwaukee Journal Sentinel	www.jsonline.com
Wisconsin State Journal (Madison)	www.madison.com

Wyoming
Douglas Budget	www.douglas-budget.com
Wyoming Tribune-Eagle	www.wyomingnews.com

College/Internships/Entry Level/Graduate School Graduates

Entry-Level
Aboutjobs.com	www.aboutjobs.com
Adguide's Employment Web Site	www.adguide.com
AfterCollege.com	www.aftercollege.com
THE BLACK COLLEGIAN Online	www.blackcollegian.com
Campus Career Center	www.campuscareercenter.com
CampusRN.com	www.campusrn.com
Canadian Association of Career Educators & Employers	www.cacee.com
Career Chase	www.careerchase.net
Career Conferences	www.careerconferences.com
Career Connections	www.resumeexpert.com
Career Explorer	http://cx.bridges.com
Careerfair.com	www.careerfair.com
College Central Network	www.collegecentral.com
CollegeGrad.com	www.collegegrad.com
College Job Board	www.collegejobboard.com
CollegeJournal.com	www.collegejournal.com
College News Online	www.collegenews.com/home_shop.asp
College PowerPrep	www.powerprep.com

Notes

Favorite sites, useful resources

College/Internships/Entry Level/Graduate School Graduates (con't)

Entry Level (Continued)

CollegeRecruiter.com	www.collegerecruiter.com
Colleges	www.colleges.com
eCampusRecruiter.com	www.ecampusrecruiter.com
EntryLevelJobs.net	www.entryleveljobs.net
Experience	www.experience.com
GetaLife.org.uk [United Kingdom]	www.getalife.co.uk
Graduating Engineer & Computer Careers Online	www.graduatingengineer.com
Gradunet [United Kingdom]	www.gradunet.co.uk
TheJobBox.com	www.thejobbox.com
job-hunt.org	www.job-hunt.org
JobPostings.net	www.jobpostings.net
Mapping Your Future	www.mapping-your-future.org
MBAGlobalNet	www.mbaglobalnet.com
MBAmatch.com [United Kingdom]	www.mbamatch.com
MBA Style Magazine	http://members.aol.com/ mbastyle/web/index.html
Monster Campus	http://campus.monster.com/
National Association of Colleges & Employers (NACE)	www.nacelink.com
National Society of Collegiate Scholars Career Connection	www.nscs.org/ CareerConnections/index.cfm
National Society of Hispanic MBAs Career Center	www.nshmba.org
New York Black MBA	www.nyblackmba.org/
OverseasJobs.com	www.overseasjobs.com
Peterson's	www.petersons.com
Princeton Review Online	www.princetonreview.com/cfe/
Prospects.ac.uk [United Kingdom]	www.prospects.ac.uk
Reference Now	www.referencenow.com
⧄ SallieMae/TrueCareers	www.truecareers.com
Search4Grads.com [United Kingdom]	www.search4grads.com
Snag A Job	www.snagajob.com
Student Affairs	www.studentaffairs.com

Internships

InternJobs.com	www.internjobs.com
Internship Programs	www.internshipprograms.com
Internships	www.internships.com
Internships4You	www.internships4you.com
Internweb	www.internweb.com
Paid Internships	www.paidinternships.com

Summer Jobs

Around Campus	www.aroundcampus.com
College Club	www.collegeclub.com

Notes

Favorite sites, useful resources

.

College/Internships/Entry Level/Graduate School Graduates (con't)

Summer Jobs (Continued)

CollegeJobs.co.uk [United Kingdom]	www.collegejobs.co.uk
CoolWorks	www.coolworks.com
NeedBeerMoney.com	www.needbeermoney.com
ResortJobs.com	www.resortjobs.com
Student Awards	www.studentawards.com
StudentJobs.gov	www.studentjobs.gov
Study Abroad	www.studyabroad.com
SummerJobs.com	www.summerjobs.com
Super College	www.supercollege.com
TechStudents.net	www.techstudents.net
Teens 4 Hire	www.teens4hire.org
TenStepsforStudents.org	www.tenstepsforstudents.org
University Links	www.ulinks.com
Youth@Work	www.youthatwork.org

College/University Affiliated

California State University - Chico	www.csuchico.edu/plc/jobs.html
Career Development Center at Rensselier Polytechnic Institute	www.cdc.rpi.edu
Case Western Reserve University	www.cwru.edu
The Catholic University of America Career Services Office	http://careers.cua.edu/
Clemson University	www.clemson.edu
Cornell Career Services	http://student-jobs.ses. cornell.edu
Drake University	www.drake.edu
Drexel University	www.drexel.edu/scdc/
Duke University Job Resources	http://career.studentaffairs.duke.edu
Emory University Rollins School of Public Health	www.sph.emory.edu/ studentservice
Foothill-De Anza Community College	www.foothill.fhda.edu
Georgia State University Career Services	www.gsu.edu/dept/admin/plc/ homepage4.html
Georgia Tech Career Services Office	www.career.gatech.edu
Loyola College	www.loyola.edu/thecareercenter/ index.html
Nova Southeastern University	www.nova.edu
Oakland University	www2.oakland.edu/ careerservices
Profiles Database	www.profilesdatabase.com
Purdue University Management Placement Office	www.mgmt.purdue.edu/ departments/gcs/
San Francisco State University Instructional Technologies	www.itec.sfsu.edu

Notes

Favorite sites, useful resources

College/Internships/Entry Level/Graduate School Graduates (con't)

College/University Affiliated (Continued)

University of Arkansas	www.uark.edu
U.C. Berkeley Work-Study Programs	http://workstudy.berkeley.edu
University of Virginia Career Planning & Placement	www.virginia.edu/~career
University of Wisconsin-Madison School of Business Career Center	www.bus.wisc.edu/career/ default1.asp
Washington and Lee University	http://www2.wlu.edu
Worcester Polytechnic Institute	www.wpi.edu

Computer
(See High Tech/Technical/Technology and Information Technology/Information Systems)

Computer-Aided Design, Manufacturing & Engineering

American Design Drafting Association	www.adda.org
Auto CAD Job Network	www.acjn.com
CAD Job Mart	www.cadjobmart.com
Computer-Aided Three-Dimensional Interactive Application Job Network	www.catjn.com
e-Architect	www.e-architect.com
IDEAS Job Network	www.ideasjn.com
Just CAD Jobs	www.justCADjobs.com
Manufacturing Jobs	www.mfgjbs.com
Manufacturing.Net	www.manufacturing.net
Pro/E Job Network	www.pejn.com
UG Job Network (Unigraphics)	www.ugjn.com

Construction (See also Engineering)

A/E/C JobBank	www.aecjobbank.com
American Society of Professional Estimators	www.aspenational.com
Bconstructive [United Kingdom]	www.bconstructive.co.uk
BigBuilderJobs.com	www.bigbuilderjobs.com
BuilderJobs.com	www.builderjobs.com
Builder Online	www.builder.hw.net
Building.com	www.building.com
Careers In Construction	www.careersinconstruction.com
CarpenterJobs.com	www.carpenterjobs.com
Construction/Careers	www.construction.com
ConstructionEducation.com	www.constructioneducation.com
Construction Gigs	www.constructiongigs.com
ConstructionJobs.com	www.constructionjobs.com
ConstructionJobsNow.co.uk [United Kingdom]	www.constructionjobsnow.co.uk
ConstructionOnly.com	www.constructiononly.com
Electrical Employment	www.cossin.com/page3.html

Notes

Favorite sites, useful resources

Construction (continued)

Engineering News Record	www.enr.com
Environmental Construction Engineering Architectural Jobs Online	www.eceajobs.com
Estimator Jobs	www.estimatorjobs.com
HelmetstoHardhats.com	www.helmetstohardhats.com
HomeBuilderJobs.com	www.bigbuildercareers.com
HVACagent.com	www.hvacagent.com
HVAC Mall	www.hvacmall.com
iHireBuildingTrades.com	www.ihirebuildingtrades.com
iHireConstruction.com	www.ihireconstruction.com
Just Construction [United Kingdom]	www.justconstruction.net
Jobsite.com	www.jobsite.com
Maintenance Engineer	www.maintenance employment.com
Materials Jobs	www.welding-engineer.com
MEPatwork.com [mechanical, electrical, plumbing]	www.mepatwork.com
Metal Working Portal	http://metal-working.tradeworlds.com
MyConstructionJobs.net	www.myconstructionjobs.net
National Association of Women in Construction	www.nawic.org
Plumbing Careers	www.plumbingcareers.com
PLUMBjob.com	www.plumbjob.com
ProjectManagerJobs.com	www.projectmanagerjobs.com
QCEmployMe.com	www.qcemployme.com
ReferWork-Jobs.com	www.referwork-jobs.com
Right of Way	www.rightofway.com
SuperintendentJobs.com	www.superintendentjobs.com
TradesJobs.com	www.tradesjobs.com
Trade Jobs Online	www.tradejobsonline.com
UtilityJobSearch.com [United Kingdom]	www.utilityjobsearch.com
Utility Jobs Online	www.utilityjobsonline.com
Welding Jobs	www.weldingjobs.com

Consultants

AndersenAlumni.net	www.andersenalumni.net
Association of Management Consulting Firms	www.amcf.org
Career Lab	www.careerlab.com
❖ Computerwork.com	www.computerwork.com
ConsultLink.com	www.consultlink.com
ConsultantsBoard.com [United Kingdom]	www.consultantsboard.com
Consulting Magazine	www.consultingmag.com
GenerationMom.com	www.generationmom.com
HotGigs.com	www.hotgigs.com
Independent Human Resource Consultants Association	www.ihrca.com/ Contract_Regular.asp

Notes

Favorite sites, useful resources

Consultants (continued)

The Independent Consultants Network	www.inconet.com
Medical Consultants Network	www.mcn.com
Top-Consultant.com	www.top-consultant.com
TrainingConsortium.com	www.trainingconsortium.com

Contract Employment/Part Time Employment (See also Search Firms)

Ants	www.ants.com
BookaTemp.co.uk [United Kingdom]	www.bookatemp.co.uk
Camp Jobs	www.campjobs.com
Camp Staff	www.campstaff.com
CanadaParttime.com [Canada]	www.canadaparttime.com
Contract Employment Weekly Jobs Online	www.ceweekly.com
Contract Engineering.com	www.contractengineering.com
Contract Job Hunter	www.cjhunter.com
Contracts247 [United Kingdom]	www.contracts247.co.uk
Creative Freelancers	www.freelancers.com
DoAAProject.com	www.doaproject.com
eMoonlighter	www.emoonlighter.com
ExperienceNet.com	www.experiencenet.com
ForContractRecruiters.com	www.forcontractrecruiters.com
FreeAgent.com	www.freeagent.com/Myhome.asp
Free Agent Nation	www.freeagentnation.com
Freelance Work X	www.freelancework exchange.com
Freelancers/TalentX	www.talentx.com
Guru.com	www.guru.com
Hands on Solutions [United Kingdom]	www.handsonsolutions.com
Homeworkers	www.homeworkers.com
HotGigs.com	www.hotgigs.com
☒ JobsinLogistics.com	www.jobsinlogistics.com
Labor Ready	www.laborready.com
LifeguardingJobs.com	www.lifeguardingjobs.com
Mediabistro	www.mediabistro.com
NeedBeerMoney.com	www.needbeermoney.com
☒ Net-Temps.com	www.net-temps.com
Roadwhore	www.roadwhore.com
Sheet Metal and Air Conditioning Contractor's Association	www.smacna.org
Snag A Job	www.snagajob.com
Sologig	www.sologig.com
Subcontract.com	www.subcontract.com
Summer Jobs	www.summerjobs.com
TelecommutingJobs	www.tjobs.com

Notes

Favorite sites, useful resources

Contract Employment/Part Time Employment (continued)

TemporarEASE.com	www.temporarease.com
Temps Online.co.uk [United Kingdom]	www.tempsonline.co.uk
Tempz	www.tempz.com
Training Consortium	www.trainingconsortium.net
U Bid Contract Contracting Portal	www.ubidcontract.com

Cosmetology

BehindtheChair.com	www.behindthechair.com
MyHBAJobs.net	www.myhbajobs.net
SalonEmployment.com	www.salonemployment.com
SalonJobStore	www.salonjobstore.com

Culinary/Food Preparation (See also Hospitality)

American Association of Brewing Chemists	www.scisoc.org
American Association of Cereal Chemists	www.scisoc.org
American Culinary Federation	www.acfchefs.org
Bakery-Net	www.bakerynet.com
BookaChef.co.uk [United Kingdom]	www.bookachef.co.uk
Careers in Food	www.careersinfood.com
Caterer.com [United Kingdom]	www.caterer.com
Chef Jobs Network	http://chefjobsnetwork.com
Escoffier Online	www.escoffier.com
FineDiningJobs.com	www.finediningjobs.com
Food And Drink Jobs.com	www.foodanddrinkjobs.com
Food Industry Jobs	www.foodindustryjobs.com
iHireChefs.com	www.ihirechefs.com
Restaurant Careers	www.restaurant-careers.com
Restaurant Jobs	www.restaurantjobs.com
SommelierJobs.com	www.sommelierjobs.com
Star Chefs	www.starchefs.com

-D-

Data Processing

Black Data Processing Association Online	www.bdpa.org
DataNewsJobs.com [Belgium]	www.datanewsjobs.com
Database Analyst	www.databaseanalyst.com
☒ Dice	www.dice.com
Jobvertise	www.jobvertise

Notes

Favorite sites, useful resources

Defense (See also Military Personnel Transitioning into the Private Sector)

AeroIndustryJobs.com	www.areoindustryjobs.com
ClearanceJobs.com	www.clearancejobs.com
ClearedConnections.com	www.clearedconnections.com
DefenseJobsBlog	www.defensejobsblog.com
The Defense Talent Network	www.defensetalent.com
⚑ Dice	www.dice.com
GovJobs.com	www.govjobs.com
IntelligenceCareers.com	www.intelligencecareers.com
National Defense Industrial Association	www.defensejobs.com
SecurityClearanceJobsBlog	www.securityclearancejobs blog.com
SpaceJobs.com	www.spacejobs.com
USDefenseJobs.com	www.usdefensejobs.com
U.S. Department of Defense	http://dod.jobsearch.org

Dental

American Dental Hygienists' Association	www.adha.org/careerinfo
California Dental Hygienists' Association	http://cdha.org/employment
DentalJobs.com	www.dentaljobs.com
Foothill College Biological & Health Sciences	www.foothill.edu/bio/jobs.shmtl
iHireDental.com	www.ihiredental.com
JobDental.com	www.jobdental.com
JobDentist.com	www.jobdentist.com
JobDentistry.com	www.jobdentistry.com
JobHygienist.com	www.jobhygienist.com
MedHunters Dental Hygiene	www.medhunters.com/jobs/ Dent_Hyg.html
Medical-Dental-Hospital Business Associateion	www.mdhbaorg
OverseasDentist.com	www.overseasdentist.com
SmileJobs.com	www.smilejobs.com

Diversity

Diversity-General

Affirmative Action Register	www.aar-eeo.com
Best Diversity Employers	www.bestdiversityemployers.com
Career Moves	www.jvsjobs.org
CommunityConnectJobs.com	www.communityconnectjobs.com
Corporate Diversity Search	www.corpdiversitysearch.com
DiversityAlliedHealth.com	www.diversityalliedhealth.com
Diversity Careers	www.diversitycareers.com
Diversity Central	www.diversityhotwire.com
Diversity Employment	www.diversityemployment.com
Diversity Events	www.diversityevents.com

Notes

Favorite sites, useful resources

Diversity (continued)

Diversity-General (continued)

DiversityInc.com	www.diversityinc.com
DiversityJobFairs.com	www.diversityjobfairs.com
Diversity Job Network	www.diversityjobnetwork.com
DiversityLink	www.diversitylink.com
Diversity Search	www.diversitysearch.com
DiversityZone.com	www.diversityzone.com
Equal Opportunity Publications, Inc.	www.eop.com
HireDiversity.com	www.hirediversity.com
IMDiversity.com	www.imdiversity.com
Jobs4Diversity.com	www.jobs4diversity.com
LeadingDiversity.com	www.leadingdiversity.com
MinnesotaDiversity.com	www.minnesotadiversity.com
The Multicultural Advantage	www.tmaonline.net
National Diversity Newspaper Job Bank	www.newsjobs.com
Society for Human Resource Management Diversity Page	www.shrm.org/diversity/

Age

Canada's Fifty-Plus	www.fifty-plus.net
Fifty On [United Kingdom]	www.fiftyon.co.uk/frameset.asp
Fifty Something Jobs	www.fiftysomethingjobs.com
Forty Plus	www.fortyplus.org
GeezerJobs.com	www.geezerjobs.com
National Commission on Aging	www.ncoa.org
RetiredBrains	www.retiredbrains.com
RetirementJobs.com	www.retirementjobs.com

Bilingual Persons

Asia-Net	www.asia-net.com
BilingualCareer.com	www.bilingualcareer.com
Bilingual-Jobs	www.bilingual-jobs.com
CHALLENGEUSA	www.challengeusa.com
Eflweb	www.eflweb.com
Euroleaders	www.euroleaders.com
Hispanic Chamber of Commerce JobCentro	www.jobcentro.com/jobcentro/ index.asp
iHispano	www.ihispano.com
⌦ LatPro	www.latpro.com
National Society of Hispanic MBAs Career Center	www.nshmba.org
SaludosWeb	www.saludos.com
Society of Hispanic Professional Engineers Career Services	www.shpe.org
Spanish JobSite	www.gojobsite.es
TopLanguageJobs.co.uk [United Kingdom]	www.toplanguagejobs.co.uk

Notes

Favorite sites, useful resources

Diversity (continued)

Ethnicity

Afro-Americ@	www.afro.com
Alianza (Latino)	www.alianza.org
Asia-Net	www.asia-net.com
AsianAvenue.com	www.asianavenue.com
Association of Latino Professionals	
in Finance & Accounting Job Postings	www.alpfa.org
Black Career Women Online	www.bcw.org
THE BLACK COLLEGIAN Online	www.blackcollegian.com
Black Data Processing Association Online	www.bpda.org
Black Enterprise Magazine Career Center	www.blackenterprise.com
Blackgeeks	www.blackgeeks.com
BlackPlanet.com	www.blackplanet.com
Black Voices	www.blackvoices.com
Black World	www.blackworld.com
The Black World Today	http://tbwt.com
Chicago Chinese Computing Professional Assn	www.cccpa.org
El Nuevo Herald	www.elherald.com
Ethnicity	www.ethnicity.com
GoldSea	www.goldsea.com
HierosGamos	www.hg.org
Hispanic American Police Command Officers	
Association	www.hapcoa.org
Hispanic Business.com	www.hispanicbusiness.com/
Hispanic Chamber of Commerce	www.jobcentro.com/jobcentro/
JobCentro	index.asp
Hispanic-Jobs.com	www.hispanic-jobs.com
Hispanic Online	www.hispaniconline.com
iHispano.com	www.ihispano.com
Job Latino	www.joblatino.com
JournalismNext.com	www.journalismnext.com
LatinoHire.com	www.latinohire.com
Latinos in Information Sciences and Technology	
Association	www.a-lista.org
⚉ LatPro	www.latpro.com
MiContacto	www.micontacto.com
MiGente.com	www.migente.com
Minorities Job Bank	www.iminorities.com
Minority Career Network	www.minoritycareernet.com
MinorityNurse.com	www.minoritynurse.com
Minority Professional Network	www.minorityprofessional
	network.com
National Association of Hispanic Nurses	
Houston Chapter	www.nahnhouston.org

Notes

Favorite sites, useful resources

Diversity (continued)

Ethnicity (continued)

National Association of African Americans in Human Resources	www.naaahr.org
National Association of Black Accountants, Inc. Career Center	www.nabainc. jobcontrolcenter.com
National Association of Hispanic Publications Online Career Center	www.nahp.org
National Black MBA Association, Inc.	www.nbmbaa.org
National Black MBA Association New York Chapter	www.nyblackmba.org
National Latino Peace Officers Association	www.nlpoa.org
National Organization of Black Law Enforcement Executives	www.noblenational.org
National Organization for Professional Advancement of Black Chemists and Chemical Engineers University of Michigan Chapter	www.engin.umich.edu/ soc/nobcche
National Society of Black Engineers	www.nsbe.org
National Society of Hispanic MBAs Career Center	www.nshmba.org
National Urban League	www.nul.org
NativeAmericanJobs.com	www.nativeamericanjobs.com
NetNoir	www.netnoir.com
Saludos Web Site	www.saludos.com
Society of Hispanic Professional Engineers Career Services	www.shpe.org
Society of Mexican American Engineers and Scientists	www.maes-natl.org
US Empleos	www.usempleos.com

Gender

The Ada Project	http://tap.mills.edu/ employment.jsp
AdvancingWomen.net	www.advancingwomen.net
American Society of Women Accountants Employment Opportunities	www.aswa.org/i4a/pages/ index.cfm?pageid=3281
Association for Women in Communications	www.womcom.org
Association for Women in Computing	www.awc-hq.org
Career Women	www.careerwomen.com
DCWebWomen	www.dcwebwomen.com
Electra	http://electra.com
Feminist Majority Foundation Career Center	www.feminist.org/911/jobs/ 911jobs.asp
Financial Women International Careers	www.fwi.org/careers/careers.htm
GetaMom.com	www.getamom.com
Healthcare Businesswomen's Association	www.hbanet.org

Notes

Favorite sites, useful resources

Diversity (continued)

Gender (continued)

JobsandMoms.com	www.jobsandmoms.com
Jobs 4 Women	http://jobs4women.com
National Association of Women in Construction	www.nawic.org
National Female Executives	www.nafe.com
National Network of Commercial Real Estate Women Job Bank	www.nncrew.org/job_bank/ job_bank_introduction_frm.html
WomenSportsJobs.com	www.womensportjobs.com
Women's Sport Services	www.wiscnetwork.com
Sistahspace	www.sistahspace.com
Society of Women Engineers Career Services	www.societyofwomenengineers .org/specialservices/ careerservices.aspx
Webgrrls International	www.webgrrls.com
Women.com	www.women.com
Women Connect.com	www.womenconnect.com
Women In Communications Washington, D.C. Chapter	www.awic-dc.org
Women in Federal Law Enforcement	www.wifle.com
WomenforHire.com	www.womenforhire.com
Women in Technology	www.worldWIT.org
Women in Technology International (WITI) 4Hire	www.witi4hire.com
Women Work! The National Network for Women's Employment	www.womenwork.org
Women's Executive Network	www.thewen.com
Women's Finance Exchange	www.wfedallas.org
WomensJobList.com	www.womensjoblist.com
WomensJobSearch.net	www.womensjobsearch.net
WomenSportsJobs.com	www.womensportjobs.com
Women's Sport Services	www.wiscnetwork.com
Women's Wear Daily	www.wwd.com
Womens-work	www.womans-work.com
Women Executives in Public Relations	www.wepr.org
Worksfm.com [United Kingdom]	www.worksfm.com

National Origin

VISA Jobs	www.h1visajobs.com/

Physical Disability

Disability Job Site	www.disabilityjobsite.com
disABLEDperson.com	www.disabledperson.com
Job Ability	www.jobability.com
Job Accommodation Network	http://janweb.icdi.wvu.edu
NBDC	www.business-disability.com

Notes

Favorite sites, useful resources

Diversity (continued)

Physical Disability (continued)

New Mobility	www.newmobility.com
Return 2 Work	www.r2w.org

Religion

Christian Jobs Online	www.christianjobs.com
Jewish Vocational Service Jobs Page	www.jvsjobs.org

Sexual Orientation

GayWork.com	www.gaywork.com
Pride Source	www.pridesource.com

Veterans

Army Career & Alumni Program	www.acap.army.mil
Blue-to-Gray	www.bluetogray.com
Center for Employment Management	www.cemjob.com
Classified Employment Web-Site	www.yourinfosource.com/ CLEWS
ClearanceJobs.com	www.clearancejobs.com
ClearedStars.com	www.clearedstars.com
Connecting Corporations to the Military Community	www.vets4hire.com
Corporate Gray Online	www.corporategrayonline.com
The Defense Talent Network	www.defensetalent.com
Green-to-Gray	www.greentogray.com
HelmetstoHardhats.com	www.helmetstohardhats.com
Hire Quality	www.hire-quality.com
HireVetsFirst.gov	www.hirevetsfirst.gov
Jobs4Vets.com	www.jobs4vets.com
Military.com	www.military.com
Military Careers	www.militarycareers.com
Military Connection	www.militaryconnection.com
Military Connections	www.militaryconnections.com
MilitaryHire.com	www.militaryhire.com
Mil2civ.com	www.mil2civ.com
MilitaryExits	www.militaryexits.com
Military JobZone	www.militaryjobzone.com
Military Spouse Corporate Career Network	www.msccn.org
Military Spouses	www.militaryspouses.com
Military Spouse Job Search	www.militaryspousejobsearch.org
MilitaryStars.com	www.militarystars.com
My Future	www.myfuture.com
Operation Transition	www.dmdc.osd.mil/ot
RecruitAirForce.com	www.recruitairforce.com

Notes

Favorite sites, useful resources

Diversity (continued)

Veterans (continued)

RecruitMarines.com	www.recruitmarines.com
RecruitMilitary.com	www.recruitmilitary.com
RecruitNavy.com	www.recruitnavy.com
Reserve Officers Association	www.roa.org/career_center.asp
Stripes.com	www.stripes.com
Transition Assistance Online	www.taonline.com
Veterans Today	www.veteranstoday.com
⌘ VetJobs.com	www.vetjobs.com
Vets of Color	www.vetsofcolor.com

-E-

Economists

American Agriculatural Economics Association	www.aaes.org
E-JOE: European Job Opportunites for Economists	http://rfe.org/JobGrant/index.html
Inomics	www.inomics.com
JobSlide.com	http://jobslide.com/directory/ FinanceIns/Economist/
JOE: Job Opportunities for Economists	http://www.eco.utexas.edu/joe/

Education/Academia

About.com	www.about.com/careers
Academe This Week	www.chronicle.com
Academic Employment Network	www.academploy.com
Academic Physician & Scientist	www.acphysci.com
Academic Position Network	www.apnjobs.com
Affirmative Action Register	www.aar-eeo.com
American Agricultural Economic Association Employment Service	www.aaea.org/classifieds
American Bankruptcy Institute Career Center	www.abiworld.org/abi careercenter
American Educational Research Association Job Openings	www.aera.net/jobposts/
American Institute of Physics Career Services	www.aip.org/careersvc
American Psychological Society Observer Job Listings	www.psychologicalscience.org/ jobs
ArtJob Online	www.artjob.com
Association for Environmental and Outdoor Education	www.aeoe.org

Notes

Favorite sites, useful resources

Education/Academia (continued)

Association of Graduate Careers
  Advisory Service [United Kingdom] — www.agcas.org.uk
The Association for Institutional Research — www.airweb.org/
  page.asp?page=2
Association of Teachers of — http://english.ttu.edu/attwtest/
  Technical Writing — default.asp
Association of University Teachers
  [United Kingdom] — www.AUT4Jobs.com
ATeacherJobSearch.com — www.ateacherjobsearch.com
Canadian Society of Biochemistry and
  Mollecular and Cellular Biologists — www.medcor.mcgill.ca/EXPMED/
  Experimental Medicine Job Listing — DOCS/index.html
ccJobsOnline.com — www.ccjobsonline.com
The Chronicle of Higher Education
  Academe This Week — http://chronicle.merit.edu/jobs
College and University Personnel Association — www.cupahr.org/
  JobLine — jobline
Community Learning Network — www.cln.org
Computing Research Association — www.cra.org/jobs/
  Job Announcements — main/cra.jobs.html
Council for Advancement & Support
  of Education Jobs Online — www.case.org/jobs
Dave's ESL Café — www.eslcafe.com
The Directory Recruitment Service — www.thedirectory.aone.net.au/
  [Australia] — page8.htm
e-Math — www.ams.org
Education America Network — www.educationamerica.net
Education Week on the Web — www.edweek.org
Education World Jobs — www.education-world.com/jobs
EducatorJob.com — www.educatorjob.com
EFLWEB: English as a Second or
  Foreign Language — www.eflweb.com
The ESL Café's Job Center — www.pacificnet.net/~sperling/
  jobcenter.html
ESL Worldwide — www.eslworldwide.com
FEcareers.co.uk [United Kingdom] — www.fecareers.co.uk
FEjobs.com [United Kingdom] — www.fejobs.com
Foothill-De Anza Community — www.fhda.edu/district/hr/
  College District — employment.html
GeoWebServices-RocketHire — www.geowebservices.com
GreatInfo.com — www.greatinfo.com/
  business_cntr/career.html
Hire-Ed — www.hireed.net
Higher Careers.com — www.highercareers.com
HigherEdJobs.com — www.higheredjobs.com

Notes

Favorite sites, useful resources

Education/Academia (continued)

History of Science Society	www.hssonline.org
Hudson Institute	www.hudson.org
Independent School Management	www.isminc.com/mm.html
International Academic Job Market [Australia]	http://jobreview.camrev.com.au
Jaeger's Ince-Math	www.ams.org/employment
JOE: Job Opportunities for Economists	www.eco.utexas.edu/joe
Jobs in Linguistics	www.linguistlist.org/ jobsindex.html
Jobs.ac.uk [United Kingdom]	www.jobs.ac.uk
K-12 Jobs	www.k12jobs.com
Massachusetts Environmental Education Society	www.massmees.org
Math-Jobs	www.math-jobs.com
The Minerals, Metals, Materials Scoiety JOM	www.tms.org/pubs/journals/JOM/ classifieds.html
MinorityNurse.com	www.minoritynurse.com
Music Library Association Job Placement	www.music.indiana.edu/ Som/placement/index.html
MyEducationJobs.net	www.myeducationjobs.net
NationJob Network-Education Job Openings	www.nationjob.com/education
National Association for College Admission Counseling Career Opportunities	www.nacac.com/classifieds.cfm
National Council of Teachers of Math Jobs	www.nctm.org
National Information Services and Systems [United Kingdom]	www.hero.ac.uk/uk/home/ index.cfm
National Teacher Recruitment	www.recruitingteachers.com
National Women's Studies Association	www.nwsa.org
New England Higher Education Recruitment Consortium	www.faculty.harvard.edu/ 01/013.html
The New Jersey Higher Education Recruitment Consortium	www.njherc.com
North American Association for Environmental Education	www.ee-link.net
Now Hiring Teachers	www.nowhiringteachers.com
PhDjobs.com	www.phdjobs.com
Phds.org	http://phds.org
PLATO	www.skillsnet.com
SchoolSpring.com	www.schoolspring.com
School Staff	www.schoolstaff.com
Superintendent Jobs	www.superintendentjobs.com
Teacher Jobs	www.teacherjobs.com
Teachers of English to Speakers of Other Languages Job Finder	www.tesol.org

Notes

Favorite sites, useful resources

Education/Academia (continued)

THESIS: The Times Higher Education Supplement InterView Service [United Kingdom]	www.thesis.co.uk
University of Illinois at Urbana-Champaign Grad School of Library & Information Science Placement Online-Library Job Service	www.lis.uiuc.edu/gslis/ job_board.html
University of Wisconsin School of Education Placement and Career Services	http://careers.soemadison. wisc.edu
University Job Bank	www.ujobbank.com

Employee Referral

ForumJobs.com	www.forumjobs.com
G2Bay.com	www.g2bay.com
H3.com	www.h3.com
HeadlessHunter.com	www.headlesshunter.com
Interview Exchange ReferredHire	www.interviewexchange.com
Jobkabob	www.jobkabob.com
Jobster	www.jobster.com
JobThread.com	www.jobthread.com
KarmaOne.com	www.karmaone.com

Energy

Energy Careers	www.energycareers.com
Drilling Research Institute Classifieds	www.drillers.com/classifieds.cfm
Electric Job.com	www.electricjob.com
Electric Net	www.electricnet.com
NukeWorker.com	www.nukeworker.com
Oil & Gas Jobs	www.earthworks-jobs.com/ comm.htm
Oil Career	www.oilcareer.com
Oil Industry Jobs	www.oilsurvey.com
Oil Job	www.oiljob.com
PennEnergyJobs.com	www.pennenergyjobs.com
Power Magazine	www.powermag.com
Power Online	www.poweronline.com
Utility Jobs Online	www.utilityjobsonline.com

Engineering

Engineering-General

A1A Jobs	www.a1ajobs.com
All4Engineers.de [Germany]	www.all4engineers.de
AmericanJobs.com	www.americanjobs.com
American Society of	www.asae.org/membership/

Notes

Favorite sites, useful resources

Engineering (continued)

Engineering-General (continued)

Career Marketplace Network	www.careermarketplace.com
Degree Hunter	www.degreehunter.com
⚲ Dice	www.dice.com
Discover Jobs	www.discoverjobs.com
Engineer.net	www.engineer.net
EngineerJobs.com	www.engineerjobs.com
Engineering Central	www.engcen.com/jobbank.htm
Engineering Classifieds	www.engineeringclassifieds.com
Engineering Giant	www.engineergiant.com
Engineering Institute of Canada	www.eic-ici.ca
Engineering Job Source	www.engineerjobs.com
EngineeringJobs.com	www.engineeringjobs.com
Engineering News Record	www.enr.com
Engineer Web	www.engineerweb.com
The Engineering Specific Career	
Advisory Problem-Solving Environment	www.ecn.purdue.edu/escape
The Engineering Technology Site [United Kingdom]	www.engineers4engineers.co.uk
iHireEngineering.com	www.ihireengineering.com
interEC.net	www.interec.net
Job Net	www.jobnet.org
Job Search for Engineers	www.interec.net
Jobs 4 Engineers	www.ajob4engineers.com
Jobs4Engineering.com	www.jobs4eng.com
MyEngineeringJobs.net	www.myengineeringjobs.net
National Society of Professional Engineers	www.nspe.org/
Employment	em-home.asp
National Technical Services Association	www.ntsa.com
Pro/E Job Network	www.pejn.com
ReferWork-Jobs.com	www.referwork-jobs.com
Tech Employment	www.techemployment.com
Worldwide Worker	www.worldwideworker.com

Aeronautical/Aviation

Aeroindustryjobs	www.aeroindustryjobs.com
Aeronautical Engineering Jobs [United Kingdom]	www.aeronauticalengineeringjobs .co.uk
Aerospace Jobs	http://hometown.aol.com/ aerojobs
AeroSpaceNews.com	www.aerospacenews.com

Agricultural

American Society of	www.asae.org/membership/
Agricultural Engineering	career.html

Notes

Favorite sites, useful resources

Engineering (continued)

Agricultural (continued)

American Society of Agricultural and
  Biological Engineers — www.asabe.org

Chemical

American Chemical Society
  cen-chemjobs.org — www.cen-chemjobs.org
American Institute of Chemical Engineers
  Career Services — www.aiche.org/careers
Chemical Engineer — www.chemicalengineer.com
National Organization for Professional
  Advancement of Black Chemists and
  Chemical Engineers — www.engin.umich.edu/
  University of Michigan Chapter —   soc/nobcche

Civil

American Society of Civil Engineers — www.asce.org
Civil Engineering Jobs — www.civilengineeringjobs.com
CIVILjobs.com — www.civiljobs.com
iCivil Engineer — www.icivilengineer.com/jobs

Construction

A/E/C Job Bank — www.aecjobbank.com
CED Magazine — www.cedmagazine.com
PlumbingCareers.com — www.plumbingcareers.com
PLUMBjob.com — www.plumbjob.com
Utility Jobs Online — www.utilityjobsonline.com

Diversity

National Society of Black Engineers — www.nsbe.org
Society of Hispanic Professional Engineers
  Career Services — www.shpe.org
Society of Mexican American Engineers
  and Scientists — www.maes-natl.org
Society of Women Engineers Career Services — www.societyofwomenengineers
  .org/specialservices/
  careerservices.aspx

Electrical/Electronics

EDN Access — www.ednmag.com
eeProductCenter — http://cmpmedia.globalspec.com
EE Times — www.eet.com
Electric Job.com — www.electricjob.com
Electric Net — www.electricnet.com
Electrical Engineer — www.electricalengineer.com

Notes
Favorite sites, useful resources

Engineering (continued)

Electrical/Electronic (continued)

ElectricalJobs — http://erecruitingsolutions/
typepad.com/electricaljobs/

Electronic News Online — www.electronicnews.com
Institute of Electrical & Electronics
  Engineers Job Site — www.ieee.org/jobs
National Electrical Contractors Association — www.necanet.org
RF Globalnet — www.rfglobalnet.com
Test & Measurement World — www.tmworld.com
UG Job Network
  (Unigraphics CAD/CAM/CAE) — www.ugjn.com
Yaps4u.net — www.yaps4u.net

Environmental

Environmental Construction Engineering
  Architectural Jobs Online — www.eceajobs.com
GeoWebServices-RocketHire — www.geowebservices.com

Industrial/Manufacturing

iHireManufacturingEngineers.com — www.ihiremanufacturing
engineers.com

Industrial Engineer — www.industrialengineer.com
NukeWorker.com — www.nukeworker.com
Plastic Pro — www.plasticpro.com
Plastics Jobs Forum.com — www.plasticsjobsforum.com
Product Design and Development Online
  Career Center — www.manufacturing.nt/dn
Power Magazine — www.powermag.com

Mechanical

American Society of Mechanical Engineers
  Career Center — www.asme.org/jobs
Jobs for Mechanical Engineers — www.mechanicalengineer.com
The Mechanic — www.the-mechanic.com/jobs.html
Mechanical Engineers Magazine Online — www.memagazine.org

Mining/Petroleum

Drilling Research Institute Classifieds — www.drillers.com/classifieds.cfm
Job Oil — www.joboil.com
The Minerals, Metals, Materials Society
  JOM — www.tms.org/pubs/journals/JOM/
classifieds.html
Oil & Gas Jobs — www.earthworks-jobs.com/
comm.htm
Oil Career — www.oilcareer.com
Oil Industry Jobs — www.oilsurvey.com

Notes

Favorite sites, useful resources

Engineering (continued)

Mining/Petroleum (continued)
Oil Job — www.oiljob.com

Software
CadJobMart — www.cadjobmart.com
Career Center @ Semiconductor Online — www.semiconductoronline.com
Computer-Aided Three-Dimensional
  Interactive Application Job Network — www.catjn.com
Semi Web — www.semiweb.com/employment

Systems
The Instrumentation, Systems and
  Automation Society Online ISA Jobs — www.isa.org/isa_es
Society for Information Display — http://www.sid.org/jobmart/jobmart.html
Systems Engineer — www.systemsengineer.com

Transportation
Right Of Way — www.rightofway.com
Roadwhore — www.roadwhore.com
Society of Automotive Engineers Job Board — www.sae.org/careers/recruitad.htm
Society of Naval Architects and Marine Engineers — www.sname.org

Other Specialty
Biomedical Engineering Society — www.bmes.org
CFD Online
  (Computational Fluid Dynamics) — www.cfd-online.com
Contract Employment Weekly — www.ceweekly.com
Contract Engineering.com — www.contractengineering.com
Graduating Engineer & Computer Careers Online — www.graduatingengineer.com
International Society for Pharmaceutical
  Engineering — www.ispe.org
National Association of Grad & Prof Students — www.nagps.org
National Association of Radio and
  Telecommunications Engineers — www.narte.org
ScientistWorld.com [United Kingdom] — www.scientistworld.com
Space Jobs — www.spacejobs.com
SPIE Web-International Society for
  Optical Engineering — www.spieworks.com
Wireless Design Online — www.wirelessdesignonline.com

Looking for a new or better job?   Looking for top talent?
Use WEDDLE's publications. Visit www.weddles.com today.

Notes

Favorite sites, useful resources

Entertainment/Acting

4 Entertainment Jobs	www.4entertainmentjobs.com
Airwaves Media Web	www.airwaves.com
Airwaves Media Web	www.airwaves.com
Answers4Dancers.com	www.answers4dancers.com
ArtJob Online	www.artjob.org
Backstage.com	www.backstage.com
CareerFilm.com	www.careerfilm.com
Casting-America	www.casting-america.com
Casting Daily	www.castingnet.com
Designer Max	www.designermax.com
Electronic Media	www.emonline.com
Entertainment Careers	www.entertainmentcareers.net
EntertainmentJobs.com	www.eej.com
Employment Network	www.employnow.com
Filmbiz.com	www.filmbiz.com
Hollywood Web	www.hollywoodweb.com
Media Communications Association International Job Hotline	www.mca-i.org
National Association of Broadcasters	www.nab.org
New England Film	www.newenglandfilm.com/ jobs.htm
Open Casting.com	www.opencasting.com
Opportunities Online [United Kingdom]	www.opps.co.uk
PlanetSharkProductions.com	www.planetsharkproductions.com
Playbill On-Line	www.playbill.com
Radio Online	www.radio-online.com
Showbizjobs.com	www.showbizjobs.com
Show Biz Data	www.showbizdata.com
Society of Broadcast Engineers	www.sbe.org
Tech TV	www.techtv.com
Theatre Jobs	www.theatrejobs.com
TVjobs.com	www.tvjobs.com
VarietyCareers.com	www.varietycareers.com
Voice of Dance	www.voiceofdance.com

Environmental

American College of Occupational and Environmental Medicine	www.acoem.org
American Water Works Association Career Center (Water Jobs)	www.awwa.org
Association for Environmental and Outdoor Education	www.aeoe.org
APSnet-Plant Pathology Online	www.apsnet.org
Earthworks	www.earthworks-jobs.com

Notes

Favorite sites, useful resources

Environmental (continued)

EE-Link: The Environmental Education Web Server	www.nceet.snre.umich.edu/jobs.html
EHScareers.com	www.ehscareers.com
EnviroNetwork	www.environetwork.com
EnvironmentalCareer Center	www.environmentalcareer.com
Environmental Career Opportunities	www.ecojobs.com
Environmental Careers Bulletin Online	www.ecbonline.com
Environmental Careers Organization	www.eco.org
Environmental Careers World	www.environmental-jobs.com
Environmental Construction Engineering Architectural Jobs Online	www.eceajobs.com
Environmental Data Interactive Exchange Job Centre [United Kingdom]	www.edie.net
Environmental Employment Pages	www.datacor.com/employment.shtml
Environmental Engineer	www.environmentalengineer.com
Environmental Jobs & Careers	www.ejobs.org
Environmental Nes	www.enn.com
EnviroWorld	www.enviroworld.com
GeoWebServices-RocketHire	www.geowebservices.com
GIS Jobs Clearinghouse	www.gjc.org
GreenBiz.com Joblink	www.greenbiz.com/jobs
Green Dream Jobs	www.sustainablebusiness.com
Job.com	www.job.com/main.html
Massachusetts Environmental Education Society	www.massmees.org
National Environmental Health Association	www.neha.org
Nevada Mining	www.nevadamining.org
North American Association for Environmental Education	www.ee-link.net
Pollution Online	www.pollutiononline.com
Power Online	www.poweronline.com
Public Works	www.publicworks.com
Pulp & Paper Online	www.pulpandpaperonline.com
Solid Waste	www.solidwaste.com
Student Conservation Association	www.thesca.org
TechSavvy.com	www.techsavvy.com
Universities Water Information Network	www.ucowr.siu.edu
Water Online	www.wateronline.com

Equipment Leasing

Equipment Leasing Association	www.elaonline.com
Jobvertise	www.jobvertise.com
Leasing News	http://64.125.68.90/LeasingNews/JobPosting.htm

Notes

Favorite sites, useful resources

Exchanges-Recruiter/Employer/Job Seeker

@Recruiter.com	www.atrecruiter.com
Avoxa.com	www.avoxa.com
Cand-ex.com	www.cand-ex.com
Dealsplit.com	www.dealsplit.com
eLance	www.elance.com
FreelancingProjects.com	www.freelancingprojects.com
Guru.com	www.guru.com
HotGigs	www.hotgigs.com
RentaCoder.com	www.rentacoder.com
Sologig.com	www.sologig.com

Executive/Management

Executive-General

Blue Steps	www.bluesteps.com
Boardseat	www.boardseat.com
⊠ CareerJournal.com	www.careerjournal.com
CFO.com	www.cfo.com
CFO Jobsite	www.cfojobsite.com
CIO	http://jobs.cio.com
CIO Wanted	http://jobs.cio.com
Exec2Exec.com [United Kingdom]	www.exec2exec.com
Execs on the Net [United Kingdom]	www.eotn.co.uk
⊠ ExecuNet	www.execunet.com
execSearches.com	www.execsearches.com
Executive Openings	www.executiveopenings.com
Executive Registry	www.executiveregistry.com
ExecutiveTalent.net	www.executivetalent.net
Executive Taskforce [New Zealand]	http://exectask.co.nz
ExecutiveOpenings.com [United Kingdom]	www.executiveopenings.com
Executive Placement Services	www.execplacement.com
ExecutivesontheWeb.com [United Kingdom]	www.executivesontheweb.com
ExecutivesOnly.com	www.executivesonly.com
NetShare	www.netshare.com
PlatinumJobs.com [United Kingdom]	www.platinumjobs.com
RiteSite.com	www.ritesite.com
Score	www.scn.org/civic/score-online
Seek Executive [Australia]	http://executive.seek.com.au/ index.asp

Management-General

American Economic Development Council	www.aedc.org
American Management Association International	www.amanet.org/

Notes

Favorite sites, useful resources

Executive/Management (continued)

Management-General (continued)

CardBrowser.com	www.cardbrowser.com
CareerFile	www.careerfile.com
Corporate Alumni	www.corporatealumni.com
Eclectic [Netherlands]	www.eclectic.nl
Futurestep	www.futurestep.com
Institute of Management &	
Administration's Supersite	www.ioma.com
Jobs.ac.uk [United Kingdom]	www.jobs.ac.uk
Jobs4Managers.com	www.jobs4managers.com
TheLadders.com	www.theladders.com
Monster Management	http://management.monster.com
Multiunitjobs.com	www.multiunitjobs.com
MyManagementJobs.net	www.mymanagementjobs.net
⇲ 6FigureJobs.com	www.6figurejobs.com
Net Expat	www.netexpat.com
PMjob.ca [Canada]	www.pmjob.ca
Stern Alumni Outreach Career	www.stern.nyu.edu
Zhaopin.com [China]	www.zhaopin.com

Career Field-Specific

CM Today	www.cmcrossroads.com/ubb threads/postlist.php?Cat=& Board=UBB27
Compliance Jobs	www.compliancejobs.com
Financial Executives Institute Career Center	www.fei.org/careers
Ft.com-Financial Times [United Kingdom]	www.ft.com
Hispanic American Police Command Officers Association	www.hapcoa.org
National Organization of Black Law Enforcement Executives	www.noblenational.org
NursingExecutives.com	www.nursingexecutives.com

Industry-Specific

American Bankers Association	http://aba.careerbank.com
American College of Healthcare Executives	http://ache.org
American College of Physician Executives	www.acpe.org
American Society of Association Executives Career Headquarters	www.asaenet.org/ careerheadquarters
boardnetUSA	www.boardnetusa.com
CFO Publishing	http://cfonet.com
HospitalityExecutive.com	www.hospitalityexecutive.com
Medical Group Management Association	www.mgma.com

Notes

Favorite sites, useful resources

Executive/Management (continued)

Industry Specific (continued)

New York Society of Association Executives Career Center	www.nysaenet.org
Women Executives in Public Relations	www.wepr.org
GxPJobs.com [United Kingdom]	www.gxpjobs.com

-F-

Fashion

Atlantic Apparel Contractors Association, Inc.	http://atlanticapparel.com/
Be The 1	www.bethe1.com
Fashion Career Center	www.fashioncareercenter.com
Fashion Group International	www.fgi.org
Fashion Net	www.fashion.net/jobs/ positionso.php
Top Fashion Jobs [United Kingdom]	www.topfashionjobs.com/ jobs.php

Feminism

FeministCampus.org	www.feministcampus.org
Feminist Majority Foundation Online	www.feminist.org
Women's Studies Database	www.inform.umd.edu/EdRes/ Topic/WomensStudies

Fiber Optics

The Fiber Optic Association	www.thefoa.org/foajobs.htm
Fiber Optic Marketplace	www.fiberoptic.com
Fiber Optics Online	www.fiberopticsonline.com

Finance & Accounting (See also Banking, Insurance)

Accounting-General

AccountancyAgeJobs.com [United Kingdom]	www.accountancyagejobs.com
AccountantJobs.com	www.accountantjobs.com
Accountant Jobs Chicago	www.accountantjobschicago.com
AccountManager.com	www.accountmanager.com
Accounting.com	www.accounting.com
Accounting & Finance Jobs	www.accountingjobs.com
Accounting Classifieds	www.accountingclassifieds.com
Accounting Jobs Online	www.accountingjobsonline.com
AccountingNet	www.accountingnet.com

Notes

Favorite sites, useful resources

Finance & Accounting (continued)

Accounting-General (continued)

Accounting Professional	www.accountingprofessional.com
AdvancingWomen.net	www.advancingwomen.net
Ambition [Australia]	www.ambition.com.au
American Accounting Association Web Placement Service	http://aaahq.org/placements/ default.cfm
American Society of Women Accountants Employment Opportunities	www.aswa.org/i4a/pages/ index.cfm?pageid=3281
AndersenAlumni.net	www.andersenalumni.net
Awesome Accountants	www.awesomeaccountants.com
Bean Brains	www.beanbrains.com
CA Magazine	www.camagazine.com
Certified Management Accountants of Canada	www.cma-canada.org
iHireAccounting	www.ihireaccounting.com
Job Serve for Accountancy [United Kingdom]	www.accountancy.jobserve.com
LocalAccountingJobs.com	www.localaccountingjobs.com
MyAccountingJobs.net	www.myaccountingjobs.net
National Association of Black Accountants, Inc. Career Center	www.nabainc. jobcontrolcenter.com
National Society of Accountants	www.nsacct.org

Accountants-Certified Public Accountants

American Association of Hispanic Certified Public Accountants	www.aahcpa.org
American Institute of Certified Public Accountants Career Center	www.cpa2biz.com/ Career/default.htm
CPA Career Center	www.aicpa.com
CPA Jobs	www.cpajobs.com
CPA Online	www.cpaonline.com/
CPANet	www.cpanet.com
Illinois CPA Society Career Center	www.icpas.org/icpas/ career-services/carsrce.asp
Institute of Management Accountants Career Center	www.imanet.org/ima/ sec.asp? TRACKID=&CID=12&DID=12
Inside Careers Guide to Chartered Accountancy [United Kingdom]	www.insidecareers.co.uk
Institute of Chartered Accountants of Alberta [Canada]	www.icaa.ab.ca/ home/index.shtml
Maryland Association of CPAs Job Connect	www.macpa.org/services/ jobconnt/index.htm
New Jersey Society of CPAs	www.njscpa.org
New York State Society of CPAs	www.nysscpa.org/classified/ main.cfm
Tennessee Society of CPA's	www.tscpa.com

Notes

Favorite sites, useful resources

Finance & Accounting (continued)

Audit

AccountantAuditor.net	www.accountantauditor.net
Audit Jobs Chicago	www.auditjobschicago.com
Audit Net	www.auditnet.org
AuditProfessional.com	www.auditprofessional.com
AuditorJobs.com	www.auditorjobs.com
Institute of Internal Auditors Online Audit Career Center	www.theiia.org/careercenter/ index.cfm
InternalAuditJobs.net [United Kingdom]	www.internalauditjobs.net

Brokerage/Investment

Annuitiesnet.com	www.annuitiesnet.com
Association for Investment Management and Research	www.cfainstitute.org
Bond Buyer	www.bondbuyer.com
BrokerHunter.com	www.brokerhunter.com
Canadian Association of Financial Planners	www.cafp.org
International Association for Registered Financial Planners	www.iarfc.org/ jservices.shtml
Investment Management and Trust Exchange	www.antaeans.com
National Venture Capital Association	www.nvca.org
New York Society of Security Analysts Career Resources	www.nyssa.org/jobs
RepsTradingPlaces.com	www.repstradingplaces.com
Securities Industry Association Career Resource Center	www.sia.com/career
Society of Actuaries	www.soa.org
Society of Risk Analysis Opportunities	www.sra.org/opptys.php
Street Jobs	www.streetjobs.com

Finance-General

American Association of Finance & Accounting	www.aafa.com/career.htm
American Bankruptcy Institute Career Center	www.abiworld.org/abi careercenter
Association of Finance Professionals Career Services	www.afponline.org/ careerservices
Association of Latino Professionals in Finance & Accounting Job Postings	www.alpfa.org
Bloomberg.com	www.bloomberg.com/fun/ jobs.html
Business Finance Magazine	www.businessfinancemag.com
Business-Money Magazine	www.business-money.com
☒ CareerBank.com	www.careerbank.com

Notes

Favorite sites, useful resources

Finance & Accounting (continued)

Finance-General (continued)

⊠ CareerJournal.com	www.careerjournal.com
CareerJournal.com Europe	www.careerjournaleurope.com
Careers in Finance	www.careers-in-finance.com
CFO.com	www.cfo.com
CFOEurope.com	www.cfoeurope.com
CFO and CPA Jobs	www.cfoandcpajobs.com
CFO Publishing	http://cfonet.com
⊠ eFinancial Careers [United Kingdom]	www.efinancialcareers.com
eFinancialCareers.fr [France]	www.efinancialcareer.fr
eFinancial Jobs	www.efinancialjobs.com
The Finance Beat	www.search-beat.com/ finance.htm
Finance and Commerce	www.finance-commerce.com
Finance Job Network	www.financialjobnet.com
Finance Job Store	www.financejobstore.com
FinanceJobs.com	www.financejobs.com
Finance Wise	www.financewise.com
Financial Executives Institute Career Center	www.fei.org/careers
Financial Executive Networking Group	www.thefeng.org
Financial Job Network	www.fjn.com
FinancialJobs.com	www.financialjobs.com
Financial Management Association International Placement Services	www.fma.org/2003placement
Financial Managers Society Career Center	www.fmsinc.org/cms/?pid=1025
Financial Positions	www.financialpositions.com
Financial Women International Careers	www.fwi.org/careers/careers.htm
Fortune	www.fortune.com
Ft.com –Financial Times [United Kingdom]	www.ft.com
GAAP Web [United Kingdom]	www.gaapweb.com
Jamie's Jobs Finance Professionals Web in California	www.jamiesjobs.com/ s?k=finance&t=1042147302061
JobWings.ca [Canada]	www.jobwings.ca
JobsFinancial.com [United Kingdom]	www.jobsfinancial.com
⊠ jobsinthemoney.com	www.jobsinthemoney.com
TheLadders.com	www.theladders.com
MyFinanceJobs.net	www.myfinancejobs.net
NationJob Network: Financial Jobs Page	www.nationjob.com/financial

Financial Analysis

Actuary.com	www.actuary.com
Alliance of Merger and Acquisition Advisors	www.advisor-alliance.com
American Association for Budget and Program Analysis	www.aabpa.org/employ.html

Notes

Favorite sites, useful resources

Finance & Accounting (continued)

Financial Analysis (continued)

Capital Markets Credit Analysts Society Resume Service	www.cmcas.org/ resumeservice.asp
CFA Institute	www.cfainstitute.org
Global Association of Risk Professionals Career Center	www.garp.com/ careercenter/index.asp
JobsinRisk.com [United Kingdom]	www.jobsinrisk.com
Risk & Insurance Management Society Careers	www.rims.org/Template.cfm? Section=JobBank1&Template=/ Jobbank/SearchJobForm.cfm
Global Association of Risk Professionals Career Center	www.garp.com/ careercenter/index.asp
Hedge Fund Intelligence LLC [United Kingdom]	www.hedgefundintelligence.com
QuantFinanceJobs.com	www.quantfinancejobs.com
QUANTster.com	www.quantster.com
Toronto Society of Financial Analysts [Canada]	www.tsfa.ca
UnderwritingJobs.com	www.uwjobs.com

Finance-Banking

American Bankers Association	http://aba.careerbank.com
BankingBoard.com	www.bankingboard.com
BankJobs	www.bankjobs.com
CreditJobs.com	www.creditjobs.com
Escrowboard.com	www.escrowboard.com
JobsinCredit.com [United Kingdom]	www.jobsincredit.com
MortgageBoard.com	www.mortgageboard.com
Mortgage Job Store	www.mortgagejobstore.com
National Banking Network	www.banking-financejobs.com
Titleboard.com	www.titleboard.com

Finance-Conptroller

Cash Management Career Center	www.amgi.com
Controller Jobs	www.controllerjobs.com

Finance-Other

Fund Raising Jobs	www.fundraisingjobs.com
IFSjobs.com	www.ifsjobs.com
MBA Careers	www.mbacareers.com
MBA-Exchange.com	www.mba-exchange.com
MBA Free Agents	www.mbafreeagents.com
MBAGlobalNet	www.mbaglobalnet.com
MBAJobs.net	www.mbajobs.net/
MBAmatch.com [England]	www.mbamatch.com

Notes

Favorite sites, useful resources

Finance & Accounting (continued)

Finance-Other (continued)

MBA Style Magazine	http://members.aol.com/ mbastyle/web/index.html
MBATalentWire.com	www.mbatalentwire.com
National Black MBA Association, Inc.	www.nbmbaa.org
National Society of Hispanic MBAs Career Center	www.nshmba.org
Real Estate Finance Jobs	www.realestatefinancejobs.com
Smart Money	www.smartmoney.com

Tax

eTaxjobs.com	www.etaxjobs.com
Tax Jobs	www.taxjobs.com
Tax Jobs Chicago	www.taxjobschicago.com
Tax-Talent.com	www.tax-talent.com

Free Lance/Free Agents

AF Work	www.allfreelancework.com
AllFreeLance.com	www.allfreelance.com
American Society of Journalists & Authors	www.freelancewritersearch.com
Editorial Freelancers Association	www.the-efa.org
eLance	www.elance.com
FreeLanceDaily.com	www.freelancedaily.com
FreeLanceMom.com	www.freelancemom.com
FreelanceWorkExchange.com	www.freelanceworkexchange .com
FreeLanceWriting.com	www.freelancewriting.com
FreeLancers Network [United Kingdom]	www.freelancers.net
FreeLancingProjects.com	www.freelancingprojects.com
Guru.com	www.guru.com
HotGigs.com	www.hotgigs.com
iFreelance.com	www.ifreelance.com
Real-Home-Employment	www.real-home-employment.com
RentaCoder.com	www.rentacoder.com
SoloGig	www.sologig.com
Training Consortium	www.trainingconsortium.net
TelecommutingJObs	www.tjobs.com

Funeral Industry/Services

Abbott and Hast Calssifieds	www.abbottandhast/ classifieds.html
FuneralNet	www.funeralnet.com
FuneralWire.com	www.funeralwire.com
National Funeral Directors Association	www.nfda.org

Notes

Favorite sites, useful resources

-G-

Gaming

BlueFoxJobs.com	www.bluefoxjobs.com
Casino Careers Online	www.casinocareers.com
CroupierLink.com	www.croupierlink.com
Game Jobs	www.gamejobs.com

General

555-1212	www.555-1212.com
About Jobs	www.aboutjobs.com
Abracat	www.abracat.com
ActiJob	www.actijob.com
Action Jobs	www.actionjobs.com
Adguide's Employment Web Site	www.adguide.com
Adquest 3D	www.adquest3d.com/main.cfm
Adsearch	www.adsearch.com
Best Local Jobs	www.bestlocaljobs.com
Advancing Women	www.advancingwomen.com
AECPII	www.aecpii.com
Alianza (Latino)	www.alianza.org
America's Employers	www.americasemployers.com
⧅ America's Job Bank	www.ajb.dni.us
American City Business Journals	www.bizjournalshire.com
AmericanJobs.com	www.americanjobs.com
American Preferred Jobs	www.preferredjobs.com
AmpleJobs	www.amplejobs.com
Ants.com	www.ants.com
Any Who	www.anywho.com
Area Jobs	www.areajobs.com
Asia-Net	www.asia-net.com
Association Job Source	www.jobsourcenetwork.com
AssociationJobBoards.com	www.associationjobboards.com
Available Jobs	www.availablejobs.com
BaseJobs.com [Canada]	www.basejobs.com
BDOJobs.com	www.bdojobs.com
Best.com	www.best.com/index1.shtml
⧅ Best Jobs USA	www.bestjobsusa.com
BigJobs.net	www.bigjobs.net
BigTimeJobs.com	www.bigtimejobs.com
Black Career Women Online	www.bcw.org
THE BLACK COLLEGIAN Online	www.blackcollegian.com
BlowSearch	www.blowsearch.com
Blue Collar Jobs	www.bluecollarjobs.com

Notes

Favorite sites, useful resources

General (continued)

Boldface Jobs	www.boldfacejobs.com
Boston Globe	www.globe.com
Branch Staff Online	www.branchstaffonline.com
Business Week Online	www.businessweek.com/careers
Career.com	www.career.com
⇗ CareerBuilder.com	www.careerbuilder.com
CareerBuzz.com	www.careerbuzz.com
CareerCast	www.careercast.com
Career Center	www.careercenter.com
CareerChase	www.careerchase.net
The Career Connection	www.career-connection.com
Career Engine	www.careerengine
Career Exchange	www.careerexchange.com
CareerExposure	www.careerexposure.com
Careerfile.com	www.careerfile.com
Career Flex	www.careerflex.com
Career Giant	www.careergiant.com
CareerJobPlanet.com [United Kingdom]	www.careerjobplanet.com
⇗ CareerJournal.com	www.careerjournal.com
Career Magazine	www.careermag.com
CareerMart	www.careermart.com
Careermetasearch.com	www.careermetasearch.com
Career Resource Center	www.careers.org
CareerShop	www.careershop.com
Career Span	http://careerspan.com
Careers.org	www.careers.org
Career Surf	http://careersurf.com
Career Talk	www.careertalk.com
CareersMVP.com	www.careersmvp.com
Chain Store Guide	www.csgis.com
Chattanooga Publishing	www.chatpub.com
Chowk	www.chowk.com
City Search.com	www.citysearch.com
Classifieds 2000	www.classifieds2000.com
Community Associations Institute	www.caionline.org
Contract Employment Connection	www.ntes.com
Contract-Jobs.com	www.contract-jobs.com
⇗ craigsList	www.craigslist.org
Creative Hotlist	www.creativehotlist.com
Customer Service Management	www.csm-us.com
Daily Digest	www.le-digest.com
Database America	www.databaseamerica.com
Delphi Forums	www.delphi.com/windowforjobs
DirectEmployers	www.directemployers.com
Direct Job	www.directjob.com

Notes

Favorite sites, useful resources

General (continued)

Direct-jobs.com	www.direct-jobs.com
Direct Mail	www.the-dma.org/cgi/jbsearch
Diversity Careers	www.diversitycareers
Diversity Employment	www.diversityemployment.com
DiversityLink	www.diversitylink.com
Diversity Search	www.diversitysearch.com
eBullpen.com	www.ebullpen.com
e-learning Jobs	www.e-learningjobs.com
ePage Internet Classifieds	http://ep.com
eCom Recruitment	www.ecomrecruitment.com
eJobResource.com	www.ejobresource.com
Employers Online	www.employersonline.com
Employmax	www.employmax.com
Employment	www.employment.com
Employment-inc.com	www.employment-inc.com
Employment 911	www.employment911.com
↘ EmploymentGuide.com	www.employmentguide.com
Employment Spot	www.employmentspot.com
Employment Weekly	www.employment-weekly.com
Employment Wizard	www.employmentwizard.com
eNeighborhoods	www.eneighborhoods.com
The EPages Classifieds	www.ep.com
Experience on Demand	www.experienceondemand.com
FillThatJob.com	www.fillthatjob.com
Finder2000	www.finder2000.com
First Market Research	http://firstmarket.com
FlipDog.com	www.flipdog.com
4 Work	www.4work.com
Fresh Jobs	www.freshjobs.com
Fun Jobs	www.funjobs.com
Future Access Employment Guide	www.futureaccess.com
Garage.com	www.garage.com
Get A Job	www.getajob.com
Get Jobs	www.getjobs.com
Go Ferret Go	www.goferretgo.com
Go Jobs	www.gojobs.com
Google.com	www.google.com
Got A Job	www.gotajob.com
Grass is Greener	www.grassisgreener.com
HeadlessHunter.com	www.headlesshunter.com
The Help Wanted Page	www.helpwantedpage.com
Help-Wanted.net	www.help-wanted.net
Hire.com	www.hire.com
Hire Web	www.hireweb.com
Hiring Network	www.hiringnetwork.com

Notes

Favorite sites, useful resources

General (continued)

Homefair	www2.homefair.com
How2FindAJob.com	www.how2findajob.com
Hot Resumes	www.hotresumes.com
Hennepin County Job Openings	www.co.hennepin.mn.us
123hire.com	www.123hire.com
Hiregate.com	www.hiregate.com
HispanicBusiness.com	www.hispanicbusiness.com
100 Hot	www.100hot.com/jobs
Hottest 100 Job Sites	www.worldhot.com
HRpal.com	www.hrpal.com
Human-Intelligence.com	www.human-intelligence.com
iHireJobNetwork	www.iHireJobNetwork.com
Ideal Jobs.com	www.idealjobs.com
InfoSpace.com	www.infospace.com
Insta Match	www.instamatch.com
International Career Employment Center	www.internationaljobs.org
International Customer Service Association Job Board	http://secure2.neology.com/ICSA/ jobs/employer/welcome.cfm
Internet Career Connection	www.iccweb.com
The Internet Job Locator	www.joblocator.com/jobs
Internet Traffic Report	www.internettrafficreport.com
Iowa Smart Idea	www.smartcareermove.com
I-resign.com	www.i-resign.com
Its Your Job Now	www.itsyourjobnow.com
Job AA	www.jobaa.com
Job Ads1	www.jobads1.com
Job Animal	www.jobanimal.com
JobBank USA	www.jobbankusa.com
Job Catalog	www.jobcatalog.com
JobCenterUSA.com	www.jobcenterusa.com
Job Choices	www.jobweb.org/jconline
Job City USA.com	www.jobcityusa.com
Job.com	www.job.com
JobDiscover.com	www.jobdiscover.com
Job Exchange	www.jobexchange.com
JobFerret.ca [Canada]	www.jobferret.ca
JobFind.com	www.jobfind.com
JobFlash.com	www.jobflash.com
Job Fly	www.jobfly.com
Job Front	www.jobfront.com
Job-Hunt	www.job-hunt.org
Job Hunt	www.jobhunt.com
Jobing.com	www.jobing.com
Job Launch	www.joblaunch.com
Job Lynx	http://joblynx.com

Notes

Favorite sites, useful resources

General (continued)

The Job Market	www.thejobmarket.com
Job Master	www.rvp.com/jh
Job Match	www.jobmatch.com
JobNewsTV.com	www.jobnewstv.com
JobNewsRadio.com	www.jobnewsradio.com
JobPilot.net	www.jobpilot.net
Job Point Connection	www.jobpoint.com
Job Safari	www.jobsafari.com
Job SAT	www.jobsat.com
Job-Search-Engine	www.job-search-engine.com
JobSeekUSA.com	www.jobseekusa.com
Job Sleuth	www.jobsleuth.com
Job Sniper	www.jobsniper.com
JobSpin.com	www.jobspin.com
Job Star	www.jobstar.org
Job Trak	www.jobtrak.com
Jobvertise	www.jobvertise.com
Job Warehouse	www.jobw.com
JobYours.com	www.jobyours.com
Jobby	www.gojobby.com
Jobs Inc.	www.jobsinc.com
Jobs+	www.jobsplus.org
Jobs America	www.us.plusjobs.com
Jobs-Careers	www.jobs-careers.com
Jobs at Corporations	www.searchbeat.com/jobs2.htm
JobsDB [Hong Kong]	www.jobsdb.com
Jobs Made Easy	www.jobsmadeeasy.com
JobsinNewEngland.com	www.jobsinnewengland.com
Jobs Online	www.jobsonline.com
Jobs-Online	www.jobs-online.net
Jobs Posted Free	www.jobspostedfree.com
Jobs on the Web	www.jobsontheweb.com
Jumbo Classifieds	www.jumboclassifieds.com
LatinoWeb	www.latinoweb.com
ꙅ LatPro	www.latpro.com
Liszt	www.liszt.com
LocalOpenings.com	www.localopenings.com
Local Staff	www.localstaff.com
Lycos City Guide	http://cityguide.lycos.com/usa
Mail.com	http://corp.mail.com
MegaJobSites	www.megajobsites.com
Meta Crawler	www.go2net.com/search.html
Minorities Job Bank	www.iminorities.com
Minority Career Network	www.minoritycareernet.com
Monitor	www.monitordaily.com

Notes

Favorite sites, useful resources

General (continued)

⚑ Monster.com	www.monster.com
My Job Search	www.myjobsearch.com
The Nando Times	www.nandotimes.com
NationCareer	www.nationcareer.com
National Diversity Newspaper Job Bank	www.newsjobs.com
NationJob Network	www.nationjob.com
NationJobSearch.com	www.nationjobsearch.com
Nationwide Consultants	www.nationwideconsultants.com
Neighbor Works Net	www.nw.org
NetNoir	www.netnoir.com
⚑ Net-Temps	www.net-temps.com
NewYorkJobs.com	www.newyorkjobs.com
NoMoreHeadhunters.com	www.nomoreheadhunters.com
NowHiring.com	www.nowhiring.com
1to1jobs.com	www.1to1jobs.com
Online-Jobs	www.online-jobs.com
Only-Jobs	www.only-jobs.com
Opportunities-inc.com	www.opportunities-inc.com
PageBites.com	www.pagebites.com
People Bank	www.peoplebank.com/pbank/owa/ pbk06w00.main
People Bonus	www.peoplebonus.com
Personnel Department	www.careermachine.com
Personnel Desk	www.personneldesk.com
Planet Recruit	www.planetrecruit.com
PlugStar.com	www.plugstar.com
Position Filler	www.positionfiller.com
Position Watch	www.positionwatch.com
Pro Hire.com	www.prohire.com
Quintessential Careers	www.quintcareers.com
RecruiterConnection	www.recruiterconnection.com
Recruiting Shark	www.recruitingshark.com
ReferTalent.com	www.refertalent.com
RegionalHelpWanted.com	www.regionalhelpwanted.com
Rep Resources	www.represources.com
ResourceOcean.com	www.resourceocean.com
Resume Blaster	www.resumeblaster.com
ResumeXPRESS	www.resumexpress.com
Resume' Net	www.resumenet.com
ResumeRabbit.com	www.resumerabbit.com
Resumes on the Web	www.resweb.com
Resunet	www.resunet.com
RetiredBrains	www.retiredbrains.com
Revolution.net	www.revolution.net
RSSJobs.com	www.rssjobs.com

Notes

Favorite sites, useful resources

General (continued)

Saludos Web Site	www.saludos.com
Searchease	www.searchease.com
See Me Resumes	www.seemeresumes.com
Select Minds	www.selectminds.com
The Sense Media Surfer	http://sensemedia.net/ employment.edge
Skill Hunter	www.skillhunter.com
Start Up Jobs	www.startupjobs.com
Start Up Zone	www.startupzone.com
Starting Point	www.stpt.com/default.asp
State Jobs	http://statejobs.com
The Sunday Paper	www.sundaypaper.com
SwapJobs.com	www.swapjobs.com
Switchboard	www.switchboard.com
Talentology	www.talentology.com
TargetedJobSites.com	www.targetedjobsites.com
Team Rewards	www.careerrewards.com
TelecommutingJobs	www.tjobs.com
Teleplaza	www.teleplaza.com
TeleportJobs.com	www.teleportjobs.com
Thingama Job	www.thingamajob.com
⚑ TopUSAJobs.com	www.topusajobs.com
Totaljobs.com	www.totaljobs.com
Tribe.net	www.tribe.net
Tripod	http://members.tripod.com
⚑ TrueCareers	www.truecareers.com
Union Jobs Clearinghouse	www.unionjobs.com
United States Department of Labor	www.dol.gov
UpSeek	www.upseek.com
US Jobs	www.usjobs.com
USA Hot Jobs	www.usahotjobs.com
USJobNet.com	www.usjobnet.com
⚑ Vault.com	www.vault.com
Vertical Net	www.verticalnet.com
Virtual Job Fair	www.jobcenter.com
Virtual Recruiting Network	www.dmpmail.com
Virtual Resume	www.virtualresume.com/vitae
Web Crawler	www.webcrawler.com
Web Reference	www.webreference.com/
Wetfeet	www.wetfeet.com
WhoHasJobs.com	www.whohasjobs.com
Womenswire	www.womenswire.com
Work at Home Digest	www.intlhomeworkers.com
WorkGiant.com	www.workgiant.com
WorkLife.com	www.worklife.com

Notes

Favorite sites, useful resources

General (continued)

Work-Web	www.work-web.com
Working.ca [Canada]	www.working.ca
The World Wide Web Employment Office	www.employmentoffice.net
WorldWorkz.com	www.worldworkz.com
⇲ Yahoo! HotJobs	www.hotjobs.com
Yep.com	www.yep.com

Graphic Arts/Electronic & Traditional (See also Journalism & Media)

3D Café	www.3dcafe.com
3Dmax	www.3dmax.com
3DSite	www.3dsite.com
Adrecruiter	www.adrecruiter.com
Advertising-PR.com	www.advertising-pr.com
American Institute of Graphic Arts	www.aiga.org
Animation Industry Database	www.aidb.com
Animation World Network	www.awn.com
Communication Arts Magazine	www.commarts.com
Communications Round Table	www.roundtable.org
CopyEditor.com	www.copyeditor.com
Coroflot	www.coroflot.com
DesignJobs.co.uk [United Kingdom]	www.designjobs.co.uk
Design Management Institute Job Bank	www.dmi.org/dmi/html/ jobbank/jobbank_d.jsp
Design Sphere Online Job Hunt	www.dsphere.net
Desktop Publishing	http://desktoppublishing.com
DigitalMediaJobs.com [United Kingdom]	www.digitalmediajobs.com
FindCreative.com	www.findcreative.com
Freelance BBS	www.freelancebs.com
GamesIndustry.biz	www.gamesindustry.biz
Graphic Artists Guild JobLine	www.gag.org/jobline/index.html
Graphic Artists Information Network	www.gain.org
Graphic Artists Monthly	www.gammag.com
Interior Design Jobs	www.interiordesignjobs.com
MediaKnowledge.com [United Kingdom]	www.mediaknowledge.com
Media Lab	www.media.mit.edu
Media Street.com	www.mediastreet.com
Mip Map	www.mipmap.com
National Assocation of Printing Ink Manufacturers	www.napim.org
New York New Media Association	www.nynma.com/jobs
PaidContent.org	www.paidcontent.org/jobs
Portfolios.com	www.portfolios.com
Print Jobs	www.printjobs.com
PrintWorkers.com	www.printworkers.com
Printing Careers	www.printingcareers.com

Notes

Favorite sites, useful resources

Graphic Arts/Electronic & Traditional (continued)

Screenprinting & Graphic Imaging Association
  International
www.sgia.org/
  employ/employ.html

Silicon Alley
www.siliconalley.com/sa/
  index.cfm

VFXWorld
www.vfxworld.com

-H-

Healthcare/Medical

Healthcare-General

Absolutely Healthcare	www.healthjobsusa.com
Allegheny County Medical Society	www.acms.org
America's Health Care Source	www.healthcaresource.com
Centers for Disease Control	www.cdc.gov
Chicago Medical Society	www.cmsdocs.org
Discover Jobs	www.discoverjobs.com
Employ Med	www.embbs.com/jobs/jobs.html
Find Medical	www.findmedical.com
FocusonHealthcare.com	www.focusonhealthcare.com
Future Med	http://ourworld.compuserve.com/ homepages/futuremed/main.htm
Georgia Department of Human Resources	www.dhrjobs.com
GovMedCareers.com	www.govmedcareers.com
GxPJobs.com [United Kingdom]	www.gxpjobs.com
Harris County Medical Society	www.hcms.org
HealthAndWellnessJobs.com	
Healthcare Businesswomen's Association	www.hbanet.org
HealthcareCareerWeb.com	www.healthcarecareerweb.com
Healthcare Hub	www.healthcarehub.com
Health Care Jobs Online	www.hcjobsonline.com
Health Care Mart	www.healthcaremart.com
Health Care Match	www.healthcarematch.com
Health Care Hiring	www.healthcarehiring.com
Healthcare/Monster	www.healthcare.monster.com
HealthCareRecruitment.com	www.healthcarerecruitment.com
Health Care Seeker	www.healthcareseeker.com
Health Careers	www.healthcareers-online.com
Health Direction	www.healthdirection.com
HealtheHire, Inc.	www.healthehire.com
HealthJobsite.com	www.healthjobsite.com
HealthJobsUSA.com	www.healthjobsusa.com
Health Network USA	www.hnusa.com
Health Seek.com	www.healthseek.com

Notes

Favorite sites, useful resources

Healthcare/Medical (continued)

Healthcare-General (continued)

HealthCare Job Store	www.healthcarejobstore.com
Healthcare Professional Jobs	www.HealthcareProfessional.com
Healthcare Source	www.healthcareresource.com
HealthCareerWeb.com	www.healthcareerweb.com
⚊ HEALTHeCAREERS	www.healthecareers.com
HealthOpps	www.healthopps.com
HireBio.com	www.hirebio.com
HireHealth.com	www.hirehealth.com
HireRX.com	www.hirerx.com
HireMedical.com	www.hiremedical.com
HireNursing.com	www.hirenursing.com
HireCentral.com	www.hirecentral.com
IndianaHealthCareers.com	www.indianahealthcareers.com
JAMACareerNet (Journal & Archives Journals of the American Medical Association)	http://jamacareernet.ama-assn.org
JobHealthCareers.com	www.jobhealthcareers.com
JobMedical.com	www.jobmedical.com
Jobscience Network	www.jobscience.com
Job Span	www.jobspan.com
Jobs4Medical.com	www.jobs4medical.com
JobsinHealth [Ireland]	www.jobsinhealth.ie
Jobs in Healthcare	www.jobsinhealthcare.com
JobsStat.com	www.jobsstat.com
Med Bulletin	http://web.medbulletin.com/webodrome/jobHome.php
Med Careers	www.medcareers.com
Med Connect	www.medconnect.com
Medhunters	www.medhunters.com
MedJobsNow.com	www.medjobsnow.com
MedicSolve.com [United Kingdom]	www.medicsolve.com
MedLaunch	www.medlaunch.com
MedMarket	www.medical-admart.com
Medical AdMart	www.medical-admart.com
Medical Design Online	www.medicaldesignonline.com
MedicalJobList.com	www.medicaljoblist.com
Medical Matrix	www.medmatrix.org/index.asp
Medical Words	www.md123.com
MedicalWorkers.com	www.medicalworkers.com
Medicenter.com	www.medicenter.com
Medi Match	www.medimatch.com
Medi-Smart	www.medi-smart.com/renal4.htm
Medimorphus.com	www.medimorphus.com
MedJobsNow.com	www.medjobsnow.com
MEDSTER.com	www.medster.com

Notes

Favorite sites, useful resources

Healthcare/Medical (continued)

Healthcare-General (continued)

MedWorking.com	www.medworking.com
Medzilla	www.medzilla.com
Modern Healthcare	www.modernhealthcare.com
MyHealthcareJobs.net	www.myhealthcarejobs.net
The National Assembly	www.nassembly.org
National Association for Health Care Recruitment	www.nahcr.com
National Rural Recruitment & Retention Network	www.3rnet.net
New England Journal of Medicine	www.nejm.org
Oklahoma State Medical Association	www.osmaonline.org
Orleans Parish Medical Society	www.opms.org
Texas Medical Association	www.texmed.org
Wisconsin Medical Society	www.wisconsinmedical society.org

Acute Care/Critical Care/Intensive Care

American Association of Critical Care Nurses	www.aacn.org
JobAcuteCare.com	www.jobacutecare.com
JobCriticalCare.com	www.jobcriticalcare.com
JobICU.com	www.jobicu.com
JobIntensiveCare.com	www.jobintensivecare.com

Addiction/Substance Abuse

Addiction Medicine Jobs	www.addictionmedicinejobs.com
Substance Abuse Jobs	www.substanceabusejobs.com

Administration/Management

American College of Healthcare Executives	http://ache.org
American College of Physician Executives	www.acpe.org
Association of Staff Physician Recruiters	www.aspr.org
CareersIntellect.com	www.careersintellect.com
College of Healthcare Information Management Executives	www.cio-chim.org/services/ serv5.asp
Healthcare Information and Management Systems	www.himss.org
Healthline Management	www.hmistl.com
Massachusetts Healthcare Human Resources Association	www.mhhra.org
Medbizpeople.com	www.medbizpeople.com
Medical Case Management Jobs	www.casemanagementjobs.com
Medical-Dental-Hospital Business Associateion	www.mdhbaorg
Medical Group Management Association	www.mgma.com
NursingExecutives.com	www.nursingexecutives.com
Radiology Business Management Association	www.rbma.org

Notes

Favorite sites, useful resources

Healthcare/Medical (continued)

Allied Health
Allied Health Jobs   www.alliedhealthjobs.com
Allied Health Opportunities Directory   www.gvpub.com
DiversityAlliedHealth.com   www.diversityalliedhealth.com
JobAlliedHealth.com   www.joballiedhealth.com

Anethesiology
American Society of PeriAnesthesia Nurses   www.aspan.org
CRNAjobs.com   www.crnajobs.com
Gas Jobs   www.gasjobs.com
IConnect2Anesthesiology.com   www.iconnect2annesthesiology
                                                       .com

Cardiology
American College of Cardiology   www.acc.org
American Associatin of Cardiovascular and
  Pulmonary Rehabilitation   www.aacvpr.org
Cardiologist Jobs   www.cardiologistjobs.com
Cardioworking.com   www.cardioworking.com
JobCardiology.com   www.jobcardiology.com

Equipment-Healthcare
American Medical Technologists   www.amtl.com
Healthcare Information and Management Systems   www.himss.org
iHireMedTechs.com   www.ihiremedtechs.com
Jobaids.com   www.jobaids.com
JobMedTech.com   www.jobmedtech.com
MDL Career Center   http://careercenter.devicelink.com
PharmaOpportunities   www.pharmaopportunites.com

Hospital
Arizona Hospital and Healthcare Association
  AZHealthJobs   www.azhha.org
CareerHospital.com   www.careerhospital.com
Colorado Health and Hospital Association   www.cha.com
Connecticut Hospital Association   www.chime.org
Hospital Hub   www.hospitaljobweb.com
Hospital Jobs Online   www.hospitaljobsonline.com
HospitalSoup.com   www.hospitalsoup.com
Hospital Web   http://neuro.www.mgh.harvard.
                                                       edu/hospitalweb.shtml

JobHospital.com   www.jobhospital.com
MedBizPeople.com   www.medbizpeople.com
Medical-Dental-Hospital Business Associateion   www.mdhbaorg
Society of Hospital Medicine Career Center   www.hospitalmedicine.org

Notes
Favorite sites, useful resources

Healthcare/Medical (continued)

International

CanMed [Canada]	www.canmed.com
DERWeb [United Kingdom]	www.derweb.co.uk
EMBL Job Vacancies [Germany]	www.embl-heidelberg.de/ ExternalInfo/Jobs
HUM-MOLGEN [Germany]	www.hum-molgen.de/positions
Medjobsuk.com [United Kingdom]	www.medjobsuk.com
Opportunities Online [United Kingdom]	www.opps.co.uk

Midwife

American College of Nurse Midwives	www.acnw.org
JobMidwife.com	www.jobmidwife.com
MidwifeJobs	www.midwifejobs.com
NMC4Jobs.com [United Kingdom]	www.nmc4jobs.com
Professional Information from the American College of Nurse-Midwives	www.midwife.org

Nurses/Nursing

Academy of Medical-Surgical Nurses	www.medsurgnurse.org
AllNurses.com	http://allnurses.com
American Academy of Ambulatory Care Nursing	www.aaacn.org
American Academy of Nurse Practitioners	www.aanp.org
American Association of Critical Care Nurses	www.aacn.org
American Association of Occupational Health Nurses	www.aaohn.org
American College of Nurse Midwives	www.acnw.org
American Nurses Association	www.nursingworld.org
American Psychiatric Nurses Association	www.apna.org
American Society of PeriAnesthesia Nurses	www.aspan.org
ANNAlink	http://anna.inurse.com
Association of Perioperative Registered Nurses Online Career Center	www.aorn.org/ Careers/default.htm
Association of Women's health, Obstetric & Neonatal Nurses	www.awhonn.org
CampusRN.com	www.campusrn.com
CareersIntellect.com	www.careersintellect.com
Dermatology Nurses' Association	www.dnanurse.org
GraduateNurse.com	www.graduatenurse.com
Guaranteed Employment Advertising & Resume Service	www.nurse-recruiter.com
HappyCareer.com	www.happycareer.com
HealthJobsUSA.com	www.healthjobsusa.com
HireNursing.com	www.hirenursing.com
Hot Nurse Jobs	www.hotnursejobs.com

Notes

Favorite sites, useful resources

Healthcare/Medical (continued)

Nurses/Nursing (continued)

iHireNursing.com	www.ihirenursing.com
JobCNA.com	www.jobcna.com
JobLPN.com	www.joblpn.com
JobLVN.com	www.joblvn.com
JobNurse.com	www.jobnurse.com
JobNursingAid.com	www.jobnursingaid.com
JobPracticalNurse.com	www.jobpracticalnurse.com
JobPracticioner.com	www.jobpracticioner.com
JobRN.com	www.jobrn.com
JobStaffNurse.com	www.jobstaffnurse.com
Locum Tenens	www.locumtenens.com
National Association of Hispanic Nurses Houston Chapter	www.nahnhouston.org
National Association of Orthopaedic Nurses	www.orthonurse.org
National League for Nursing	www.nln.org
National Rural Recruitment & Retention Network	www.3rnet.net
Nurse Career	www.nursecareer.com
Nurse Director Jobs	www.directorofnursingjobs.com
NurseJobShop.com	www.nursejobshop.com
Nurse Manager Jobs	www.nursemanagerjobs.com
NurseTown.com	www.nursetown.com
NurseUniverse.com	www.nurseuniverse.com
Nurse Zone	www.nursezone.com
Nurseserve [United Kingdom]	www.nurseserv.co.uk
Nurses for a Healthier Tomorrow	www.nursesource.org
Nursing Center	www.nursingcenter.com
NursingExecutives.com	www.nursingexecutives.com
Nursing Hands	www.nursinghands.com
NursingJobs.com	www.nursingjobs.com
NursingMatters.com	www.nursingmatters.com
Nursing Spectrum Career Fitness Online	www.nursingspectrum.com
PDCforNurses.com	www.pdcfornurses.com
Psychiatric Nurse Jobs	www.psychiatricnursejobs.com
RN.com	www.rn.com
Society of Gastroenterology Nurses & Associates	www.sgna.org
TravelNursing.com	www.travelnursing.com
TravelNursingUSA.com	www.travelnursingusa.com

OBGYN

AdvancedPracticeJobs.com	www.advancedpracticejobs.com
American Association of Gynecologic Laproscopists	www.aagl.com

Notes

Favorite sites, useful resources

Healthcare/Medical (continued)

OBGYN (continued)

American College of Obstetricians and Gynecologists	www.acog.org
JobOBGYN.com	www.jobobgyn.com
OBGYNCareer.com	www.obgyncareer.com
Obstetric Jobs	www.obstetricjobs.com

Pediatrics

JobPediatrics.com	www.jobpediatrics.com
Pediatric Jobs	www.pediatricjobs.com

Pharmacist/Pharmacy (See also Pharmaceutical)

American Association of Pharmaceutical Scientists	www.aaps.org
American Pharmaceutical Association	www.aphanet.org
Association for Applied Human Pharmacology [Germany]	www.agah-web.de
CareersIntellect.com	www.careersintellect.com
Cen-ChemJobs.org	www.cen-chemjobs.org
HireHealth.com	www.hirehealth.com
HireRX.com	www.hirerx.com
iHirePharmacy.com	www.ihirepharmacy.com
International Society for Pharmaceutical Engineering	www.ispe.org
Pharmaceutical Rep Jobs	www.pharmaceuticalrepjobs.com
PharmacyWeek	www.pharmacyweek.com
PharmaOpportunities	www.pharmaopportunites.com
RPh on the Go	www.rphonthego.com
RPhRecruiter	www.rphrecruiter.com
RxCareerCenter	www.rxcareercenter.com
Rx Immigration	www.rximmigration.com
RxWebportal	www.rxwebportal.com

Physical Therapy/Occupational Therapy

American Academy of Cardiovascular and Pulmonary Rehabilitation	www.aacvpr.org
American Association of Occupational Health Nurses	www.aaohn.org
American College of Occupational and Environmental Medicine	www.acoem.org
American Occupational Therapy Association	www.aota.org
American Physical Therapy Association	www.apta.org
American Society of Clinical Pharmacology and Therapeutics	www.ascpt.org
PhysicalTherapist.com	www.physicaltherapist.com

Notes

Favorite sites, useful resources

Healthcare/Medical (continued)

Physical Therapy/Occupational Therapy (continued)

Physical Therapist Jobs	www.physicaltherapistjobs.com
PT Central	www.ptcentral.com
Rehab Options	www.rehaboptions.com
TherapyJobs.com	www.therapyjobs.com

Physicians/Physician Assistants

Academic Physician & Scientist	www.acphysci.com
American Academy of Family Physicians	www.fpjobsonline.org
American Academy of Physician Assistants	www.aapa.org
American College of Chest Physicians	www.chestnet.org
American College of Emergency Physicians	www.acep.org
American College of Physicians	www.acponline.org/careers
American College of Physician Executives	www.acpe.org
American Medical Association	
Journal of the AMA (JAMA)	
Physician Recruitment Ads	www.ama-assn.org
California Academy of Family Physicians	www.fpjobsonline.org
CareersIntellect.com	www.careersintellect.com
Colorado Academy of Family Physicians	www.fpjobsonline.org
Doc Job	www.docjob.com
Doc on the Web	www.webdoc.com
DoctorWork.com	www.doctorwork.com
Ed Physician	www.edphysician.com
Florida Academy of Family Physicians	www.fpjobsonline.org
Georgia Academy of Family Physicians	www.fpjobsonline.org
iHirePhysicians.com	www.ihirephysicians.com
Illinois Academy of Family Physicians	www.fpjobsonline.org
JobMD.com	www.jobmd.com
JobPhysician.com	www.jobphysician.com
MD Job Site	www.mdjobsite.com
Missouri Academy of Family Physicians	www.fpjobsonline.org
National Rural Recruitment & Retention Network	www.3rnet.net
New England Journal of Medicine Career Center	www.nejmjobs.org
New York State Academy of Family Physicians	www.fpjobsonline.org
Pennsylvania Academy of Family Physicians	www.fpjobsonline.org
Physician Work	www.physicianwork.com
Physician's Employment	www.physemp.com
Practice Link	www.practicelink.com
Profiles Database	www.profilesdatabase.com
Texas Academy of Family Physicians	www.fpjobsonline.org
UO Magazine	www.uoworks.com
Web MD	www.webmd.com
Wisconsin Academy of Family Physicians	www.fpjobsonline.org

Notes

Favorite sites, useful resources

Healthcare/Medical (continued)

Psychology/Psychiatry/Mental Health

American Counseling Association	www.counseling.org
American Psychiatric Association	www.psych.org
American Psychiatric Nurses Association	www.apna.org
American Psychological Association	
Monitor Classified Advertising	www.apa.org/ads
American Psychological Society	
ObserverJob Listings	www.psychologicalscience.org
American Psychological Society	www.psychologicalscience.org
iHireMentalHealth.com	www.ihirementalhealth.com
iHireTherapy.com	www.ihiretherapy.com
JobPsychiatry.com	www.jobpsychiatry.com
JobPsychology.com	www.jobpsychology.com
Mental Health Jobs	www.mentalhealthjobs.com
Mental Health Net	www.mentalhelp.net
National Association of School Psychologists	www.naspcareercenter.org
Psychiatric Nurse Jobs	www.psychiatricnursejobs.com
Psychiatrist Jobs	www.psychiatristjobs.com
Psychologist Jobs	www.psychologistjobs.com
Social Psychology Network	www.socialpsychology.org

Radiology/Radiologic Technicians

American Healthcare Radiology Administrators	www.ahraonline.org
American Registry of Diagnostic Medical	
Sonographers	www.ardms.org
American Registry of Radiologic Technologists	www.arrt.org
American Society of Radiologic Technologists	www.asrt.org
AuntMinnie.com	www.auntminnie.com
iHireRadiology.com	www.ihireradiology.com
JobRadiology.com	www.jobradiology.com
NukeWorker.com	www.nukeworker.com
Radiological Society of North America	www.rsna.org
Radiology Business Management Association	www.rbma.org
RadWorking.com	www.radworking.com
RTJobs.com	www.rtjobs.com
Society of Diagnostic Medical Sonographers	www.sdms.org
Society of Nuclear Medicine	www.snm.org

Research

American Society for Clinical Laboratory Science	www.ascls.org
American Society for Clinical Pathology	www.ascp.org
American Society of Clinical Pharmacology	
and Therapeutics	www.ascpt.org
Association for Applied Human Pharmacology	
[Germany]	www.agah-web.de

Notes

Favorite sites, useful resources

Healthcare/Medical (continued)

Research (continued)

Association of Clinical Reseach Professionals
  Career Center — www.acrpnet.org
BC Biotechnology Alliance [Canada] — www.biotech.bc.ca/bcba
BioStaticianjobs.com — www.biostaticianjobs.com
Biotechemployment.com — www.biotechemployment.com
Biotechnology Industry Organization — www.bio.org/welcome.html
Canadian Society of Biochemistry and
  Mollecular and Cellular Biologists
  Experimental Medicine Job Listing — www.medcor.mcgill.ca/EXPMED/
  DOCS/index.html
History of Science Society — www.hssonline.org
Institute of Clinical Research [United Kingdom] — www.instituteofclinical
  research.org
JAMACareerNet [Journal & Archives Journals
  of the American Medical Association] — http://jamacareernet.ama-
  assn.org
PharmaVillage.com [United Kingdom] — www.pharmavillage.com
Texas Healthcare & Bioscience Institute — www.thbi.org

Specialties-Other

American Academy of Dermatology — www.aad.org
American Academy of Professional Coders — www.aapc.com
American Associatin of Cardiovascular and
  Pulmonary Rehabilitation — www.aacvpr.org
American Association of Medical Assistants — www.aama-ntl.org
American Association of Neuromuscular &
  Electrodiagnostic Medicine — www.aanem.org
American Association of Respiratory Care — www.aarc.org
American Association for Medical
  Transcription — www.aamt.org
American College of Occupational and
  Environmental Medicine — www.acoem.org
American Dietetic Association — www.eatright.org
American Industrial Hygiene Association — www.aiha.org
American College of Allergy, Asthma &
  Immunology — www.acaai.org
American College of Preventive Medicine — www.acpm.org
American College of Rheumatology — www.rheumatology.org
American Gastroenterological Association — www.GICareerSearch.com
American Geriatrics Society — www.americangeriatrics.org
American Society of Ichthyologists
  and Herpetologists — http://199.245.200.110/
American Society for Microbiology — www.asm.org
CancerJobs.net [United Kingdom] — www.cancerjobs.net
College of American Pathologists — www.cap.org
EHScareers.com — www.ehscareers.com

Notes

Favorite sites, useful resources

Healthcare/Medical (continued)

Specialties-Other (continued)

Emergency Medicine Residents Association	www.emra.org
FieldMedics.com	www.fieldmedics.com
HIV Medicine Association	www.hivma.org
iHireMedicalSecretaries.com	www.ihiremedicalsecretaries.com
iHireNutrition.com	www.ihirenutrition.com
Infectious Diseases Society of America	www.idsa.org
JobDiagnostics.com	www.jobdiagnostics.com
JobDietician.com	www.jobdietician.com
JobEKG.com	www.jobekg.com
JobEmergency.com	www.jobemergency.com
JobHematology.com	www.jobhematology.com
JobHomeHealth.com	www.jobhomehealth.com
JobHospice.com	www.jobhomehealth.com
JobImaging.com	www.jobimaging.com
JobImmunology.com	www.jobimmunology.com
JobLaboratory.com	www.joblaboratory.com
JobsMRI.com	www.jobsmri.com
JobNeonatal.com	www.jobneonatal.com
JobOncology.com	www.joboncology.com
Job Opportunities in Entomology	www.colostate.edu/Entomology/ jobs/jobs.html
JobParamedic.com	www.jobparamedic.com
JobPathology.com	www.jobpathology.com
JobPrimaryCare.com	www.jobprimarycare.com
JobTelemetry.com	www.jobtelemetry.com
JobTherapy.com	www.jobtherapy.com/ Entomology/jobs/jobs.html
JobX-ray.com	www.jobx-ray.com
MedBizPeople.com	www.medbizpeople.com
Medical Consultants Network	www.mcn.com
MedicalSalesJobs.com	www.medicalsalesjobs.com
MedicalSecretaryJobs.com	www.medicalsecretary.com
National Environmental Health Association	www.neha.org
North American Spine Society	www.spine.org
Renal World	www.renalworld.com

Students/Recent Graduates

CampusRN.com	www.campusrn.com
Career Espresso	www.sph.emory.edu/ studentservice
The College of Education & Human Development at the University of Minnesota	http://education.umn.edu/sps/career
Degree Hunter	www.degreehunter.com
Profiles Database	www.profilesdatabase.com

Notes

Favorite sites, useful resources

Healthcare/Medical (continued)

Surgery/Surgeons/Surgical Nurses

Academy of Medical-Surgical Nurses	www.medsurgnurse.org
American Association of Neurological Surgeons	www.aans.org
American College of Foot and Ankle Surgeons	www.acfas.org
American College of Surgeons	www.facs.org
American Society of General Surgeons	www.theasgs.org
JobSurgeon.com	www.jobsurgeon.com
JobTransplant.com	www.jobtransplant.com
American Association of Oral & Maxillofacial Surgeons	www.aoms.org

High Tech/Technical/Technology

The Ada Project	http://tap.mills.edu/ employment.jsp
AmericanJobs.com	www.americanjobs.com
Association for Educational Communications and Technology Job Center	www.aect.org
Career Net	www.careernet.com
Contract Employment Weekly	www.ceweekly.com
CyberMediaDice.com [India]	www.cybermediadice.com
High Technology Careers	www.hightechcareers.com
Infoworks - The Computer Job Center	www.IT123.com
IrishDev.com [Ireland]	www.irishdev.com
ITSystemsJobsNow.com	www.itsystemsjobsnow.com
Job Authority	www.jobauthority.com
Job Searching - Technical	http://jobsearchtech. miningco.com
JobsInSearch.com	www.jobsinsearch.com
JustTechnicalJobs [United Kingdom]	www.justtechnicaljobs.net
TheLadders.com	www.theladders.com
Latinos in Information Sciences and Technology Association	www.a-lista.org
LookTech.com	www.looktech.com
Metro Atlanta High Tech Personnel Association	http://mahtpa.hom. mindspring.com
New Dimensions in Technology, Inc.	www.ndt.com
New Mexico High Tech Job Forum	www.nmtechjobs.com
Passport Access	www.passportaccess.com
PickaJob.com	www.pickajob.com
RecruTech.ca [Canada]	www.recrutech.ca
ScientistWorld.com [United Kingdom]	www.scientistworld.com
Society for Technical Communications	www.stc.org
TechJobsOnline.com	www.techjobsonline.com
TechJobsScotland	www.techjobscotland.com

Notes

Favorite sites, useful resources

High Tech/Technical/Technology (continued)

TechStudents.net — www.techstudents.net
Technical Recruiter — www.technicalrecruiter.com
TechResults — www.techresults.com
US Tech Jobs — www.ustechjobs.net
Virtual Job Fair — http://careerexpo.jobing.com

Hospitality (See also Culinary/Food Preparation)

Hospitality-General
AnyWorkAnywhere.com [United Kingdom] — www.anyworkanywhere.com
Avero — www.averoinc.com/
BlueFoxJobs.com — www.bluefoxjobs.com
Hcareers — www.hcareers.com
Hospitality Net Virtual Job Exchange [Netherlands] — www.hospitalitynet.nl
Hospitality Online — www.hospitalityonline.com
HospitalityRecruitment.co.uk [United Kingdom] — www.hospitalityrecruitment.co.uk
iHireHospitality.com — www.ihirehospitality.com
iHireHospitalityServices.com — www.ihirehospitalityservices.com
Job Monkey — www.jobmonkey.com
MyHospitalityJobs.net — www.myhospitalityjobs.net

Food Preparation
BookaChef.co.uk [United Kingdom] — www.bookachef.co.uk
Careers in Food — www.careersinfood.com
Caterer.com [United Kingdom] — www.caterer.com
CatererGlobal.com [United Kingdom] — www.catererglobal.com
FineDiningJobs.com — www.finediningjobs.com
Food and Drink Jobs — www.foodanddrinkjobs.com
FoodIndustryJobs.com — www.foodindustryjobs.com
MyFoodJobs.net — www.myfoodjobs.net
Restaurant Careers — www.restaurant-careers.com
Restaurant Job Site — www.restaurantjobsite.com
Restaurant Jobs — www.restaurantjobs.com
SommelierJobs.com — www.sommelierjobs.com
StarChefs — www.starchefs.com

Hotel
American Hotel and Lodging Association — www.ahla.com/careers
Hotel Jobs — www.hoteljobs.com
Hotel Jobs Network — www.hoteljobsnetwork.com
Hotel-Restaurant Jobs — www.hotel-restaurantjobs.com
LuxuryHotelJobs.com — www.luxuryhoteljobs.com

Notes

Favorite sites, useful resources

Hospitality (continued)

Management
Executive Placement Services	www.execplacement.com
HospitalityExecutive.com	www.hospitalityexecutive.com
Restaurant Mangement Jobs	www.restaurantmgmtjobs.com
Restaurant Manager Job Site	www.restaurantmgrjobsite.com

Resorts
Cooljobs	http://cooljobs.com
CoolWorks.com	www.coolworks.com
HospitalityAdventures.com	www.hospitalityadventures.com
Resortjobs.co.uk [United Kingdom]	www.resortjobs.co.uk

Travel
American Society of Travel Agents	www.astanet.com
TravelJobSearch.com [United Kingdom]	www.traveljobsearch.com

Other Speciality
Casino Careers Online	www.casinocareers.com
International Association of Conference Centers Online	www.iacconline.com/home.cfm
Lifeguardingjobs.com	www.lifeguardingjobs.com
MeetingJobs.com	www.meetingjobs.com
Museum Jobs	www.museumjobs.com
ScottishHospitalityJobs.com [Scotland]	www.scottishhospitalityjobs.com
Showbizjobs.com	www.showbizjobs.com
SkiingtheNet	www.skiingthenet.com

Hourly Workers (See also Classifieds-Newspaper)

⇲ EmploymentGuide.com	www.employmentguide.com
GrooveJob.com	www.groovejob.com
Monster JobMatch	www.jobmatch.com
SnagaJob.com	www.snagajob.com
TemporarEASE.com	www.temporarease.com
YouApplyHere.com	www.youapplyhere.com

Human Resources (See also Recruiters' Resources)

Human Resources-General
American Management Association International	www.amanet.org/start.htm
HR Connections	www.hrjobs.com
HRjob.ca [Canada]	www.hrjob.ca
HR Job Net	www.hrjobnet.com
HR-Jobs	www.hr-jobs.net

Notes

Favorite sites, useful resources

Human Resources (continued

Human Resources-General (continued)

HR Professionals	http://hrpro.org/main.html
HR Staffers	www.hrstaffers.com
HR World	www.hrworld.com
HRIM Mall	www.hrimmall.com
HRM Jobs	www.hrmjobs.com
Human Resources.org	www.humanresources.org
iHireHR.com	www.ihirehr.com
Jobs4HR.com	www.jobs4hr.com
TheLadders.com	www.theladders.com
NationJob Network: Human Resources Job Page	www.nationjob.com/hr
NewHRJobs.com	www.newhrjobs.com
■ Society for Human Resource Management HRJobs	www.shrm.org/jobs
TCM.com's HR Careers	www.tcm.com/hr-careers
Workforce Online	www.workforceonline.com

Assessment/Evaluation/Selection

American Evaluation Association	www.eval.org
Business Test Publishers Association [United Kingdom]	www.assessmentjobs.com

Compensation & Benefits

BenefitsLink	www.benefitslink.com
International Foundation of Employee Benefit Plans Job Postings	www.ifebp.org/jobs/default.asp
Salary.com	www.salary.com
WorkersCompensation.com	www.workerscompensation.com
World at Work Job Links (American Compensation Association)	www.worldatwork.org

Consulting

Human Resource Independent Consultants (HRIC) On-Line Job Leads	www.hric.org/ hric/hrcaopp1.html
Independent Human Resource Consultants Association	www.ihrca.com/ Contract_Regular.asp

Diversity

Career Center for Workforce Diversity	www.eop.com
DiversityCareers.com	www.diversitycareers.com
DiversityInc.com	www.diversityinc.com
DiversityWorking.com	www.diversityworking.com
IMDiversity.com	www.imdiversity.com
WorkplaceDiversity.com	www.workplacediversity.com

Notes

Favorite sites, useful resources

Human Resources (continued

Industry Specific

Cable and Telecommunications Human Resources Association	www.cthra.com
College and University Personnel Association JobLine	www.cupahr.org/jobline
HRS Jobs	www.hrsjobs.com
Massachusetts Healthcare Human Resources Association	www.mhhra.org
Media Human Resource Association	www.shrm.org/mhra/index.asp
National Association of Colleges & Employers (NACE)	www.nacelink.com

Information Systems

HRISjobs.com	www.hrisjobs.com
International Association for Human Resource Information Management Job Central	http://ihr.hrdpt.com

Recruiting

Academy of Healthcare Recruiters	www.academyofhealthcarerecruiters.com
Alliance of Medical Recruiters	www.physicianrecruiters.com/amrapp.htm
American Staffing Association	www.staffingtoday.net
Arizona Technical Recruiters Association	www.atraaz.org/pages/recruiterjobopenings.html
Association of Executive Search Consultants	www.aesc.org
Association of Financial Search Consultants	www.afsc-jobs.com
Association of Staff Physician Recruiters	www.aspr.org
California Staffing Professionals	www.catss.org
Canadian Technical Recruiters Network	www.ctrn.org
Colorado Technical Recruiters Network	www.ctrn.org
Delaware Valley Technical Recruiters Network	www.dvtrn.org
Electronic Recruiters Exchange	www.erexchange.com
Houston High Tech Recruiters Network	www.hhtrn.org
Illinois Recruiters Association	www.illinoisrecruiters.org
International Association of Corporate and Professional Recruitment	www.iacpr.org
Minnesota Technical Recruiters Network	www.mntrn.com
National Association of Executive Recruiters	www.naer.org
National Association for Health Care Recruitment	www.nahcr.com
National Association of Legal Search Consultants	www.nalsc.org
National Association of Personnel Services	www.napsweb.org
National Association of Physician Recruiters	www.napr.org

Notes

Favorite sites, useful resources

Human Resources (continued

Recruiting (continued)

National Insurance Recruiters Association
  Online Job Database   www.nirassn.com/positions.cfm
National Technical Staffing Association   www.ntsa.com
New Jersey Metro Employment Management
  Association   www.njmetroema.org
New Jersey Staffing Association   www.njsa.com
New Jersey Technical Recruiters Alliance   www.njtra.org
Northeast Human Resource Association   www.nehra.org
Northwest Recruiters Association   www.nwrecruit.org
OnrecJobs.com [United Kingdom]   www.onrecjobs.com
Personnel Management Association of
  Western New England   www.hrmawne.org
Recruiters Network   www.recruitersnetwork.com
RecruitingJobs.com   www.recruitingjobs.com
The Regional Technical Recruiter's Association   www.rtra.com
Southeast Employment Network   www.senetwork.com
Technical Recruiters Network   www.trnchicago.org
Texas Association of Staffing   www.texasstaffing.org
Washington Area Recruiters Network   www.warn.net
WEDDLE's Newsletters, Guides
  & Directory   **www.weddles.com**

Regional

Atlanta Human Resources Association   www.ahraonline.com/
California Human Resources Professionals   www.keyhrjobs.com
Central Iowa Chapter, SHRM   http://cishrm.org/
Chesapeake Human Resources
  Association   www.chra.com
Dallas Human Resource Management
  Association   www.dallashr.org
Houston Human Resource Management
  Association   www.hhrma.org/default.shtml
Howard County Human Resources Society   www.hocohrs.org
HRMA Resource Bank   www.hrma.org/bank
Human Resource Association of
  Broward County   www.hrabc.org
Human Resource Association of
  Central Indiana   www.hraci.org
Human Resource Association of
  Greater Kansas City   http://hrma-kc.org
Human Resource Association of   http://members.aol.com/hraob/
  Greater Oak Brook   main.htm
Human Resource Association
  of the National Capital Area Job Bank Listing   http://hra-nca.org/job_list.asp

Notes

Favorite sites, useful resources

Human Resources (continued

Regional (continued)

Human Resource Association of New York	www.nyshrm.org
Human Resource Management	http://hrmamm.com/jobpostings/
Association of Mid Michigan Job Postings	index.php
Human Resources Online [Russia]	www.hro.ru
Illinois Association of Personnel Services	www.searchfirm.com
JobsinSearch [United Kingdom]	www.jobsinsearch.com
Metro Atlanta High Tech Personnel	http://mahtpa.hom.
Association	mindspring.com
Navigator Online	www.lwhra.org
New Jersey Human Resource	
Planning Group	www.njhrpg.org
Northeast Human Resource Association	www.nehra.org
Northeast Human Resource Association	www.nehra.org
Ohio State Council (SHRM)	www.ohioshrm.org
Personnel Management Association of	
Western New England	www.hrmawne.org
Pittsburgh Personnel Association	ww.ppapitt.org
The Portland Human Resource Management Assn	www.pdxhr.org
Professionals in Human Resource Association	www.pihra.org/capirasn/
Career Center	careers.nsf/home?open
Sacremento Area Human Resources Association	www.sahra.org
SHRM Atlanta	www.shrmatlanta.org
SHRM Jacksonville	www.shrmjax.org
Tri-State Human Resource Management Assn	www.tristatehr.org
Tulsa Area Human Resources Association	www.tahra.org

Training & Development

American Society for	
Training & Development Job Bank	http://jobs.astd.org
Instructional Systems Technology Jobs	http://education.indiana.edu/ist/
	students/jobs/joblink.html
International Society for Performance	
Improvement Job Bank	www.ispi.org
Training Consortium	www.trainingconsortium.net
Training Forum	www.trainingforum.com
Trainingjob.com	www.trainingjob.com
TrainingProviderJobs.co.uk [United Kingdom]	www.trainingproviderjobs.co.uk
The Training SuperSite	www.trainingmag.com
WillTrainJobs.com	www.willtrainjobs.com

Other Specialty

New Jersey Human Resource	
Planning Group	www.njhrpg.org
OD Network On-line	www.odnetwork.org

Notes

Favorite sites, useful resources

-I-

Industrial/Manufacturing

American Chemical Society Rubber Division	www.rubber.org
American Forest & Paper Association	www.afandpa.org/careercenter
Association of Industrial Metalizers, Coaters & Laminators	www.aimcal.org
Auto Glass Magazine	www.glass.org
CastingJobs.com	www.castingjobs.com
CoatingCareers.com	www.coatingcareers.com
COBRA	www.technologysource.com
Drilling Research Institute	www.drillers.com
Epro.com	www.epro.com
Energy Careers	www.energycareers.com
Finishing.com	www.finishing.com
FM Link-Facilities Management	www.fmlink.com
HVACagent.com	www.hvacagent.com
iHireManufacturingEngineers.com	www.ihiremanufacturing engineers.com
Iron & Steel Society	www.issource.org
Jobwerx	www.jobwerx.com
ManufacturingJob.com	www.manufacturingjob.com
Manufacturing Job Store	www.manufacturingjobstore.com
ManufacturingJobs.com	www.manufacturingjobs.com
MDL CareerCenter	http://careercenter.devicelink.com
MoldingJobs.com	www.moldingjobs.com
MyManufacturingJobs.net	www.mymanufacturingjobs.net
National Association of Industrial Technology	www.nait.org
National Defense Industrial Association	www.defensejobs.com
Network Glass Jobs	www.glassjobs.net
OilCareer.com	www.oilcareer.com
The Oil Directory	www.oildirectory.com
Petroleum Services Association of Canada Employment	www.psac.ca
Power Builder Journal	www.sys-con.com/pbdj/
Semicon	www.semicon.com
Semicon Bay	www.semiconbay.com
Sheet Metal and Air Conditioning Contractor's Association	www.smacna.org
Society of Petrologists & Well Log Analysts Job Opportunities	www.spwla.org
Subseaexplorer	www.subseaexplorer.com
SwissCNCJobs.com	www.swisscncjobs.com
TextileJobs.net	www.textilejobs.net
UtilityJobSearch.com [United Kingdom]	www.utilityjobsearch.com

Notes

Favorite sites, useful resources

Information Technology/Information Systems
Software, Hardware, Middleware, Client server, Web specialists

Information Technology-General

15 Seconds Job Classifieds	www.15seconds.com/
A1A Computer Jobs Mailing List	www.a1acomputerpros.net
A-Z Internet Jobs	www.a-zjobs.com
Ace thee Interview	www.acetheinterview.com
The Ada Project	http://tap.mills.edu/ employment.jsp
AD&A Software Jobs Home Page	www.softwarejobs.com
The Advanced Computing Systems Association	http://usenix.org
Advisor Zone	www.advisorzone.com
AS400 Network	www.iseriesnetwork.com
Association for Computing Machinery Career Resource Center	http://acpinternational.org
Association for Educational Communications and Technology Job Center	www.aect.org
Association of Internet Professionals National Job Board	www.association.org
Association of Legal Information Systems Managers Job Listings	www.alism.org/jobs.htm
Asynchrony	www.asynchrony.com
Avatar Magazine	www.avatarmag.com
Beeline.com	www.beeline.com
Brain Buzz	www.cramsession.com
Brain Power	www.brainpower.com
CanadaIT.com	www.canadait.com
Canada Job	www.canadajob.com
CardBrowser.com	www.cardbrowser.com
CareerFile	www.careerfile.com
Career Magic	www.careermagic.com
Career Marketplace Network	www.careermarketplace.com
Career Shop	www.careershop.com
Cert Review	www.itspecialist.com
CIO	http://jobs.cio.com
CM Today (Configuration Management)	www.cmcrossroads.com/ubb threads/postlist.php?Cat=&
CNET's Ultimate ISP Guide	www.cnet.com/content/reports/ special/ISP/index.html
Cobol Jobs	www.coboljobs.com
Comforce	www.comforce.com
⧆ ComputerJobs.com	www.computerjobs.com
⧆ Computerwork.com	www.computerwork.com
Computing Research Association Job Announcements	www.cra.org/jobs/ main/cra.jobs.html

Notes

Favorite sites, useful resources

Information Technology/Information Systems (continued)

Information Technology-General (continued)

Contract Employment Weekly	www.ceweekly.com
CREN	www.computingresources.com
CRN	www.channelweb.com/ sections/careers
Cyberking Employment	www.cyberkingemployment.com
Data Masters	www.datamasters.com
DevBistro.com	www.devbistro.com
Developers.Net	www.developers1.net
Devhead	www.zdnet.com/devhead
⊠ DICE	www.dice.com
Digital Cat's	http://human.jobcats.com
Digital City	http://home.digitalcity.com/ employment
Discover Jobs	www.discoverjobs.com
Dr. Dobb's	www.ddj.com
Domino Pro	www.dominopro.com
E-Cruiter	www.ecruiter.com
Eclectic [Netherlands]	www.eclectic.nl
eContent	www.ecmag.net
Educause	www.educause.edu
EE Times	www.eet.com
eLance	www.elance.com
Embedded.com	www.embedded.com
Emergit	www.emergit.com
eMoonlighter	www.emoonlighter.com
The Engineering Technology Site [United Kingdom]	www.engineers4engineers.co.uk
e-itwizards.com	www.e-itwizards.com
ePro.com	www.epro.com
eWork Exchange	www.ework.com
FatJob.com	www.fatjob.com
Free Agent	www.freeagent.com
GisaJob.com [United Kingdom]	www.gisajob.com
Gurus.com.au [Australia]	www.gurus.com.au
GxPJobs.com [United Kingdom]	www.gxpjobs.com
H1B Sponsors	www.h1bsponsors.com
Hands on Solutions	www.handsonsolutions.com
Hardware-Jobs	www.hardware-jobs.net
Hi-Tech Careers	www.careermarthi-tech.com
Hi-Tech Club	www.hitechclub.com
Hightech-Jobs	www.high-tech-Jobs.net
High Technology Careers	www.hightechcareers.com
Hire Ability	www.hireability.com
Hot Dispatch	www.hotdispatch.com
Humanys.com	www.humanys.com

Notes

Favorite sites, useful resources

Information Technology/Information Systems (continued)

Information Technology-General (continued)

Huntahead	www.huntahead.com
InfiNet	www.infi.net
InformationWeek Career	www.informationweek.com/career
Informant Communications Group, Inc.	www.informant.com/icgmags.asp
In the Middle [United Kingdom]	www.inthemiddle.co.uk
Information Professionals	www.bring.com
Informix Jobs	www.premierjobs.com
Intega Online [United Kingdom]	www.intega.co.uk
Inter City Oz	http://interoz.com
Internet.com	http://jobs.internet.com
iSmart People	www.ismartpeople.com
ITcareers.com	www.itcareers.com
IT Classifieds	www.itclassifieds.com
IT Firms	www.itfirms.com
IT Hideout	www.hideout.com
TheITJobBoard.com [United Kingdom]	www.theitjobboard.com
IT Job Scooter	www.itjobscooter.com
ITjobs.ca [Canada]	www.itjobs.ca
IT Jobs Online	www.itjobsonline.com
ITonlinejobs.com	www.itonlinejobs.com
IT Solutions 2000	www.itsolutions2000.com
ITSystemsJobsNow.com	www.itsystemsjobsnow.com
IT Talent	www.ittalent.com
IT webForum	www.it-webforum.com
ITCV [United Kingdom]	www.itcv.co.uk
JV Search	www.jvsearch.com
Job Ads	www.jobads.com
Job Authority	www.jobauthority.com
JobCircle.com	www.jobcircle.com
Job Domain [United Kingdom]	www.jobdomain.co.uk
JobEngine	www.jobengine.com
The JobFactory	www.jobfactory.com
Job Island	www.jobisland.com
Job Net America	www.jobnetamerica.com
Job Serve	www.jobserve.com
JobUniverse.com	www.jobuniverse.com
JobWarehouse.com	www.jobwarehouse.com
Job Warriors	http://jobwarriors.com
Job Webs	www.jobwebs.com
JobsDB	www.jobsdbusa.com
Jobs4IT.com	www.jobs4it.com
Jobs-net	www.jobs-net.com
Jobs-Network	www.jobs-network.com

Notes

Favorite sites, useful resources

Information Technology/Information Systems (continued)

Information Technology-General (continued)

Just Tech Jobs	www.justtechjobs.com
KR Solutions [United Kingdom]	www.kr-solutions.co.uk/index.php
Lan-Jobs	www.lan-jobs.net
Latinos in Information Sciences and Technology Association	www.a-lista.org
Lotus Notes Jobs	www.lotusnotesjobs.com
Mojolin	www.mojolin.com
MoreGeeks.com	www.moregeeks.com
MyITJobs.net	www.myitjobs.net
Neo Soft	www.neosoft.com
NerdsWanted.com	www.nerdswanted.com
Nerdworkz	www.nerdworkz.com
Net Mechanic	www.netmechanic.com
OperationIT	www.operationIT.com
Oxygen [United Kingdom]	www.oxygenonline.co.uk
PC World	www.pcworld.com
People Bonus	www.peoplebonus.com
PeopleOnline [Brazil]	www.peopleonline.com
PeopleSoft-Resources.com	www.peoplesoft-resources.com
PLACEUM 2000	www.placeum.com
Professional Exchange	www.professional-exchange.com/indexie.htm
Real-Time Magazine [Belgium]	www.realtime-info.be/encyc/magazine/magazine.htm
Real-Time Engineering	www.realtime-engineering.com
Road Techs	www.roadtechs.com
SAS Institute	www.sas.com/usergroups
Securityportal.com	www.securityportal.com
Semiconductor Jobs	www.semiconductorjobs.net
Skills Village	www.skillsvillage.com
Smarter Work	www.smarterwork.com
Soft Moonlighter	www.softmoonlighter.com
Software-Jobs	www.software-jobs.net
Society of Computer Professionals Online	www.comprof.com
SoftwareJobLink	www.softwarejoblink.com
Southern California Electronic Data Interchange Roundtable	www.scedir.org/html/jobs.html
staffITnow	www.staffitnow.com
Swift Jobs	www.swiftjobs.com
Tech-Engine	www.tech-engine.com
Tech Expo USA	www.techexpousa.com
TechEmployment.com	www.techemployment.com
Techie Gold	www.techiegold.com

Notes

Favorite sites, useful resources

Information Technology/Information Systems (continued)

Information Technology-General (continued)

Tech Job Bank	www.techjobbank.com
TechJobs	www.tech-jobs.net
TechResults	www.techresults.com
Tech Target	www.techtarget.com
TechWeb	www.techweb.com
Technology Jobs	www.technology-jobs.net
Techs	www.techs.com
VAR Business	www.channelweb.com/ sections/careers/jobboard.asp
Virtual Job Fair	http://careerexpo.jobing.com
Wireless Developers	www.wirelessdevnet.com
Work Exchange	www.workexchange.com
Element K Journals	www.elementkjournals.com

AS400

Just AS/400 Jobs	www.justas400jobs.com
News400.com	www.news400.com

Baan

BaanBoard.com	www.baanboard.com
The Baan Fan Club	www.baanfans.com
Just BAAN Jobs	www.justbaanjobs.com

C++

C++ Jobs	www.cplusplusjobs.com
C++ Report	www.creport.com
C++ Users Group Job Links	www.hal9k.com/cug/jobs.htm
C Plus Plus Jobs	www.cplusplusjobs.com
Just C Jobs	www.justcjobs.com

Cobol

The Cobol Center	www.infogoal.com/cbd/ cbdjob.htm
CobolJobs.com	www.coboljobs.com
Just Cobol Jobs	www.justcoboljobs.com
Matt's Perfect COBOL Employment World	http://members.home.net/ doormatt/jobs.html

Cold Fusion

Atlanta Cold Fusion	www.acfuq.org
Austin Cold Fusion	http://cftexas.outer.net/jobs.cfm
CF Programmers	www.cfprogrammers.com
Chicago Area Cold Fusion	www.chicfuq.org/jobs
Cold Fusion Advisor	www.cfadvisor.com

Notes

Favorite sites, useful resources

Information Technology/Information Systems (continued)

Cold Fusion (continued)

ColdFusion Support Forums

www.adobe.com/cfusion/ webforums/forum/index.cfm? forumid=1

House of Fusion

www.houseoffusion.com

Just Cold Fusion Jobs

www.justcoldfusionjobs.com

New England Allaire Developers

www.cfuqboston.com/index.cfm

Database

Database Analyst

www.databaseanalyst.com

Database Jobs

www.databasejobs.com

DataNewsJobs.com [Belgium]

www.datanewsjobs.com

DBA Support

http://ora.dbasupport.com

Learn ASP

www.learnasp.com

International DB2 Users Group

www.idug.org

Just DB2 Jobs

www.justdb2jobs.com

LazyDBA.com

www.lazydba.com

Delphi

Delphi Jobs

www.delphijobs.com

Just Delphi Jobs

www.delphijobs.com

Electric Data Interchange

EDI Jobs Online

www.edijobsonline.com

EDI Coordinators & Consultants
  Clearinghouse

www.friend-edi.com

Just Exchange Jobs

www.justexchangejobs.com

Southern California Electronic Data
  Interchange Roundtable

www.scedir.org/html/jobs.html

ERP

ERP Assist

www.erpassist.com

ERP Central

www.erpcentral.com

ERP Fan Club

www.erpfans.com

ERP Jobs [Canada]

www.erp-jobs.com

ERP People

www.erp-people.com

ERP Professional

www.erpprofessional.com

ERP Software

www.erpsos.com

The ERP Supersite

www.techra.com

Geographic Information Systems

GIScareers.com

www.giscareers.com

GISjobs.com

www.gisjobs.com

GIS Jobs Clearinghouse

www.gjc.org

GISuser.com

www.gisuser.com

Notes

Favorite sites, useful resources

Information Technology/Information Systems (continued)

Java

All-Java-Jobs	www.all-java-jobs.com
Digital Cat	http://human.javaresource.com
Java Jobs	www.javajobs.com
Java Jobs Online	www.javajobsonline.com
Java World	www.javaworld.com
jGuru	www.jguru.com
Just Java Jobs	www.justjavajobs.com
Team Java	www.teamjava.com

Lotus Notes

Association of ex-Lotus Employees	www.axle.org/ careerframeset.html
Just Notes Jobs	www.justnotesjobs.com
Lavatech	www.lotusnotes.com
Lotus Notes Jobs	www.lotusnotesjobs.com

MacIntosh

MacDirectory Job Opportunities	www.macdirectory.com
MacTalent.com	www.mactalent.com
The Mac Trading Post	www.mymac2u.com/ themactradingpost
MacWorld [United Kingdom]	www.macworld.co.uk/jobfinder
Macnologist	www.macnologist.com

Network/LAN/WAN

iHireNetworkAdministrators.com	www.ihirenetwork administrators.com
Just Netware Jobs	www.justnetwarejobs.com
Just Networking Jobs	www.justnetworkingjobs.com
LAN Jobs	www.lanjobs.com
Network Engineer.com	www.networkengineer.com
Network World Fusion	www.nwfusion.com

Oracle

Just Oracle Jobs	www.justoraclejobs.com
Orafans.com	www.orafans.com
Orca—The Oracle Job Site	www.theoraclejobsite.com
Oracle Contractor Database	www.cois.com/houg/con.html
Oracle Fan Club	www.oraclefans.com
Oracle Fans	www.oraclefans.com
Oracle Job Network	www.oracjobs.com
Oracle Jobs Network	www.orajobs.com/postjb1.htm
Oracle Professional	www.oracleprofessional.com
OraSearch.com	www.orasearch.com

Notes

Favorite sites, useful resources

Information Technology/Information Systems (continued)

PeopleSoft

Jobs for Programmers — www.prgjobs.com/Jobs.cfm/ PeopleSoft

Just People Soft Jobs — www.justpeoplesoftjobs.com

People Soft Fans — www.peoplesoftfans.com

People Soft Links — http://peoplesoftassist.com/ peoplesoft_links.htm

PSoftPros.com — www.psoftpros.com

Power Builder

Just Power Builder Jobs — www.justpowerbuilderjobs.com

Power Builder Jobs — www.powerbuilderjobs.com

Power Builder Journal — www.sys-con.com/pbdj/

Programming

iDevjobs.com — www.idevjobs.com

iHireProgrammers.com — wwwihireprogrammers.com

Jobs for Programmers — www.prgjobs.com

Programming-Webmaster — www.programming.com

Programming Jobs — www.programmingjobs.com

Programming-Services — www.programming-services.com

RentaCoder.com — www.rentacoder.com

SoftwareJoblink.com — www.softwarejoblink.com

Superexpert — www:superexpert.com

SAP

A1A Computer Jobs Mailing List — www.a1acomputerpros.net

Just SAP Jobs — www.justsapjobs.com

SAP Club — www.sapclub.com

The SAP Fan Club — www.sapfans.com

SAPInfo.net — www.sapinfo.net

The SAP Job Board [Europe] — www.thesapjobboard.com

SAP Professional Organization — www.sap-professional.org

SAP Solutions — www.sap.com

The Spot 4 SAP — www.thespot4sap.com

Unix

Donohue's RS/6000 & UNIX Employment Site — www.s6000.com

Just UNIX Jobs — www.justunixjobs.com

Unix Guru Universe — www.ugu.com

UNIX admin search — www.unixadminsearch.com

Unix Review — www.unixreview.com

Unix World — www.networkcomputing.com/ unixworld/unixhome.html

Notes

Favorite sites, useful resources

Information Technology/Information Systems (continued)

Visual Basic
Just VB Jobs   www.justvbjobs.com
V Basic Search   www.vbasicsearch.com
VB Code Guru   http://codeguru.earthweb.com/vb
Visual Basic Jobs   www.visualbasicjobs.com

Unix
Donohue's RS/6000 & UNIX
  Employment Site   www.s6000.com
Just UNIX Jobs   www.justunixjobs.com
Unix Guru Universe   www.ugu.com
UNIX admin search   www.unixadminsearch.com
Unix Review   www.unixreview.com
Unix World   www.networkcomputing.com/
                                                      unixworld/unixhome.html

Visual Basic
Just VB Jobs   www.justvbjobs.com
V Basic Search   www.vbasicsearch.com
VB Code Guru   http://codeguru.earthweb.com/vb
Visual Basic Jobs   www.visualbasicjobs.com

Web
B2B Frontline.com   www.b2bfrontline.com
CGI Resource Index   www.cgi-resources.com
DevBistro.com   www.devbistro.com
HTML Writers Guild HWG-Jobs   www.hwg.org/lists/hwg-jobs
I-Advertising   http://internetadvertising.org
JobsInSearch.com   www.jobsinsearch.com
Just E-Commerce Jobs   www.juste-commercejobs.com
Just Web Jobs   www.justwebjobs.com
Search Hound   www.searchhound.com
SGML/XML Jobs   www.eccnet.com/xmlug
Site Experts   www.siteexperts.com
US Internet Industry   www.usiia.org
Web Jobs USA   www.webjobsusa.com
Web Programming Jobs   www.webprogrammingjobs.com
Web Site Builder   www.websitebuilder.com
XMLephant   www.xmlephant.com

Windows
BHS Job Center   www.bhs.com/jobs2
Information NT   www.informationnt.com
Just NT Jobs   www.justntjobs.com
Just Windows Jobs   www.justwindowsjobs.com

Notes

Favorite sites, useful resources

Information Technology/Information Systems (continued)

Windows (continued)

NTPRO	www.ntpro.org/jobbank.html
Swynk.com	www.swynk.com
Windows NT Resource Center	www.bhs.com/default.asp

Other Specialty

American Statistical Association Statistics Career Center	www.amstat.org/careers
Association for Women in Computing	www.awc-hq.org
Axaptajobs.com	www.axaptajobs.com
Black Data Processing Association Online	www.bdpa.org
Blackgeeks	www.blackgeeks.com
BroadbandCareers.com	www.broadbandcareers.com
Carolina Computer Jobs	www.carolinacomputerjobs.com
Common Switzerland	www.common.ch
Controller Jobs	www.controllerjobs.com
CyberMediaDice.com [India]	www.cybermediadice.com
Donohue's RS/6000 & UNIX Employment Site	www.s6000.com
Ed Barlow's Sysbase Stuff	www.edbarlow.com
Electronic Media Online	www.emonline.com
Florida NACCB	www.floridanaccb.org
IrishDev.com [Ireland]	www.irishdev.com
ITmoonlighter.com	www.itmoonlighter.com
Just Access Jobs	www.justaccessjobs.com
Just ASP Jobs	www.justaspjobs.com
Just Fox Pro Job	www.foxprojobs.com
Just Help Desk Jobs	www.justhelpdeskjobs.com
Just Informix Jobs	www.justinformixjobs.com
Just JD Edwards Jobs	www.justjdedwardsjobs.com
Just Mainframe Jobs	www.justmainframejobs.com
Just OLAP Jobs	www.justolapjobs.com
Just Perl Jobs	www.justperljobs.com
Just Progress Jobs	www.justprogressjobs.com
Just Project Manager Jobs	www.justprogram managerjobs.com
Just Q A Jobs	www.justqajobs.com
Just Security Jobs	www.justsecurityjobs.com
Just Siebel Jobs	www.justsiebeljobs.com
Just SQL Server Jobs	www.justsqlserverjobs.com
Just Sybase Jobs	www.justsybasejobs.com
Just Tech Sales Jobs	www.justtechsalesjobs.com
Just Telephony Jobs	www.justelephonyjobs.com
Lapis Software	www.lapis.com
Midrange Computing Institute	www.midrangecomputing.com
MVShelp.com	www.mvshelp.com

Notes

Favorite sites, useful resources

Information Technology/Information Systems (continued)

Other Specialty (continued)

NACCB - Dallas - Ft. Worth Chapter	www.dfw-naccb.org
Project Manager	www.projectmanager.com
See Beyond	www.seebeyond.com
Software Contractor's Guild	www.scguild.com
Software Developer	www.softwaredeveloper.com
Software Engineer	http://softwareengineer.comIn
Software & IT Sales Employment Review	www.salesrecruits.com
Software QA and Testing Resource Center	www.softwareqatest.com
Tech Writers	www.techwriters.com
Technical Communicator	www.technical communicator.com
University of Maryland Computer Science Grads	www.cs.umd.edu/users
Texas A&M University Computer Science Grads	www.cs.tamu.edu/Resumes
User Group News	www.ugn.com/index.html
Women in Information Technology	www.worldWIT.org
Women in Technology International (WITI) 4Hire	www.witi4hire.com

Insurance

Alliance of Merger and Acquisition Advisors	www.advisor-alliance.com
Actuary.com	www.actuary.com
ActuaryJobs.com	www.actuaryjobs.com
American Institute for Chartered Property Casualty Underwriters	www.aicpcu.org
Chartered Property Casualty Underwriters	www.cpcusociety.org
4 Insurance Jobs	www.4insurancejobs.com
Global Association of Risk Professionals Career Center	www.garp.com/ careercenter/index.asp
IFSjobs.com	www.ifsjobs.com
iHireInsurance.com	www.ihireinsurance.com
INSData	www.insdata.com
Insurance File	www.insfile.com
The Insurance Job Bank	www.iiin.com/html/jobs.html
InsuranceWorks.com [Canada]	www.insuranceworks.com
Life Career Retreat	www.lifecareer.com
LIMRA International	www.limra.com
National Insurance Recruiters Association Online Job Database	www.nirassn.com
NationJob Network: Financial, Accounting and Insurance Jobs Page	www.nationjob.com/financial
Property and Casualty	www.propertyandcasualty.com
Risk Info	www.riskinfo.com

Notes

Favorite sites, useful resources

Insurance (continued)

Risk & Insurance Management Society
  Careers

www.rims.org/Template.cfm?
  Section=JobBank1&Template=/
  Jobbank/SearchJobForm.cfm

Ultimate Insurance Jobs   www.ultimateinsurancejobs.com
UnderwritingJobs.com   www.underwritingjobs.com

International

International-General
AnyWorkAnywhere.com   www.anyworkanywhere.com
Community Learning Network   www.cln.org
Empowered Network   http://empowerednetworks.com
Expat Exchange   www.expatexchange.com
EscapeArtist.com
Financial Job Network   www.financialjobnetwork.com
FT.com -Financial Times   www.ft.com
Global Workplace   www.global-workplace.com
Humanys.com   www.humanys.com
International Academic Job Market   http://jobreview.camrev.com.au
International Jobs Center   www.internationaljobs.org
International Personnel Management Association   www.ipma-hr.org
International Society for Molecular
  Plant-Microbe Interactions   www.ismpinet.org/career
International Union of Food   www.iuf.org
JobsAbroad.com   www.jobabroad.com
Jobs in Higher Education   http://volvo.gslis.utexas.edu/
  Geographical Listings   ~acadres/jobs/index.html
Jobs 4 All   www.jobs4all.com
Net Expat   www.netexpat.com
Oil Online   www.oilonline.com
OneWorld.net   www.oneworld.net/section/
  involved

OverseasJobsExpress   www.overseasjobs.com
Packinfo-World   www.packinfo-world.com
The Internet Pilot to Physics   http://physicsweb.org/TIPTOP
Sales & Marketing Executives International   www.smei.org/
  Career Center   careers/index.shtml
Space Jobs   www.spacejobs.com
Top Jobs   www.topjobs.co.uk

Africa-General
AfricaJob.com   www.africajob.com
AfricaJobsSite.com   www.africajobsite.com
AfricaJobs.net   www.africajobs.net
FindaJobinAfrica.com   www.findajobinafrica.com

Notes

Favorite sites, useful resources

International (continued)

Africa-General (continued)
Job Searching for Africa	www.sas.upenn.edu/ African_Studies/Home_Page/ menu_job_srch.html
Kazinow.com	www.kazinow.com

Argentina
Bumeran.com	www.bumeran.com
Empleate.com	www.empleate.com
Laborum.com	www.laborum.com
MineJobs.com	www.minejob.com
TipTopJob.com	www.tiptopjob.com
Zeezo.com	www.zeezo.com

Asia-General
Asia Inc.	www.asia-inc.com
Asia-Net	www.asia-net.com
Asia Wired	www.asiawired.com
Asiaco Jobs Center	http://jobs.asiaco.com
Asianpro.com	http://asianpro.com
CareerJournal Asia	www.careerjournalasia.com
Career Next	www.careernext.com
E4Asia	www.e4asia.com
Job Asia	www.jobasia.com
JobsDB	www.jobsdb.com
Job Street	www.jobstreet.com
Panda Career	www.pandacareer.com
Wang & Li Asia Resources Online	www.wang-li.com

Australia
Ambition	www.ambition.com.au
The Australian Resume Server	www.herenow.com.au
CareerOne	www.careerone.com.au
Careers On Line	www.careersonline.com.au
Edonline.com.au	www.edonline.com.au
Employment Opportunities In Australia	www.employment.com.au
Fairfax Market	http://market.fairfax.com.au
Gurus.com.au	www.gurus.com.au
International Academic Job Market	http://jobreview.camrev.com.au
Jobwire.com.au	www.jobwire.com.au
JobsDB	www.jobsdb.com
Learn SA	www.nexus.edu.au/learnsatext/ default.htm
LinkedMe	www.linkme.com.au
MyCareer.com.au	www.mycareer.com.au

Notes

Favorite sites, useful resources

International (continued)

Australia (continued)

Queensland Department of Primary Industries	www.dpi.qld.gov.au/cft
SEEK	www.seek.com.au
WorkingIn.com	www.workingin.com

Austria

Austria.at	www.austria.at
JobsinAustria.at	www.jobsinaustria.at

Bangladesh

JobsDB	www.jobsdb.com

Belgium

DataNewsJobs.com	www.datanewsjobs.com
JobsCareer.be	www.jobs-career.be
Organic Chemistry Jobs Worldwide	www.organicworldwide.net/jobs/ jobs.html
StepStone	www.stepstone.com

Bermuda

Bermuda Biological Station for Research, Inc.	www.bbsr.edu
BermudaJobs.com	www.bermudajobs.com

Brazil

PeopleOnline	www.peopleonline.com
Zeezo	http://brazil.zeezo.com/jobs.htm

Caribbean

CaribCareer.com	www.caribcareer.com
Caribbean JobFair	www.caribbeanjobfair.com
EscapeArtist	www.escapeartist.com
JobsintheSun.com	www.jobsinthesun.com
TropicJobs.com	www.tropicjobs.com

Canada

ACREQ	www.cre.qc.ca
ActiJob	www.actijob.com
AdminJob.ca	www.adminjob.ca
Agricultural Employment in British Columbia	www.island.net/~awpb/emop/ startag.html
Atlantic Canada Careers	www.brainstalent.com
BaseJobs.com	www.basejobs.com
Battlefords Job Shop	www.battlefordsjobshop.ca

Notes

Favorite sites, useful resources

International (continued)

Canada (continued)

BC Biotechnology Alliance	www.bcbiotech.ca
Brains Talent	www.brainstalent.com
CACEE Work Web	www.cacee.com/index.html
Calgary Job Shop	www.calgaryjobshop.ca
CallCenterJob.ca	www.callcenterjob.ca
CanadaIT.com	www.canadait.com
Canada Job Search	www.canadajobsearch.com
CanadaParttime.com	www.canadaparttime.com
Canada's Fifty-Plus	www.fifty-plus.net
Canadian Association of Career Educators & Employers	www.cacee.com
Canadian Careers	www.canadiancareers.com
Canadian Jobs Catalogue	www.kenevacorp.mb.ca
Canadian Relocation Systems	http://relocatecanada.com
Canadian Resume' Centre	www.canres.com
Canadian Society of Biochemistry and Mollecular and Cellular Biologists Experimental Medicine Job Listing	www.medcor.mcgill.ca/EXPMED/ DOCS/index.html
Canadian Technical Recruiters Network	www.ctrn.com
Canjobs.com	www.canjobs.com
CanMed	www.canmed.com
CareerBridge	www.careerbridge.com
CareerBuilder	www.careerbuilder.ca
Career Exchange	www.careerexchange.com
Career Internetworking	www.careerkey.com
Circuit Match	www.circuitmatch.com
Eastern Ontario Job Shop	www.easternontariojobshop.ca
Edmonton Job Shop	www.edmontonjobshop.ca
Electronic Labour Exchange	www.ele-spe.org
Employxpress	www.employxpress.com
Globe and Mail	www.theglobeandmail.com
Grande Prairie Job Shop	www.grandprairiejobshop.ca
Hcareers.com	www.hcareers.ca
HeadHunt.com	www.headhunt.com
HRjob.ca	www.hrjob.ca
Human Resource Professionals Association of Ontario	www.hrpao.org
InfoPresseJobs.com	www.infopressejobs.com
Institute of Chartered Accountants of Alberta	www.icaa.ab.ca/ home/index.shtml
InsuranceWorks.com	www.insuranceworks.com
ITjob.ca	www.itjob.ca
Jobboom	www.jobboom.com
JobPostings.ca	www.jobpostings.ca

Notes

Favorite sites, useful resources

International (continued)

Canada (continued)

Job Shark	www.jobshark.com
Job Toaster	www.jobtoaster.com
JobWings.com	www.jobwings.com
Jobs	www.jobs.ca
KW Job Shop	wwww.kwjobshop.ca
LegalJob.ca	www.legaljob.ca
Lethbridge Job Shop	www.lethbridgejobshop.ca
Medicine Hat Job Shop	www.medicinehatjobshop.ca
Net @ccess	http://netaccess.on.ca
New Brunswick Job Shop	www.newbrunswickjobshop.ca
Newfoundland Labrador Job Shop	www.newfoundland labradorjobshop.ca
Nova Scotia Job Shop	www.novascotiajobshop.ca
Ottawa Area Computer Job Links Page	http://regionalhelpwanted.com/ home/164.htm?SN=164&
Ottawa Job Shop	www.ottawajobshop.ca
Paralegaljob.ca	www.paralegaljob.ca
Payroll Jobs	www.payrolljobs.com
Petroleum Services Association of Canada	www.psac.ca
PMjob.ca	www.PMjob.ca
Prince Albert Job Shop	www.princealbertjobshop.ca
Prince George Job Shop	www.princegeorgejobshop.ca
PubliPac.ca	www.publipac.ca
RecruitersCafe.com	www.recruiterscafe.com
Recrutech.ca	www.recrutech.ca
Red Deer Job Shop	www.reddeerjobshop.ca
Regina Job Shop	www.reginajobshop.ca
RetailJob.ca	www.retailjob.ca
SalesRep.ca	www.salesrep.ca
Saskatoon Job Shop	www.saskatoonjobshop.ca
SCWIST Work Pathfinder	www.harbour.sfu.ca/scwist/ pathfinder/index.htm
Sympatico Work Place	http://workplace.sympatico.ca
TCM.com's HR Careers	www.tcm.com/hr-careers
Thompson Okanagan Job Shop	www.thompsonokanagan jobshop.ca
Toronto Job Shop	www.torontojobshop.ca
Toronto Jobs	www.toronto-jobs.com
Toronto Society of Financial Analysts	www.tsfa.ca
Tourism Work Web	www.tourismworkweb.com
Vancouver Job Shop	www.vancouverjobshop.ca
Vancouver Jobs	www.vancouver-jobs.com
Victoria Job Shop	www.victoriajobshop.ca
Winnipeg Job Shop	www.winnipegjobshop.ca

Notes

Favorite sites, useful resources

International (continued)

Canada (continued)
Working.ca   www.working.ca
Winnipeg Job Shop   www.winnipegjobshop.ca
⚄ Workopolis   www.workopolis.com

Caribbean
CaribbeanJobs.com   www.caribbeanjobs.com
CaribbeanJobsOnline.com   www.caribbeanjobsonline.com
JobsintheSun.com   www.jobsinthesun
ResortJobs.com   www.resortjobs.com
TropicJobs.com   www.tropicjobs.com

Chile
Bumeran.com   www.bumeran.com
ChileTech.com   www.chiletech.com
Empleate.com   www.empleate.com
Laborum.com   www.laborum.com
TipTopJob.com   www.tiptopjob.com
Zeezo   http://chile.zeezo.com/
                                                santiago-de-chile/jobs.htm

China
Asiaco Job Center   http://jobs.asiaco.com
AsiaOne Careers   www.asiaonecareers.com
CareerWise at Dragonsurf.com   www.dragonsurf.com/
                                                CareerWise/index.cfm

CC-Jobs.com   www.cc-jobs.com
BeijingJob.com   www.beijingjob.com
ChinaHR.com   www.chinahr.com
DragonSurf.com   www.dragonsurf.com
51job.com   www.51job.com
JobSquare   www.jobsquare.com
JobsDB   www.jobsdb.com
Zaobao   http://careers.zaobao.com
Zhaopin   www.zhaopin.com

Colombia
Empleate.com   www.empleate.com
Laborum.com   www.laborum.com
TipTopJob.com   www.tiptopjob.com

Czech Republic
HotJobs.cz   www.hotjobs.cz
Jobs.cz   www.jobs.cz
Prace.cz   www.prace.cz

Notes

Favorite sites, useful resources

International (continued)

Denmark
Job-Index	www.jobindex.dk
+Jobs Danmark	www.denmark.plusjobs.com
StepStone	www.stepstone.com

Europe-General
AuPair In Europe	www.planetaupair.com/ aupaireng.htm
CareerJournal Europe	www.careerjournaleurope.com
CVO Online	www.cvogroup.com
◪ eFinancial Careers	www.efinancialcareers.com
E-JOE: European Job Opportunites for Economists	http://rfe.org/JobGrant/index.html
EUjobzone.com	www.eujobzone.com
Euroleaders	www.euroleaders.com
The European Network	www.theeuropeannetwork.com
Jobline International	www.jobline.org
Job Pilot	www.jobpilot.com
Job Universe	www.jobuniverse.com
Russoft.org	www.russoft.org
The SAP Job Board	www.thesapjobboard.com
StepStone	www.stepstone.com
SupplyChainRecruit.com	www.supplychainrecruit.com
TipTopJob.com	www.tiptopjob.com
Wideyes	www.wideyes.co.uk

Finland
StepStone	www.stepstone.com

France
ANPE.fr	www.anpe.fr
BlogEmploi	www.blogemploi.com
Cadremploi.fr	www.cadremploi.fr
CEGOS Worldwide	www.cegos.fr
Cooptin.com	www.cooptin.com
DialJob.com	www.dialjob.com
eFinancialCareers.fr	www.efinancialcareers.fr
eMailJob.com	www.emailjob.com
JobPilot.fr	www.jobpilot.fr
KelJob.com	www.keljob.com
Les Echos	http://emploi.lesechos.fr
Monster.fr	www.monster.fr
StepStone	www.stepstone.com

Notes

Favorite sites, useful resources

International (continued)

Germany

All4Engineers.de	www.all4engineers.de
Arbeitslife.de	www.arbeitslife.de
Association for Applied Human Pharmacology	www.agah-web.de
CallCenterProfi.de	www.callcenterprofi.de
City Jobs	www.cityjobs.com
EMBL Job Vacancies	www.embl-heidelberg.de/ ExternalInfo/Jobs
Financial Times Deutschland	www.positionnet.de
Germany-USA	www.germany-usa.com
ICjobs	www.icjobs.de
JobBerlin.com	www.jobberlin.com
Jobdoo.de	www.jobdoo.de
JobDumping.de	www.jobdumping.de
Jobline	www.jobline.de
JobLinks	http://cip.physik.uni-wuerzburg.de
JobPilot.de/Monster	www.jobpilot.de
JobScout 24	www.jobscout.de
JobStairs.de	www.jobstairs.de
JobUniverse.de	www.computerwoche.de/ stellenmarkt.html
Jobware.de	www.jobware.de
Monster.de	www.monster.de
Stellenanzeigen.de	www.stellenanzeigen.de
StepStone	www.stepstone.com
uJob.de	www.ujob.de
Undertool.de	www.undertool.de
Virtueller Arbeitsmarkt	www.arbeitsagentur.de
WorkingOffice.de	www.workingoffice.de
Worldwide Jobs	www.worldwidejobs.de

Guam

The Jobs Guam Job Search Site	www.post-a-job.com/ allJobs/United_States/ Guam/Guam.html
Job Search in Guam	www.worldtenant.com/ jobs/guam.htm

Hong Kong

CareerWise at Dragonsurf.com	www.dragonsurf.com/ CareerWise/index.cfm
Hong Kong Jobs	www.hkjobs.com
Hong Kong Standard	www.hkstandard.com
JobsDB	www.jobsdb.com
Monster.com.hk	www.monster.com.hk

Notes

Favorite sites, useful resources

International (continued)

Hungary
CVO Online	www.cvogroup.com
Profession.hu	www.profession.hu

India
BPOJobSite.com	www.bpojobsite.com
CareerBuilderIndia.com	www.careerbuilderindia.com
Career India	www.careerindia.com
Career Mosaic India	www.careermosaicindia.com
Cyber India Online	www.ciol.com
CyberMediaDice.com	www.cybermediadice.com
HindJob.com	www.hindjob.com
Ikerala	www.ikerala.com
JobStreet.com	www.jobstreet.com
Jobs Ahead	www.jobsahead.com
JobsDB	www.jobsdb.com
MonsterIndia	www.monsterindia.com
Nasscom.org	www.nasscom.org
Naukri.com	www.naukri.com
Net Pilgrim	www.recruitmentindia.com
People.com	www.people.com
RegisterJobs.com	www.registerjobs.com
The Times of India	www.timesjobs.com
Win Jobs	www.winjobs.com

Ireland
Corporate Skills	www.irishjobs.com
Hcareers	www.hcareers.co.uk
IFSCjobs.com	www.ifscjobs.com
IrishDev.com	www.irishdev.com
Irishjobs	www.irishjobs.ie
The Irish Jobs Page	www.exp.ie
JobSearchNI.com	www.jobsearchni.com
JobsinHealth.com	www.jobsinhealth.com
Loadzajobs.co.uk	www.loadzajobs.co.uk
Northern Ireland Jobs	www.nijobs.com
RecruitIreland.com	www.recruitireland.com
TotalJobs.com	www.totaljobs.com

Israel
The Jerusalem Post	http://info.jpost.com/C005/ IsraelJobs/
JobNet Israel	www.jobnet.co.il
Marksman	www.marksman.co.il
MyRecruiter.com	www.myrecruiter.com

Notes

Favorite sites, useful resources

International (continued)

Italy
JobOnline.it	www.jobonline.it
TalentManager	www.talentmanager.it
StepStone	www.stepstone.com

Jamaica
CarribeanJobs.com	www.carribeanjobs.com
JobsintheSun.com	www.jobsinthesn.com
SplashJamaica.com	www.splashjamaica.com

Japan
Career Forum	www.careerforum.net
Daijob.com	www.daijob.com
enjapan.com	www.enjapan.com
Japanese Jobs	www.japanesejobs.com
Job Easy	www.jobeasy.com
NAUKRI	www.naukri.com
O Hayo Sensei	www.ohayosensei.com/ classified.html
Tokyo Classified	www.tokyoclassified.com
WorkinJapan	www.workinjapan.com

Korea
Asiaco Jobs Center	http://jobs.asiaco.com/ southkorea/
Job Korea [not in English]	www.jobkorea.co.kr
JobLink	www.joblink.kr
Peoplenjob	www.peoplenjob.com

Latin America
Asiaco Jobs Center	http://jobs.asiaco.com/ latinamerica/
Bumeran	www.bumeran.com
⊠ LatPro	www.latpro.com

Luxembourg
LuxJobs	www.luxjobs.lu
Monster.lu	www.monster.lu
StepStone	www.stepstone.com

Malaysia
JobStreet.com	www.jobstreet.com
JobsDB	www.jobsdb.com
StarJobs Online	www.star-jobs.com

Notes

Favorite sites, useful resources

International (continued)

Mexico
ChambaMex.com	www.chambamex.com
Laborum.com	www.laborum.com

Middle East
GulfJobSites.com	www.gulfjobsites.com

Netherlands
City Jobs	www.cityjobs.com
CV Market	www.cvmarket.nl
EEGA	www.eega.nl
Hospitality Net Virtual Job Exchange	www.hospitalitynet.nl
Jobs Netherland	www.jobs.nl
NationaleVacaturebank.nl	www.nationalevacaturebank.nl
TotalJobs.nl	www.totaljobs.ne
Van Zoelen Recruitment	www.vz-recruitment.nl/ uk/indexuk.htm

New Zealand
Executive Taskforce	http://exectask.co.nz
Job.co.nz	www.job.co.nz
JobStuff.co.nz	www.jobstuff.co.nz
KiwiCareers	www.kiwicareers.govt.nz
Nzjobs	www.nzjobs.co.nz
RealContacts.com	www.realcontacts.com
WorkingIn.com	www.workingin.com

Norway
FNN Jobb	www.finn.no
StepStone	www.stepstone.com

Peru
EC – Jobshark	www.ec-jobshark.com.pe
Empleate.com	www.empleate.com
Laborum.com	www.laborum.com
TipTopJob.com	www.tiptopjob.com
Zeezo	http://peru.zeezo.com/jobs.htm

Philippines
JobStreet Philippines	http://ph.jobstreet.com/
JobsDB	www.jobsdb.com
Jobs.NET	www.jobs.net
Philippines Employment Center	www.asiadragons.com/ philippines/employment/
Philippines Jobs	http://philippinejobs.ph/

Notes

Favorite sites, useful resources

International (continued)

Poland
Praca.Gazeta.pl   www.praca.gazeta.pl
Pracui.pl   www.pracui.pl

Portugal
StepStone   www.stepstone.com
Super Emprego   http://superemprego.sapo.pt

Scotland
InternalAuditJobs.net   www.internalauditjobs.net
Jobsword   www.jobsword.co.uk/
                                                  scotland.html
ScotCareers.co.uk   www.scotcareers.co.uk
ScotlandJobs.net   www.scotlandjobs.net
ScottishHospitalityJobs.com   www.scottishhospitalityjobs.com
ScottishJobs.com   www.scottishjobs.com
ScottishLegalJobs.com   www.scottishlegaljobs.com
TechJobsScotland   www.techjobscotland.com
TotalJobs.com   www.totaljobs.com
WorkWithUs.org   www.workwithus.org/people/

Singapore
JobStreet.com   www.jobstreet.com
JobsDB   www.jobsdb.com
9to5Asia.com   www.careermastery.com
Singapore and Asean Job Resume
  Database   www.siam.net/jobs
Singapore Jobs Directory   www.jobs.com.sg
SingaporeJobsOnline.com   www.singaporejobsonline.com

Slovakia
Profesia.sk   www.profesia.sk

South Africa
Best Jobs South Africa   www.bestjobsza.com/dr-job.htm
BioCareers.co.za   www.biocareers.co.za
CareerClassifieds South Africa   www.careerclassifieds.co.za/
CareerJunction   www.careerjunction.co.za
Jobs.co.za   www.jobs.co.za

Spain
InfoEmpleo.com   www.infoempleo.com
InfoJobs.net   www.infojobs.net
Laboris.net   www.laboris.net
Monster Espania   www.monster.es

Notes

Favorite sites, useful resources

International (continued)

Spain (continued)
Spanish-Living.com	www.spanish-living.com/ Jobs-offers.htm
Zeezo	http://spain.zeezo.com/jobs.htm

Sweden
JobbSverige AB	www.jobbsverige.se
Dagens Industri	www.di.se
Shortcut	www.shortcut.nu
StepStone	www.stepstone.com

Switzerland
Common Switzerland	www.common.ch
JobPilot.ch	www.jobpilot.ch
JobScout24.ch	
Jobs.ch	www.jobs.ch
LeTemps.ch	www.letemps.ch
Math-Jobs.ch	www.math-jobs.ch
Monster.ch	www.monster.ch
StepStone	www.stepstone.com
TopJobs.ch	www.topjobs.ch

Taiwan
CareerWise at Dragonsurf.com	www.dragonsurf.com/ CareerWise/index.cfm
JobSlide.com	www.jobslide.com/directory/ Country/Taiwan/
JobsDB	www.jobsdb.com

Thailand
JobsDB	www.jobsdb.com

United Kingdom
AccountancyAgeJobs.com	www.accountancyagejobs.com
AccountingWeb	www.accountingweb.co.uk
Aeronautical Engineering Jobs	www.aeronauticalengineeringjobs .co.uk
AllHousingJobs.co.uk	www.allhousingjobs.co.uk
ArtsJobsOnline.com	www.artsjobsonline.com
Association of Graduate Careers Advisory Service	www.agcas.org.uk
Association of Online Recruiters	www.rec.uk.com
Association of University Teachers	www.AUT4Jobs.com
Aston University	www.aston.ac.uk
Bconstructive	www.bconstructive.co.uk

Notes

Favorite sites, useful resources

International (continued)

United Kingdom (continued)

BigBlueDog.com	www.bigbluedog.com
BlowSearch.com	www.blowsearch.com
BookaChef.co.uk	www.bookachef.co.uk
BookaTemp.co.uk	www.bookatemp.co.uk
BUBL Employment Bulletin Board	http://bubl.ac.uk
Business Test Publishers Association	www.assessmentjobs.com
Business Web Directory	www.businessdirectory.com
Call Centres	www.searchcallcentre.co.uk
CanaryWharfJobs.com	www.canarywharfjobs.com
CancerJobs.net	www.cancerjobs.net
Career-Ahead	www.career-ahead.co.uk
CareerJobPlanet.com	www.careerjobplanet.com
CareersinLogistics.co.uk	www.careersinlogistics.co.uk
CareersInRecruitment.com	www.careersinrecruitment.com
Caterer.com	www.caterer.com
CatererGlobal.com	www.catererglobal.com
Change Jobs	www.changejobs.co.uk
CharityJob.co.uk	www.charityjob.co.uk
ChemPeople.com	www.chempeople.com
Citifocus	www.citifocus.co.uk
CityJobs	www.citijobs.co.uk
CollegeJobs.co.uk	www.collegejobs.co.uk
Commserve	www.commserve.co.uk
Computer Staff	www.computerstaff.net
Confidential IT	www.confidentialit.com
ConstructionJobsNow.co.uk	www.constructionjobsnow.co.uk
Consultants on the Net	www.consultantsonthenet.com
ConsultantsBoard.com	www.consultantsboard.com
The CV Index Directory	www.cvindex.com
CVServices.net	www.cvspecial.co.uk
CWJobs.co.uk	www.cwjobs.co.uk
Cyberia	www.cyberiacafe.net/jobs
CyberKing Employment	www.cyberkingemployment.com
CYMRU Prosper Wales	www.cpw.org.uk
Datascope Recruitment	www.datascope.co.uk
DERWeb	www.derweb.co.uk
DesignJobs.co.uk	www.designjobs.co.uk
DHA Resourcing Solutions	www.d-h-a.net
DigitalMediaJobs.com	www.digitalmediajobs.com
Discover Me	www.discoverme.com
DMjobs.co.uk	www.dmjobs.co.uk
Do-It	www.do-it.org.uk
Dot Jobs	www.dotjobs.co.uk
dotJournalism	www.journalism.co.uk

Notes

Favorite sites, useful resources

International (continued)

United Kingdom (continued)

EasyJobs.com	www.easyjobs.com
Easyline.co.uk	www.easyline.co.uk
Edie's Environmental Job Centre	www.edie.net
Eteach.com	www.eteach.com
Education-Jobs	www.education-jobs.co.uk
EFL Web	www.eflweb.com
e-job	www.e-job.net
Employment Postions Abroad	www.ecaltd.com/default.asp
ENDS	www.endsco.uk/jobs
The Engineering Technology Site	www.engineers4engineers.co.uk
Eplace.co.uk	www.eplace.co.uk
Escape Artist	www.escapeartist.com
Euro London	www.eurolondon.com
Exec2Exec.com	www.exec2exec.com
Execs on the Net	www.eotn.co.uk
ExecutiveOpenings.com	www.executiveopenings.com
ExecutivesontheWeb.com	www.executivesontheweb.com
FEcareers.co.uk	www.fecareers.co.uk
FEjobs.com	www.fejobs.com
50Connect.co.uk	www.50connect.co.uk
First Choice Recruitment	www.first-choice-uk.co.uk
1st Job	www.1stjob.co.uk
1st 4 UK HR Jobs	www.1st4ukhrjobs.co.uk
Fish4IT	www.fish4it.co.uk
Fish4Jobs	http://jobs.fish4.co.uk
Fledglings	www.fledglings.net
Football-jobs.com	www.football-jobs.com
FootieJobs.com	www.footiejobs.com
4 Weeks	www.4weeks.com
FreeLancers Network	www.freelancers.net
Freelawyer	www.freelawyer.coluk
Free-Recruitment.com	www.free-recruitment.com
G2legal	www.g2legal.co.uk
GAAPWeb.com	www.gaapweb.com
GetaLife.org.uk	www.getalife.org.uk
GetHeadHunted	www.getheadhunted.co.uk
GisaJob.com	www.gisajob.com
GoJobSite	www.jobchannel.com
GoldJobs.com	www.goldjobs.com
Go Partnership Limited	www.gogogo.org
The Guardian Observer	http://recruitnet.guardian.co.uk
Gisajob	www.gisajob.com
Go Job Site	www.gojobsite.com
Goldensquare.com	www.goldensquare.com

Notes

Favorite sites, useful resources

International (continued)

United Kingdom (continued)

Graduate-jobs.com	www.graduate-jobs.com
GraduateLink	www.graduatelink.com
Gradunet	www.gradunet.co.uk
Grapevine Jobs	www.grapevinejobs.co.uk
GrocerJobs.co.uk	www.grocerjobs.co.uk
GTNews	www.gtnews.com
The Guardian Jobs	www.guardian.co.uk/jobs
GxPJobs.com	www.gxpjobs.com
Hands on Solutions	www.handsonsolutions.com
Hcareers	www.hcareers.co.uk
Hedge Fund Intelligence LLC	www.hedgefundintelligence.com
HospitalityRecruitment.co.uk	www.hospitalityrecruitment.co.uk
Hotcourses.com	www.givemeajob.co.uk
HotJobsandCareers	www.hotjobsandcareers.com
Hot Recruit	www.hotrecruit.co.uk
Hotel Jobs	www.hotel-jobs.co.uk
HR Staff	www.hrstaff.co.uk
Hy-phen	www.hy-phen.com
Gradvacs.com	www.gradvacs.com
InAutomotive.com	www.inautomotive.com
In the Middle	www.inthemiddle.co.uk
The Independent Consultants Network	www.inconet.com
InHR	www.inhr.co.uk
InRetail	www.inretail.co.uk
Institute of Clinical Research	www.instituteofclinical research.org
Intega Online	www.intega.co.uk
InternalAuditJobs.net	www.internalauditjobs.net
I-Resign.co	www.i-resign.com/uk/ home/default.asp
TheITJobBoard.com	www.theitjobboard.com
IT List	www.itlist.co.uk
It's A People Thing!	www.itsapeoplething.com
ITCV	www.itcv.co.uk
Jim Finder	www.jimfinder.com
Jobs4a.com	www.jobs4a.com
Job4me.com	wwwjob4me.com
Jobcentre Plus	www.jobcentreplus
Jobcorner	www.jobcorner.com
JobChannel	www.jobchannel.tv
Job Domain	www.jobdomain.co.uk
Job Finder	www.jobfinder.com
Job Force	www.jobforce.com
Job Jobbed	www.jobjobbed.com

Notes

Favorite sites, useful resources

International (continued)

United Kingdom (continued)

Job Magic	www.jobmagic.net
Job Magnet	www.jobmagnet.co.uk
JobMax.co.uk	www.jobmax.co.uk
Job-opps.co.uk	www.job-opps-co.uk
JobPilot UK	www.jobpilot.co.uk
JobScout	www.jobscout.co.uk
Job Search UK	www.jobsearch.co.uk
JobseekersAdvice.com	www.jobseekersadvice.com
Job Serve	www.jobserve.com
Jobshark.com	www.jobshark.co.uk
Job Shop	www.workweb.co.uk
JobSite UK	www.jobsite.co.uk
Job-surf.com	www.job-surf.com
JobTrack Online	www.jobtrack.co.uk
Job Watch	www.jobwatch.co.uk
Jobworld UK	www.jobworld.oc.uk
jobbies.com	www.jobbies.com
Jobs.ac.uk	www.jobs.ac.uk
Jobs-at	www.jobs-at.co.uk
Jobs.co.uk	www.jobs.co.uk
Jobsandadverts.com	www.jobsandadverts.com
Jobs-Chesire.co.uk	www.jobs-chesire.co.uk
JobsinCredit.com	www.jobsincredit.com
JobsFinancial.com	www.jobsfinancial.com
Jobsgopublic	www.jobsgopublic.co.uk
Jobsin.co.uk	www.jobsin.co.uk
Jobs Jobs Jobs	www.jobsjobsjobs.co.uk
Jobs in Marketing	www.jobs-in-marketing.co.uk
Jobs-Merseyside.co.uk	www.jobs-merseyside.co.uk
Jobs-Northeast.co.uk	www.jobs-northeast.co.uk
JobsinRisk.com	www.jobsinrisk.com
JobsinSearch.com	www.jobsinsearch.com
Jobs-Southeast.co.uk	www.jobs-southeast.co.uk
Jobs.telegraph.co.uk	www.appointments-plus.com
Jobs Unlimited	www.jobsunlimited.co.uk
JobsWithBalls.com	www.jobswithballs.com
Johnston Vere	www.johnstonvere.com
Just Construction	www.justconstruction.net
Just Engineers	www.justengineers.net
Just Go Contract!	www.gocontract.com
Just Graduates	www.justgraduates.net
Just Rail	www.justrail.net
JustSalesandMarketing.net	www.justsalesandmarketing.net
JustTechnicalJobs	www.justtechnicaljobs.net

Notes

Favorite sites, useful resources

International (continued)

United Kingdom (continued)

KillerJobs.com	www.killerjobs.com
KR Solutions	www.kr-solutions.co.uk/index.php
Laser Computer Recruitment	www.laserrec.co.uk
Leisure Recruit Ltd	www.leisurerecruit.com
Leisure Opportunities	www.leisureopportunities.co.uk
Local Government Jobs	www.lgjobs.com
LocalJobSearch.co.uk	www.localjobsearch.co.uk
Locum Group Recruitment	www.locumgroup.co.uk
The London Biology Network	www.biolondon.co.uk
London Careers	www.londoncareers.net
London Jobs	www.londonjobs.co.uk
LookTech.com	www.looktech.com
Mandy.com	www.mandy.com
Marine Recruitment Co.	www.marine-recruitment.co.uk
MediaKnowledge.com	www.mediaknowledge.com
MedicSolve.com	www.medicsolve.com
Medjobsuk.com	www.medjobsuk.com
MightyMatch.com	www.mightymatch.com
Milkround Online	www.milkround.co.uk
Monster.com UK	www.monster.co.uk
Mycvonline UK	www.mycvonline.co.uk
My9to5.com	www.my9to5.com
My Oyster	www.myoyster.com
National Health Service	www.nhs.uk/jobs
National Information Services and Systems	www.hero.ac.uk/uk/home/index.cfm
Net J	www.netjobs.co.uk
NewMonday.co.uk	www.newmonday.co.uk
NHS Jobs	www.jobs.nhs.uk
Nixers.com	www.nixers.com
NMC4Jobs.com	www.nmc4jobs.com
Northwest Workplace	www.northwestworkplace.com
Nurseserve	www.nurseserv.co.uk
Oil Careers	www.oilcareers.com
Online Context UK	www.onlinecontentuk.org
OnlineMarketingJobs.com	www.onlinemarketingjobs.com
OnrecJobs.com	www.onrecjobs.com
PharmaVillage.com	www.pharmavillage.com
Phee Farrer Jones Consultancy	www.pheefarrerjones.co.uk
PhoneAJob	www.phoneajob.com
Planet Recruit	www.planetrecruit.co.uk
PlatinumJobs.com	www.platinumjobs.com
Prospects.ac.uk	www.prospects.ac.uk
PTO People	www.ptopeople.co.uk

Notes

Favorite sites, useful resources

International (continued)

United Kingdom (continued)

PublicJobs-Northwest.co.uk	www.publicjobs-northeast.co.uk
OutdoorStaff	www.outdoorstaff.co.uk
Oxygen	www.oxygenonline.co.uk
Qworx.com	www.qworx.com
Recruitment-Consultant.com	www.recruitment-consultant.com
Recruitment Jobz	www.recruitmentjobz.com
Recruitment-Marketing	www.recruitment-marketing.co.uk
Redgoldfish.co.uk	www.redgoldfish.co.uk
Resourcing International Consulting	www.cyber-cv.com
Resortjobs.co.uk	www.resortjobs.co.uk
RetailChoice.com	www.retailchoice.com
RetailHomepage.co.uk	www.retailhomepage.co.uk
RetailMoves.com	www.retailmoves.com
SalesWise.co.uk	www.saleswise.co.uk
ScientistWorld.com	www.scientistworld.com
Search4Grads.com	www.search4grads.com
Searching the Universe	www.oconnell.co.uk
SimplyLawJobs.com	www.simplylawjobs.com
Simply Sales and Marketing	www.simplysalesandmarketing. co.uk
SkillsArena.com	www.skillsarena.com
Smarter Work	www.smarterwork.com
SmugOne.com	www.smugone.com
StepStone	www.stepstone.com
THESIS: The Times Higher Education Supplement InterView Service	www.thesis.co.uk
Talent Manager	www.talentmanager.com
Tandem-World.com	www.tandem-world.com
Temps Online	www.tempsonline.co.uk
Tempz	www.tempz.com
ThisIsJobs	www.thisisjobs.co.uk
TipTopJob.com	www.tiptopjob.com
TiscaliJobSearch.co.uk	www.tiscalijobsearch.com
Top Contracts	www.topcontacts.com
Top Jobs	www.topjobs.net
Top Jobs On the Net	www.topjobs.co.uk
TopLanguageJobs.co.uk	www.toplanguagejobs.co.uk
TotalJobs.com	www.totaljobs.com
TrainingProviderJobs.co.uk	www.trainingproviderjobs.co.uk
TravelJobSearch.com	www.traveljobsearch.com
UK Graduate Careers	www.gti.co.uk
UKjobs2004.com	www.ukjobs2004.com
Workthing.com	www.workthing.com
Worksfm.com	www.worksfm.com

Notes

Favorite sites, useful resources

International (continued)

Venezuela
MeQuieroIr.com   www.mequieroir.com

Vietnam
JobStreet.com   www.jobstreet.com
JobsAbroad   www.jobsabroad.com/
     Vietnam.cfm
VietnamWorks.com   www.vietnamworks.com

Wales
JobsinWales.com   www.databaseforjobs.com
JobsWales.co.uk   www.jobswales.co.uk
WelshJobs.com   www.welshjobs.com

Investment/Brokerage

Annuitiesnet.com   www.annuitiesnet.com
Association for Investment
  Management and Research   www.cfainstitute.org
Bond Buyer   www.bondbuyer.com
BrokerHunter.com   www.brokerhunter.com
Canadian Association of Financial Planners   www.cafp.org
❆ CareerBank.com   www.careerbank.com
❆ eFinancialCareers.com [United Kingdom]   www.efinancialcareers.com
International Association for Registered   www.iarfc.org/
  Financial Planners   jservices.shtml
Investment Management and Trust
  Exchange   www.antaeans.com
National Association of Securities
  Professionals Current Openings   www.nasphq.com/career.html
National Association of Securities   www.naspatlanta.com/
  Professionals (Atlanta) Current Openings   career.html
National Association of Securities
  Professionals (New York) Underground Railroad   www.nasp-ny.org
Securities Industry Association
  Career Resource Center   www.sia.com/career
National Venture Capital Association   www.nvca.org
New York Society of Security Analysts
  Career Resources   www.nyssa.org/jobs
RepsTradingPlaces.com   www.repstradingplaces.com
Securities Industry Association
  Career Resource Center   www.sia.com/career
Society of Actuaries   www.soa.org
Society of Risk Analysis Opportunities   www.sra.org/opptys.php
Street Jobs   www.streetjobs.com

Notes

Favorite sites, useful resources

-J-

Job Fairs Online

Job Dex	www.jobdex.com
OilCareerFair	www.oilcareerfair.com
MedJobsNow.com	www.medjobsnow.com
Professional Exchange	www.professional-exchange.com/ indexie.htm

Journalism & Media (See also Graphic Arts)

Airwaves Job Services	www.airwaves.com
American Society of Journalists & Authors	www.freelancewritersearch.com
Animation Industry Database	www.aidb.com
Animation World Network	www.awn.com
Association of Electronic Journalists	www.rtnda.org
Association for Women in Communications	www.womcom.org
Association for Women in Communcations WDC Chapter	www.awic-dc.org
Communications Roundtable	www.roundtable.org
Copy Editor	www.copyeditor.com/ Copy/copy_jobs_jobboard.asp
Copy Editor Newsletter	www.copyeditorjobs.com
Coroflot	www.coroflot.com
Creative Freelancers	www.freelnacers.com
DigitalMediaJobs.com [United Kingdom]	www.digitalmediajobs.com
dotJournalism [United Kingdom]	www.journalism.co.uk
Editor & Publisher	www.mediainfo.com
eFront.com	www.efront.com
eLance.com	www.elance.com
Electronic Media Online	www.emonline.com
FreeLanceWriting.com	www.freelancewriting.com
GamesPress.com	www.gamespress.com
GrapevineJobs [United Kingdom]	www.grapevinejobs.co.uk
Guru.com	www.guru.com
HTML Writers Guild HWG-Jobs	www.hwg.org/lists/hwg-jobs
I-Advertising	http://internetadvertising.org
International Association of Business Communicators Career Centre	www.iabc.com
JobLink for Journalists	http://ajr.newslink.org/joblink.html
JournalismJob.com	www.journalismjob.com
Journalism Jobs	www.journalismjobs.com
JournalismNext.com	www.journalismnext.com
Mandy.com	www.mandy.com/1/filmtvjobs.ctm
MassMediaJobs.com	www.massmediajobs.com

Notes

Favorite sites, useful resources

Journalism & Media (continued)

Mediabistro	www.mediabistro.com
Media Communications Association International Job Hotline	www.mca-i.org
Media Human Resource Association	www.shrm.org/mhra/index.asp
MediaKnowledge.co.uk [United Kingdom]	www.mediaknowledge.co.uk
Medialine	www.medialine.com
MediaRecruiter.com	www.mediarecruiter.com
National Alliance of State Broadcasters Associations CareerPage	www.careerpage.org
National Diversity Newspaper Job Bank	www.newsjobs.com
National Writers Union Job Hotline	www.nwu.org/hotline
NationJob Advertising and Media Jobs Page	www.nationjob.com/media
New York New Media Association	www.nynma.org
News Jobs	www.newsjobs.com
Newspaper Association of America Newspaper CareerBank	www.naa.org/careerbank
OnlineMarketingJobs.com [United Kingdom]	www.onlinemarketingjobs.com
PaidContent.org	www.paidcontent.org/jobs
Print Jobs	www.printjobs.com
R & R Online	www.rronline.com
Radio Ink Help Wanted	www.radioinkhelpwanted.com
Silicon Alley Connections	www.salley.com
Society for Technical Communications	www.stc.org
StaffWriters Plus, Inc.	www.staffwriters.com
Technical Communicator	www.technical communicatior.com
TelecommutingJobs	www.tjobs.com
TV Jobs	www.tvjobs.com
Ultimate TV	www.ultimatetv.com
VFXWorld	www.vfxworld.com
Webmonkey Jobs	www.hotwired.com/dreamjobs
Workinpr.com	www.workinpr.com
The Write Jobs	www.writerswrite.com/jobs
The Write Jobs for The Writers Write	www.writerswrite.com/jobs
Writer's SunOasis	www.sunoasis.com
WritersWeekly.com	www.writersweekly.com

-L-

Law/Legal

AACN Career Opportunites	www.acca.com/jobline
Alliance of Merger and Acquisition Advisors	www.advisor-alliance.com

Notes

Favorite sites, useful resources

Law (continued)

American Association of Law Libraries
  Job Placement Hotline   www.aallnet.org/hotline
American Bankruptcy Institute Career Center   www.abiworld.org/abi
        careercenter
American Bar Association   www.abanet.org
American Corporate Counsel Association   www.acca.com
American Immmigration Lawyers Association   www.aila.org
Association of Legal Information
  Systems Managers Job Listings   www.alism.org/jobs.htm
Attorney Jobs   www.attorneyjobs.com
Attorney Pages   http://attorneypages.com
Barry University of Orlando   www.uo.edu
Bench & Bar   www.mnbar.org/bbclass.htm
Corporate Legal Times   www.insidecounsel.com
Counsel.net   www.counel.net
Degree Hunter   www.degreehunter.com
eAttorney.com   www.eattorney.com
Elite Consultants   www.eliteconsultants.com
Emplawyernet   www.emplawyernet.com
Find Law Careers   www.findlaw.com
Find Law Job   www.findlawjob.com
4 Paralegals   www.4paralegals.com
G2legal [United Kingdom]   www.g2legal.co.uk
Greedy Associates   www.greedyassociates.com
HeadHunt.com [Canada]   www.headhunt.com
Hieros Gamos Legal
  Employment Classified   www.hg.org/employment.html
iHireLegal   www.ihirelegal.com
Infirmation   www.infirmation.com
Intelproplaw   www.intelproplaw.com
International Association for Commercial
  and Contract Management   www.iaccm.com
The International Lawyers Network   www.lawinternational.com
JobLinks for Lawyers   htttp://home.sprynet.com/
    ~ear2ground
JobsLawInfo.com   http://jobs.lawinfo.com
TheLadders.com   www.theladders.com
Law.com   www.law.com
Law Bulletin   www.lawbulletin.com
LawCrossing   www.lawcrossing
Law Forum   www.lawforum.net
Law Guru   www.lawguru.com
Law Info   www.lawinfo.com
Law Jobs   www.lawjobs.com
Law Match   http://lawmatch.com

Notes

Favorite sites, useful resources

Law (continued)

Law Office	www.lawoffice.com
Law Source	http://lawsource.com
Lawyers – About.com	http://lawyers.about.com
Lawyers Weekly Jobs	www.lawyersweeklyjobs.com
The Legal Career Center Network	www.thelccn.com
The Legal Employment Search Site	www.legalemploy.com
Legal Gate	www.legalgate.com
Legal Hire	www.legalhire.com
LegalJob.ca [Canada]	www.legaljob.ca
Legal Job Store	www.legaljobstore.com
Legal Report	www.legalreport.com
Legal Search Network	wwwlegalsearchnetwork.com
Legal Serve	www.legalserve.com
Legal Staff	www.legalstaff.com
MyLegalJobs.net	www.mylegaljobs.net
National Association of Legal Assistants	www.nala.org
National Employment Lawyers Association	www.nela.org
National Federation of Paralegal Associations Career Center	www.paralegals.org/display common.cfm?an=20
National Paralegal	www.nationalparalegal.org
Nationwide Process Servers Association	www.processservers association.com
New Hampshire Legal Assistance	www.nhla.org
Paralegal Classifieds	www.paralegalclassifieds.com
Paralegaljob.ca [Canada]	www.paralegaljob.ca
PatentJobs.com	www.patentjobs.com
Piper Pat	www.piperpat.co.nz
RegulatoryCareers.com	www.regulatorycareers.com
ScottishLegalJobs.com [Scotland]	www.scottishlegaljobs.com
SimplyLawJobs.com [United Kingdom]	www.simplylawjobs.com
Trial Lawyers for Public Justice	www.tlpj.com

Law Enforcement

American Society for Law Enforcement Training	www.aslet.org
The Blue Line: Police Opportunity Monitor	www.theblueline.com
Cop Spot	www.cop-spot.com
High Technology Crime Investigation Association	www.htcia.org
Hispanic American Police Command Officers Association	www.hapcoa.org
iHireLawEnforcement.com	www.ihirelawenforcement.com
LawEnforcementJobs.com	www.lawenforcementjob.com
National Black Police Association	www.blackpolice.org

Notes

Favorite sites, useful resources

Law Enforcement (continued)

National Organization of Black Law Enforcement
  Executives   www.noblenational.org
National Latino Peace Officers Association   www.nlpoa.org
TechLawAdvisor.com Job Postings   www.techlawadvisor.com/jobs
Women in Federal Law Enforcement   www.wifle.com

Library & Information Science

American Association of Law Libraries
  Job Placement Hotline   www.aallnet.org/hotline
American Library Association
  Library Education and Employment
  Menu Page   www.ala.org/education
Art Libraries Society of North America JobNet   http://arlisna.org/jobs.html
BUBL Employment Bulletin Board
  [United Kingdom]   http://bubl.ac.uk
LibraryJobPostings.org   www.libraryjobpostings.org
LisJobs.com   www.lisjobs.com
Media Central   www.mediacentral.com/careers
Special Libraries Association   www.sla.org

Linguistics

Academic Job Openings in Applied Linguistics   http://aaaljobs.lang.uiuc.edu/
Jobs in Linguistics   www.linguistlist.org/
     jobsindex.html
Linguistic Enterprises   http://web.gc.cuny.edu/
     dept/lingu/enter/
The Linguist List   http://linguistlist.org/jobs/
     index.html

Logistics

CareersinLogistics.co.uk [United Kingdom]   www.careersinlogistics.co.uk
Energy Careers   www.energycareers.com
FM Link-Facilities Management   www.fmlink.com
Jobstor.com   www.jobstor.com
Jobs4Trucking.com   www.jobs4trucking.com
◙ JobsinLogistics.com   www.jobsinlogistics.com
LogisticsJobShop.com [United Kingdom]   www.logisticsjobshop.com
Logistics World   www.logisticsworld.com
MaintenanceEmployment.com   www.maintenance
     employment.com
RoadWhore.com   www.roadwhore.com
SupplyChainBrains.com   www.supplychainbrains.com

Notes

Favorite sites, useful resources

Logistics (continued)

SupplyChainJobs.com www.supplychainjobs.com
SupplyChainRecruit.com [Europe] www.supplychainrecruit.com
Truckdriver.com www.truckdriver.com
Virtual Logistics Directory www.logisticsdirectory.com

-M-

Military Personnel Transitioning into the Private Sector

Army Career & Alumni Program www.acap.army.mil
Blue-to-Gray www.bluetogray.com
Center for Employment Management www.cemjob.com
Classified Employment Web-Site www.yourinfosource.com/
 CLEWS
ClearanceJobs.com www.clearancejobs.com
ClearedStars.com www.clearedstars.com
Connecting Corporations to the
 Military Community www.vets4hire.com
Corporate Gray Online www.corporategrayonline.com
The Defense Talent Network www.defensetalent.com
Green-to-Gray www.greentogray.com
HelmetstoHardhats.com www.helmetstohardhats.com
Hire Quality www.hire-quality.com
HireVetsFirst.gov www.hirevetsfirst.gov
Jobs4Vets.com www.jobs4vets.com
Marine Executive Association www.marineea.org
Military.com www.military.com
Military Careers www.militarycareers.com
Military Connection www.militaryconnection.com
Military Connections www.militaryconnections.com
MilitaryHire.com www.militaryhire.com
Mil2civ.com www.mil2civ.com
MilitaryExits www.militaryexits.com
Military JobZone www.militaryjobzone.com
Military Spouse Corporate Career Network www.msccn.org
Military Spouses www.militaryspouses.com
Military Spouse Job Search www.militaryspousejobsearch.org
MilitaryStars.com www.militarystars.com
My Future www.myfuture.com
Operation Transition www.dmdc.osd.mil/ot
RecruitAirForce.com www.recruitairforce.com
RecruitMarines.com www.recruitmarines.com
RecruitMilitary.com www.recruitmilitary.com

Notes

Favorite sites, useful resources

Military Personnel Transitioning into the Private Sector (continued)

RecruitNavy.com   www.recruitnavy.com
Reserve Officers Association   www.roa.org/career_center.asp
Stripes.com   www.stripes.com
Transition Assistance Online   www.taonline.com
☑ VetJobs.com   www.vetjobs.com
Vets of Color   www.vetsofcolor.com

Modeling

ModelService.com   www.modelservice.com
OneModelPlace.com   www.onemodelplace.com
Supermodel.com   www.supermodel.com

Music

FilmMusic.net   www.filmmusic.net
The Internet Music Pages   www.musicpages.com
Key Signature [United Kingdom]   www.keysignature.co.uk
MusicJObsOnline.net   www.musicjobsonline.net
MusiciansBuyLine.com   www.musiciansbuyline.com/
    music_jobs_avail.html

-N-

Networking

ContactSpan   www.contactspan.com
Eurekster   www.eurekster.com
LinkedIn   www.linkedin.com
LinkedMe [Australia]   www.linkme.com.au
Monster Networking   www.monster.com
RealContacts   www.realcontacts.com
Ryze Business Networking   www.ryze.com
Spoke   www.spoke.com

Non-Profit

AllHousingJobs.co.uk [United Kingdom]   www.allhousingjobs.co.uk
boardnetUSA   www.boardnetusa.com
Career Action Center   www.careeraction.org
CharityJob.co.uk [United Kingdom]   www.charityjob.co.uk
Chronicle of Philanthropy   www.philanthropy.com
Community Career Center   www.nonprofitjobs.org
DotOrgJobs.com   www.dotorgjobs.com
The Foundation Center   www.fdncenter.org

Notes

Favorite sites, useful resources

Non-Profit (continued)

411 Fundraising	www.411fundraising.com
Fundraising Jobs	www.fundraisingjobs.com
Georgia Center for Nonprofits	www.gcn.org
Good Works	www.essential.org
Idealist	www.idealist.org
Internet Nonprofit Center	www.nonprofits.org
International Service Agencies	www.charity.org
Localstaff.com	www.localstaff.com
The National Assembly	www.nassembly.org
Non Profit Career Network	www.nonprofitcareer.com
Nonprofit Charitable Organizations	www.nonprofit.about.com
Non Profit Employment	www.nonprofitemployment.com
Non-Profit Marketing	www.cob.ohio-state.edu/~fin/ Nonprofit.htm
Nonprofit Times	www.nptimes.com
Opportunity Nocs	www.opnocsne.org
Philanthropy News Network Online	www.pnnonline.org/jobs
Social Service	www.socialservice.com
Tripod	www.tripod.com
VolunteerMatch	www.volunteermatch.org/

-O-

Outdoors/Recreation/Sports

The Amateur Coaching Connection	www.tazsports.com
AnyWorkAnywhere.com [United Kingdom]	www.anyworkanywhere.com
Association for Environmental and Outdoor Education	www.aeoe.org
C.O.A.C.H.	www.coachhelp.com
CoachingJobs.com	www.coachingjobs.com
Coaching Staff	www.coachingstaff.com
CoachingTalent.com	www.coachingtalent.com
Cool Works	www.coolworks.com/showme
Cruise Job Link	www.cruisejoblink.com
Equimax	www.equimax.com
FitnessJobs.com	www.fitnessjobs.com
Football-jobs.com [United Kingdom]	www.football-jobs.com
FootieJobs.com [United Kingdom]	www.footiejobs.com
Great Summer Jobs	www.gsj.petersons.com
Horticultural Jobs	www.horticulturaljobs.com
Jobs In Sports	www.jobsinsports.com
JobsWithBalls.com [United Kingdom]	www.jobswithballs.com
Leisure Recruit Ltd [United Kingdom]	www.leisurerecruit.com

Notes

Favorite sites, useful resources

Outdoors/Recreation/Sports (continued)

Leisure Opportunities [United Kingdom]	www.leisureopportunities.co.uk
Lifeguarding Jobs	www.lifeguardingjobs.com
NascarCareers.com	www.nascarcareers.com
National Sports Employment News	www.sportsemployment.com
NCAA	http://ncaa.thetask.com/market/ jobs/browse.html
Northeast Athletic Job Link	www.bright.net/~joblink
Online Sports Career Center	www.onlinesports.com/ careercenter.html
Outdoor Job Net	www.outdoornetwork.com/ jobnetdb/default.html
OutdoorStaff [United Kingdom]	www.outdoorstaff.co.uk
Pet-Sitters.biz	www.pet-sitters.biz
PGA.com	www.pga.com
Resort Jobs	www.resortjobs.com
Resortjobs.co.uk [United Kingdom]	www.resortjobs.co.uk
Skiing the Net	www.skiingthenet.com
SportLink	www.sportlink.com
Sportscasting Jobs	www.sportscastingjobs.com
SportsJobs.com	www.sportsjobs.com
SummerJobs.com	www.summerjobs.com
TAZsport.com	www.tazsport.com
Tennis Jobs	www.tennisjobs.com
Travel Jobz	www.traveljobz.net
WomenSportsJobs.com	www.womensportjobs.com
Women's Sport Services	www.wiscnetwork.com

-P-

Packaging for Food & Drug

Association of Industrial Metalizers, Coaters & Laminators	www.aimcal.org
Composite Can & Tube Institute	www.cctiwdc.org
Foodservice.com	http://foodservice.com
Institute of Food Science & Technology	www.ifst.org
Supermarket News	www.supermarketnews.com
Technical Association of the Pulp & Paper Industry Jobline	www.tappi.org/index.asp? ip=-1&ch=14&rc=-1

Pharmaceutical

Academy of Managed Care Pharmacy	www.amcp.org
American Academy of Pharmaceutical Physicians	www.aapp.org

Notes

Favorite sites, useful resources

Pharmaceutical (continued)

American Association of Pharmaceutical
  Sales Professionals   www.pharmaceuticalsales.org
American Association of Pharmaceutical
  Scientists   www.aaps.org
American College of Clinical Pharmacology   www.accp1.org
American College of Clinical Pharmacy   www.accp.com
American Pharmaceutical Association   www.aphanet.org
American Society of Clinical Pharmacology
  and Therapeutics   www.ascpt.org
American Society of
  Health-System Pharmacists   www.ashp.com
American Society of Pharmacognosy   www.phcog.org
Association for Applied Human Pharmacology
  [Germany]   www.agah-web.de
The Biomedical Engineering Network   www.bmenet.org
Board of Pharmaceutical Specialties   www.bpsweb.org
Carefree Pharmaceutical Returns   http://members.aol.com/
                                                           ajnovotny/cpr2.htm
Cen-ChemJobs.org   www.cen-chemjobs.org
ChemPharma.org   www.chempharma.org
Drug Discovery Online   www.drugdiscoveryonline.com
Drug Information Association
  Employment Opportunities   www.diahome.org/docs/Jobs/
                                                           Jobs_index.cfm
Georgia Pharmacy Association   www.gpha.org
HireHealth.com   www.hirehealth.com
HireRX.com   www.hirerx.com
iHirePharmacy.com   www.ihirepharmacy.com
Institute of Clinical Research [United Kingdom]   www.instituteofclinical
                                                           research.org
International Pharmajobs   www.pharmajobs.com
International Society for Pharmaceutical
  Engineering   www.ispe.org
JobPharmaceuticals.com   www.jobpharmaceuticals.com
JobPharmacist.com   www.jobpharmacist.com
JobPharmacy.com   www.jobpharmacy.com
JobMedicine.com   www.jobmedicine.com
Michigan Pharmacists Association   www.mipharm.com
Missouri Pharmacy Association   www.morx.com
MyDrugJobs.net   www.mydrugjobs.net
National Association of Boards of Pharmacy   www.nabp.net
National Association of Pharmaceutical
  Sales Representatives   www.napsronline.org
Pharmaceutical Job Site   www.pharmaceuticaljobsite.com
PharmaceuticalJobsUSA.com   www.pharmaceuticaljobsusa.com
Pharmaceutical Rep Jobs   www.pharmaceuticalrepjobs.com

Notes

Favorite sites, useful resources

Pharmaceutical (continued)

PharmacyChoice.com	www.pharmacychoice.com
PharmacyWeek	www.pharmacyweek.com
PharmaOpportunities	www.pharmaopportunites.com
Pharmasys	www.pharmweb.com
PharmaVillage.com [United Kingdom]	www.pharmavillage.com
RPh on the Go	www.rphonthego.com
RPhrecruiter.com	www.rphrecruiter.com
Rx Career Center	www.rxcareercenter.com
Rx Immigration	www.rximmigration.com
RxWebportal	www.rxwebportal.com

Physics

American Institute of Physics Career Services	www.aip.org/careersvc
Board of Physics & Astronomy	www.nas.edu/bpa
Institute of Physics	www.iop.org
JobLinks [Germany]	http://cip.physik.uni-wuerzburg.de/Job/
Optics.org	http://optics.org/home.ssi
Physics Jobs Online	www.tp.umu.se/TIPTOP/FORUM/JOBS
Plasma Gate [Israel]	http://plasma-gate.weizmann.ac.il

Printing & Bookbinding

The Bookbinders Guild of New York Job Bank	www.bbgny.org/guild/jb.html
Digital Printing and Imaging Association Employment Exchange (with the Screenprinting & Graphic Imaging Association International)	www.sgia.org/employ/employ.html
Graphic Artists Information Network	www.gain.org
National Association for Printing Leadership	www.napl.org
PressTemps	www.presstemps.com
Printing Impressions	www.piworld.com

Public Sector/Government

The Blue Line: Police Opportunity Monitor	www.theblueline.com
Centers for Disease Control	www.cdc.gov
Civil Jobs	www.civiljobs.com
Cop Spot	www.cop-spot.com
Defense Jobs	www.defensejobs.com
DEM Job	www.demjob.com
Fed World	www.fedworld.gov
Federal Job Search	www.federaljobsearch.com

Notes

Favorite sites, useful resources

Public Sector/Government (continued)

FederalJobs	www.federaljobs.net
Federal Jobs Digest	www.jobsfed.com
FRS	www.fedjobs.com
GetaGovJob.com	www.getagovjob.com
GetaLife.org.uk [United Kingdom]	www.getalife.org.uk
GOP Job	www.gopjob.com
Governmentjobs.com	www.governmentjobs.com
GovernmentSecurity.org	www.governmentsecurity.org/ jobs.php
GovMedCareers.com	www.govmedcareers.com
High Technology Crime Investigation Association	www.htcia.org
HRS Federal Job Search	www.hrsjobs.com
Intelligence Careers	www.intelligencecareers.com
Internet Job Source	http://statejobs.com
Jobsgopublic [United Kingdom]	www.jobsgopublic.co.uk
Jobs In Government	www.jobsingovernment.com
Military.com	www.military.com
NASA Jobs	www.nasajobs.nasa.gov
National Association of Hispanic Publications Online Career Center	www.nahp.org
NavyJobs.com	www.navyjobs.com
NHS Jobs [United Kingdom]	www.jobs.nhs.uk
Poli Temps	www.politemps.com
Police Employment	www.policeemployment.com
Political Resources	http://politicalresources.com
PoliticalStaffing.com	www.politicalstaffing.com
Public Service Employees	www.pse-net.com
PWJobZone	http://jobs.publishersweekly.com
RegulatoryCareers.com	www.regulatorycareers.com
Security Jobs Network	www.securityjobs.net
StudentJobs.gov	www.studentjobs.gov
TenStepsforStudents.org	www.tenstepsforstudents.org
Transportation Security Administration	www.tsa.gov
United States Department of Labor	www.dol.gov
US Air Force Careers	www.af.mil/careers
◪ USAJOBS/U.S. Office of Personnel Management	www.usajobs.opm.gov

Publishing

American Journalism Review Online	www.newslink.org/joblink.html
The Bookbinders Guild of New York Job Bank	www.bbgny.org/guild/jb.html
CopyEditor.com	www.copyeditor.com
Council of Literary Magazines & Presses	www.clmp.org/jobs/jobs.html
Editorial Freelancers Association	www.the-efa.org

Notes

Favorite sites, useful resources

Publishing (continued)

Fulfillment Management Association, Inc.	www.fmanational.org
MediaKnowledge.com [United Kingdom]	www.mediaknowledge.com
MyPublishingJobs.net	www.mypublishingjobs.net
National Writer's Union Job Hotline	www.nwu.org/hotline/index.com
PrintWorkers.com	www.printworkers.com
PrioritySearch.com	www.prioritysearch.com

Purchasing

BuyingJobs.com	www.buyingjobs.com
Institute for Supply Management Career Center	www.ism.ws/ CareerCenter/index.cfm
Manufacturing-Engineering-Jobs.com	www.manufacturing-engineering-jobs.com
SupplyChainRecruit.com	www.supplychainrecruit.com

-Q-

Quality/Quality Control

iHireQualityControl.com	www.ihirequalitycontrol.com
I Six Sigma	www.isixsigma.com
Just QA Jobs	www.justqajobs.com
QA-Jobs	www.qa-jobs.com
QCEmployMe.com	www.qcemployme.com
Quality America	www.qualityamerica.com
Quality Today [United Kingdom]	www.qualitytoday.co.uk
Software QA and Testing Resource Center	www.softwareqatest.com

-R-

Real Estate

American Real Estate Society	www.aresnet.org/ARES/jobs/ currjobs.html
Apartment Careers	www.apartmentcareers.com
California Mortgage Brokers Association Career Center	www.cambweb.org
Commercial Real Estate Jobs	www.loopnet.com/asp/jobs/ index.asp
Escrowboard.com	www.escrowboard.com
FacilitiesJobs.com	www.facilitiesjobs.com
iHireRealEstate.com	www.ihirerealestate.com

Notes

Favorite sites, useful resources

Real Estate (continued)

Institute of Real Estate Management Job Bulletin	www.irem.org/sec1ins.cfm?sec =iremfirst&con=iremjobs-intro. cfm&par=
Job Directories	www.inrealty.com/rs/jobs.html
Jobsite.com	www.jobsite.com
Leasing Jobs	www.leasingjobs.com
Loan Closer Jobs	www.loancloserjobs.com
Loan Originator Jobs	www.loanoriginatorjobs.com
Loop Net	www.loopnet.com
MortgageBoard.com	www.mortgageboard.com
Mortgage Job Market	www.jobmag.com
Mortgage Jobstore	www.mortgagejobstore.com
NACORE International	www.nacore.com
National Network of Commercial Real Estate Women Job Bank	www.nncrew.org/job_bank/ job_bank_introduction_frm.html
NewHomeSalesJobs.com	www.newhomesalesjobs.com
Pike Net	www.pikenet.com
Real Estate Best Jobs	www.realestatebestjobs.com
Real Estate Careers	www.restatecareer.com
Real Estate Finance Jobs	www.realestatefinancejobs.com
Real Estate Job Store	www.realestatejobstore.com
Real Estate Lenders Association	www.rela.org
Real Jobs	www.real-jobs.com
SelectLeaders.com	www.selectleaders.com
Titleboard.com	www.titleboard.com

Recruiters Resources

AbsoluteHire.com	www.absolutehire.com
Academy of Healthcare Recruiters	www.academyofhealthcare recruiters.com
AIRS Directory	www.airsdirectory.com
Alliance of Medical Recruiters	www.physicianrecruiters.com/ amrapp.htm
American Staffing Association	www.staffingtoday.net
Arizona Technical Recruiters Association	www.atraaz.org/pages/ recruiterjobopenings.html
Association of Executive Search Consultants	www.aesc.org
Association of Financial Search Consultants	www.afsc-jobs.com
Association of Staff Physician Recruiters	www.aspr.org
Atlanta Human Resources Association	www.harb.net/ahra
BackgroundBureau.com	www.backgroundbureau.com
BrainHunter	www.brainhunter.com
The Breckenridge Group, Inc.	www.breckenridgegroup.com
California Staffing Professionals	www.catss.org

Notes

Favorite sites, useful resources

Recruiters Resources (continued)

Canadian Technical Recruiters Network	www.ctrn.org
Career Highway.com	www.careerhighway.com
Career MetaSearch	www.careermetasearch.com
Cheezhead.com	www.cheezhead.com
Colorado Technical Recruiters Network	www.ctrn.org
CyberEdit	www.cyberedit.com
DataFrenzy.com	www.datafrenzy.com
Defense Outplacement Referral System	www.dmdc.osd.mil/dors
Delaware Valley Technical Recruiters Network	www.dvtrn.org
Drake Beam Morin	www.dbm.com/dbm.html
Electronic Recruiters Exchange	www.erexchange.com
Employment Management Association	www.shrm.org/ema/index.html
eQuest	www.joblauncher.com
ExecutiveResumes.com	www.executiveresumes.com
Free-For-Recruiters	www.free-for-recruiters.com
FreeResumeSites.com	www.freeresumesites.com
Global Media	www.globalmedia recruitment.com
GotResumes.com	www.gotresumes.com
H3.com	www.h3.com
Houston High Tech Recruiters Network	www.hhtrn.org
Human Resource Management Center	www.hrmc.com
Illinois Association of Personnel Services	www.searchfirm.com
Interbiznet.com	www.interbiznet.com/hrstart.html
International Association of Corporate and Professional Recruitment	www.iacpr.org
Investment Positions	www.investmentpositions.com
Its Your Job Now	www.itsyourjobnow.com
Jobster.com	www.jobster.com
KarmaOne	www.karmaone.org
Lead411.com	www.lead411.com
Lee Hecht Harrison	www.careerlhh.com
Metro Atlanta High Tech Personnel Association	http://mahtpa.hom. mindspring.com
Minnesota Technical Recruiters Network	www.mntrn.com
MovingCenter.com	www.movingcenter.com
Nasscom.org	www.nasscom.org
National Association of Executive Recruiters	www.naer.org
National Association for Health Care Recruitment	www.nahcr.com
National Association of Legal Search Consultants	www.nalsc.org
National Association of Personnel Services	www.napsweb.org
National Association of Physician Recruiters	www.napr.org
National Insurance Recruiters Association Online Job Database	www.nirassn.com/positions.cfm

Notes

Favorite sites, useful resources

Recruiters Resources (continued)

National Technical Staffing Association	www.ntsa.com
New Jersey Metro Employment Management Association	www.njmetroema.org
New Jersey Staffing Association	www.njsa.com
New Jersey Technical Recruiters Alliance	www.njtra.org
Northeast Human Resource Association	www.nehra.org
Northwest Recruiters Association	www.nwrecruit.org
NowHiring.com	www.nowhiring.com
Personnel Management Association of Western New England	www.hrmawne.org
Pittsburgh Personnel Association	ww.ppapitt.org
The Portland Human Resource Management Assn	www.pdxhr.org
Professionals in Human Resource Association Career Center	www.pihra.org/capirasn/ careers.nsf/home?open
Project S.A.M.E.	http://netrecruiter.net/ projsame.html
Project S.A.V.E.	www.cluffassociates.com/ projectsave.htm
PubliPac.ca [Canada]	www.publipac.ca
RecruitUSA	www.recruitusa.com
Recruiters Alliance	www.recruitersalliance.com
Recruiters Café	www.recruiterscafe.com
Recruiters for Christ	www.edmondspersonnel.com
Recruiters Network	www.recruitersnetwork.com
Recruiters Online Network	www.recruitersonline.com
Recruiting.com	www.recruiting.com
RecruitingJobs.com	www.recruitingjobs.com
RecruitingMastery.com	www.recruitingmastery.com
Recruitment-Marketing [United Kingdom]	www.recruitment-marketing.co.uk
The Regional Technical Recruiter's Association	www.rtra.com
ResumeBlaster	www.resumeblaster.com
ResumeXPRESS	www.resumexpress.com
Resume-Link	http://resume-link.com
Resume Monkey	www.resumemonkey.com
Resume Network	www.resume-network.com
ResumeRabbit.com	www.resumerabbit.com
Resumes on the Web	www.resweb.com
Resume Workz	www.resumeworkz.com
Russoft.org	www.russoft.org
Sacremento Area Human Resources Association	www.sahra.org
San Francisco Bay Area ASA	www.sfasa.org/joblist.html
Semco	www.semcoenterprises.com
SHRM Atlanta	www.shrmatlanta.org
SHRM Jacksonville	www.shrmjax.org
SkillsArena.com [United Kingdom]	www.skillsarena.com

Notes

Favorite sites, useful resources

Recruiters Resources (continued)

The Smart POST Network	www.smartpost.com
■ Society for Human Resource Management	
HRJobs	www.shrm.org/jobs
Southeast Employment Network	www.senetwork.com
SplitIt.com	www.splitit.com
SplitJobs.com	www.splitjobs.com
Taleo (iLogos)	www.taleo.com
Technical Recruiters Network	www.trnchicago.org
Texas Association of Staffing	www.texasstaffing.org
Tiburon Group	www.tiburongroup.com
Top Echelon Recruiters	www.topechelon.com
UpSeek	www.upseek.com
VacancyFinder.co.uk [United Kingdom]	www.vacancyfinder.co.uk
Virtual-Edge	www.virtual-edge.net
Virtual Relocation	www.virtualrelocation.com
Washington Area Recruiters Network	www.warn.net
WebHire Network	www.webhire.com
WEDDLE's Newsletters, Guides	
& Directory	**www.weddles.com**
Wisconsin Technical Recruiters Network	www.witrn.org
You Achieve	www.youachieve.com
ZillionResumes.com	www.zillionresumes.com

Recruitment Advertising-Non-Newspaper Print & Online

Adsearch	www.adsearch.com
Advertising Age's Online Job Bank	http://adage.com
American Journalism Review Online	www.newslink.org/joblink.html
American Medical Association	
Journal of the AMA (JAMA)	
Physician Recruitment Ads	www.ama-assn.org
American Psychological Association	
Monitor Classified Advertising	www.apa.org/ads
Association for Computing Machinery	
Career Resource Center	http://acpinternational.org
Bernard Hodes Group	www.hodes.com
Cell Press Online	www.cellpress.com
Chronicle of Higher Education	
Academe This Week	http://chronicle.merit.edu/jobs
Chronicle of Philanthropy	http://philanthropy.com/
CMPnet	www.cmpnet.com
Contract Employment Weekly Jobs Online	www.ceweekly.com
Engineering News Record	www.enr.com
The ePages Classifieds	www.ep.com
Heart Advertising	www.career.com

Notes

Favorite sites, useful resources

Recruitment Advertising-Non-Newspaper Print & Online (continued)

InformationWeek Career	www.informationweek.com/ career
ITWorld.com's IT Careers	www.itcareers.com
E&P Classifieds	http://epclassifieds.com/EPM/ home.html
Louisville Internet Business Directory	www.beyondbis.com/lsvdir.html
Main Street On-Line Classifieds Service	http://classifieds.maine.com
Oil Online	www.oilonline.com
Online Help Wanted	www.ohw.com
Prospect City	www.prospectcity.com
Shaker Advertising	www.shaker.com
SocietyGuardian.co.uk [United Kingdom]	http://.society.guardian.co.uk
Star Recruiting	www.starrecruiting.net
THESIS: The Times Higher Education Supplement InterView Service [United Kingdom]	www.thesis.co.uk
TMP Worldwide	www.tmp.com

Regional-USA

Alabama

AlabamaJobs.com	www.alabamajobs.com
Alabama Live	www.alabamalive.com
Alabama's Job Bank	www.dir.state.al.us/es
AuburnOpelikaHelpWanted.com	www.auburnopelika helpwanted.com
Biotechnology Association of Alabama	www.bioalabama.com
BirminghamHelpWanted.com	www.birmingham helpwanted.com
Birmingham News	www.bhnews.com
DothanHelpWanted.com	www.dothanhelpwanted.com
HuntsvilleHelpWanted.com	www.huntsvillehelpwanted.com
Huntsville Times	www.htimes.com
Links to Television Sites	http://webcom.net/~klg/ alabama_tv_jobs.html
MobileHelpWanted.com	www.mobilehelpwanted.com
Mobile Register Online	www.mobileregister.com
Montgomery Advertiser	www.montgomeryadvertiser.com
MontgomeryAreaHelpWanted.com	www.montgomeryarea helpwanted.com
The Tuscaloosa News	www.tuscaloosanews.com

Alaska

ADN	www.adn.com
Alaska Fishing Jobs	www.fishingjobs.com
AlaskaJobs.com	www.alaskajobs.com

Notes

Favorite sites, useful resources

Regional-USA (continued)

Alaska (continued)
Alaska's Job Bank   www.labor.state.ak.us/esjobs/
                                                        Jobs

AlaskaJobFinder.com   www.alaskajobfinder.com
Anchorage Daily News   www.adn.com/classads/ads/
                                                        today/employment_index.html
AnchorageHelpWanted.com   www.anchoragehelpwanted.com
Fairbanks Daily News   http://fairbanks.abracat.com
FairbanksHelpWanted.com   www.fairbankshelpwanted.com
Frontiersman   www.frontiersman.com/class
I Love Alaska   www.ilovealaska.com/
                                                        alaskajobs
Juneau Empire   www.juneauempire.com
KodiackHelpWanted.com   www.kodiackhelpwanted.com
Nome Nugget   www.nomenugget.com

Arizona
Arizona Daily Sun (Flagstaff)   www.azdailysun.com
ArizonaFamily.com   www.arizonafamily.com
Arizona Hospital and Healthcare Association
  AZHealthJobs   www.azhha.org
ArizonaJobs.com   www.arizonajobs.com
AZ-Jobs   www.az-jobs.com
The Daily Courier (Prescott)   www.prescottaz.com
East Valley Tribune (Mesa)   www.arizonatribune.com
HelpWantedPhoenix.com   www.helpwantedphoenix.com
Jobing.com   www.jobing.com
LocalCareers.com   www.localcareers.com
Pheonix Employment   www.phoenixemployment.com
Phoenix Jobs   www.phoenixjobs.com
Phoenix News Times   www.phoenixnewstimes.com
Phoenix One Stop Career Center   www.ci.phoenix.az.us
SierraVistaHelpWanted.com   www.sierravistahelpwanted.com
Today's News-Herald (Lake Havasu City)   www.havasunews.com
TucsonHelpWanted.com   www.tucsonhelpwanted.com
Work in Arizona   www.workinarizona.com

Arkansas
ARHelpWanted.com   www.arhelpwanted.com
Arkansas Democrat (Little Rock)   www.ardemgaz.com
Arkansas Human Resources Association   www.ahra.org
ArkansasJobs.com   www.arkansasjobs.com
Arkansas Jobs   www.arjobs.com
Benton Courier   www.bentoncourier.com
HotSpringsHelpWanted.com   www.hotspringshelpwanted.com

Notes

Favorite sites, useful resources

Regional-USA (continued)

Arkansas (continued)

JonesboroHelpWanted.com	www.jonesborohelpwanted.com
Jonesboro Sun	www.jonesborosun.com
LittleRockHelpWanted.com	www.littlerockhelpwanted.com
Ozark Spectator	www.ozarkspectator.com
RiverValleyHelpWanted.com	www.rivervalleyhelpwanted.com
The Sentinel-Record (Hot Springs)	www.hotsr.com
TexarkanaHelpWanted.com	www.texarkanahelpwanted.com
University of Arkansas	www.uark.edu
What A Job	www.whatajob.com

California

680 Careers.com	www.680careers.com
Abag	www.abag.ca.gov
Association for Environmental and Outdoor Education	www.aeoe.org
BAJobs	www.bajobs.com
BakersfieldHelpWanted.com	www.bakersfieldhelpwanted.com
Bay Area Bioscience Center	www.bayareabioscience.org
Bay Area Careers	www.bayareacareers.com
BayAreaClassifieds.com	www.bayareaclassifieds.com
BayAreaHelpWanted.com	www.bayareahelpwanted.com
California Academy of Family Physicians	www.fpjobsonline.org
California Agricultural Technical Institute ATI-Net AgJobs	www.atinet.org/jobs.asp
CaliforniaCoastHelpWanted.com	www.californiacoast helpwanted.com
California Dental Hygienists' Association Employment Opportunities	www.cdha.org/employment/ index.html
California Human Resources Professionals	www.keyhrjobs.com
California Job Network	www.cajobs.com
CaliforniaJobs.com	www.californiajobs.com
California Journalism Online	www.csne.org
California Mortgage Brokers Association Career Center	www.cambweb.org
California Separation Science Society	www.casss,org
California State University - Chico	www.csuchico.edu/plc/jobs.html
CentralCaliforniaHelpWanted.com	www.centralcalifornia helpwanted.com
CentralCoastHelpWanted.com	www.centralcoast helpwanted.com
CentralValleyHelpWanted.com	www.centralvalley helpwanted.com
ChicoHelpWanted.com	www.chicohelpwanted.com
Coastline	www.ventura.com

Notes

Favorite sites, useful resources

Regional-USA (continued)

California (continued)

⚡ craigslist	www.craigslist.com
DesertHelpWanted.com	www.deserthelpwanted.com
Fat Job	www.fatjob.com
FinancialJobs.com	www.financialjobs.com
Foothill-De Anza Community College	www.foothill.fhda.edu
Forty Plus	www.fortyplus.org
Go Job Zone	www.gojobzone.com
HelpWantedSanDiego.com	www.helpwantedsandiego.com
HighDesertHelpWanted.com	www.highdeserthelpwanted.com
Hispanic-Jobs.com	www.hispanic-jobs.com
HireDiversity.com	www.hirediversity.com
Human Resource Independent Consultants (HRIC) On-Line Job Leads	www.hric.org/ hric/hrcaopp1.html
InlandEmpireHelpWanted.com	www.inlandempire helpwanted.com
JobConnect.org	www.jobconnect.org
Job Meister	www.jobmeister.com
LA Working World	www.workingworld.com
LocalCareers.com	www.localcareers.com
LosAngelesHelpWanted.com	www.losangeleshelpwanted.com
Los Angeles Times	www.latimes.com
MercedHelpWanted.com	www.mercedhelpwanted.com
Mercury Center	www.sjmercury.com
Mercury News (San Jose)	www.bayarea.com
ModestoHelpWanted.com	www.modestohelpwanted.com
MontereyBayHelpWanted.com	www.montereybay helpwanted.com
NACCB Southern California Chapter	www.socal-naccb.org
Netcom	www.netcom.com
NorthBayCareers.com	www.northbaycareers.com
NorthBayHelpWanted.com	www.northbayhelpwanted.com
Orange County Register	www.ocregister.com
Palo Alto Weekly	www.service.com/PAW/ home.html
Professionals in Human Resource Association Career Center	www.pihra.org/capirasn/ careers.nsf/home?open
Presidio Jobs	www.presidio-jobs.com
ReddingHelpWanted.com	www.reddinghelpwanted.com
Sacramento Bee	www.sacbee.com
SacramentoHelpWanted.com	www.sacramentohelpwanted.com
Sacramento Human Resource Management Association	www.shrma.org
Sacramento Recruiter	www.sacramentorecruiter.com
San Diego Careers	www.sandiegocareers.com

Notes

Favorite sites, useful resources

Regional-USA (continued)

California (continued)

San Diego Jobs	www.sandiegojobs.com
San Diego Software Industry Council	www.sdsic.org
San Francisco Chronicle	www.sfgate.com
San Francisco Bay Area American Statistical Association	www.sfasa.org/joblist.html
San Francisco Bay Area Job Hub	www.jobhub.com
San Francisco State University Instructional Technologies	www.itec.sfsu.edu
Sonic Net	www.sonic.net/employment
SonomaCountyHelpWanted.com	www.sonomacounty helpwanted.com
SouthBayHelpWanted.com	www.southbayhelpwanted.com
Southern California	www.so-cal-jobs.com
Southern California Electronic Data Interchange Roundtable	www.scedir.org/html/jobs.html
StocktonHelpWanted.com	www.stocktonhelpwanted.com
SutterButtesHelpWanted.com	www.sutterbutteshelpwanted.com
University of California- Berkeley Work-Study Programs	http://workstudy.berkeley.edu
The Valley Exchange	www.thevalleyexchange.com

Colorado

Aspen Daily News	www.aspendailynews.com
CareersColorado.com	www.careerscolorado.com
Colorado Academy of Family Physicians	www.fpjobsonline.org
Colorado Computerwork	http://colorado.computer work.com
Colorado Health and Hospital Association	www.cha.com
Colorado Human Resource Association Online	www.chra.org
ColoradoJobs.net	www.coloradojobs.net
Colorado Online Job Connection	www.peakweb.com
ColoradoSpringsHelpWanted.com	www.coloradosprings helpwanted.com
Colorado Springs Independent	www.csindy.com
Colorado Springs Society for Human Resource Management	www.csshrm.org
Colorado Technical Recruiters Network	www.ctrn.org/ctrn.org
The Daily Sentinel (Grand Junction)	www.gjsentinel.com
Denver Post	www.denverpost.com
Durango Herald	www.durangoherald.com
HighCountryHelpWanted.com	www.highcountry helpwanted.com
Inside Denver	www.insidedenver.com/jobs

Notes

Favorite sites, useful resources

Regional-USA (continued)

Colorado (continued)

NorthernColoradoHelpWanted.com — www.northerncolorado helpwanted.com

RockyMountainHelpWanted.com — www.rockymountain helpwanted.com

State of Colorado — www.state.co.us

WesternSlopeHelpWanted.com — www.westernslope helpwanted.com

Connecticut

The Advocate (Stamford) — www.stamfordadvocate.com
Connecticut's BioScience Cluster — www.curenet.org
Connecticut Hospital Association — www.chime.org
ConnecticutJobs.com — www.connecticutjobs.com
CT High Tech — www.cthightech.com
CT Jobs — www.ctjobs.com
Danbury News-Times — www.newstimes.com
EasternCTHelpWanted.com — www.easterncthelpwanted.com
Fairfield, CT Jewish Jobs — www.jewishjobs.com
FairfieldCountyHelpWanted.com — www.fairfieldcounty helpwanted.com

FairfieldCountyJobs.com — www.fairfieldcountyjobs.com
GetCTJobs.com — www.getctjobs.com
HartfordCountyJobs.com — www.hartfordcountyjobs.com
Hartford Courant — www.ctnow.com
HartfordHelpWanted.com — www.hartfordhelpwanted.com
New England Job — www.jobct.com
NewHavenCountyJobs.com — www.newhavencountyjobs.com
NewHavenHelpWanted.com — www.newhavenhelpwanted.com
New Haven Register — www.newhavenregister.com
NewLondonCountyJobs.com — www.newlondoncountyjobs.com
Tri-StateJobs.com — www.tristatejobs.com
Waterbury Republican American — wws.rep-am.com

Delaware

DelawareJobs.com — www.delawarejobs.com
Delaware Online — http://jobs.delawareonline.com/ index.shtml

Delaware Valley Technical Recruiters Network — www.dvtrn.org
Delaware's Employment — www.delmarweb.com
DelmarvaHelpWanted.com — www.delmarvahelpwanted.com
Dover Post — www.doverpost.com
HelpWantedDelaware.com — www.helpwanteddelaware.com
JobCircle — www.jobcircle.com
JobNet — www.jobnet.com

Notes

Favorite sites, useful resources

Regional-USA (continued)

Delaware (continued)
The News Journal (Wilmington)   www.delawareonline.com
Opportunity Center, Inc.   www.oppctr.com
Tri-State Human Resource Management Assn   www.tristatehr.org
Virtual Career Network   www.vcnet.net

District of Columbia
The Catholic University of America   http://careers.cua.edu/studalum/
  Career Services Office   progserv.htm
dcaccountingjobs.com   www.dcaccountingjobs.com
DC Job Source   http://dcjobsource.com
DC Registry   www.dcregistry.com
DCWebWomen   www.dcwebwomen.org
DistrictofColumbiaJobs.com   www.districtofcolumbiajobs.com
HelpWantedDC.com   www.helpwanteddc.com
Human Resource Association
  of the National Capital Area Job Bank Listing   http://hra-nca.org/job_list.asp
JobFetch.com   www.jobfetch.com
WashingtonJobs.com   www.washingtonjobs.com
The Washington Post   www.washingtonpost.com
Washington Times   www.washtimes.com

East Coast
East Bay Works   www.eastbayworks.org
East Coast Jobs   www.eastcoastjobs.net
Planet Tech   www.planet-tech.net

Florida
1-Jobs.com   www.1-jobs.com
BioFlorida   www.bioflorida.com
Central Florida Human Resource Association   www.cfhra.org
CoastalHelpWanted.com   www.coastalhelpwanted.com
DaytonaHelpWanted.com   www.daytonahelpwanted.com
EmeraldCoastHelpWanted.com   www.emeraldcoast
                                          helpwanted.com

Florida Academy of Family Physicians   www.fpjobsonline.org
Florida CareerLINK   www.floridacareerlink.com
FloridaCareers.com   www.FloridaCareers.com
Florida Jobs   www.floridajobs.com
Florida Jobs Online!   www.florida-jobs-online.com
Florida-Jobs.net   www.florida-jobs.net
Florida NACCB   www.floridanaccb.org
Florida Times Union (Jacksonville)   www.jacksonville.com
FloridianJobs.com   www.floridianjobs.com

Notes

Favorite sites, useful resources

Regional-USA (continued)

Florida (continued)

GainesvilleOcalaHelpWanted.com	www.gainesvilleocala helpwanted.com
HeartlandHelpWanted.com	www.heartlandhelpwanted.com
Human Resource Association of Broward County	www.hrabc.org
JacksonvilleHelpWanted.com	www.jacksonville helpwanted.com
Miami Herald	www.miami.com
Miami Jobs	www.miami-jobs.net
NorthFloridaHelpWanted.com	www.northfloridahelpwanted.com
Nova Southeastern University	www.nova.edu
OrlandoHelpWanted.com	www.orlandohelpwanted.com
Orlando Jobs	www.orlando-jobs.com
Orlando Sentinel	www.orlandosentinel.com
PanamaCityHelpWanted.com	www.panamacity helpwanted.com
PensacolaHelpWanted.com	www.pensacola helpwanted.com
Pensacola News Journal	www.pensacolanews times.com
RhinoMite	www.jobing.com/?chang=local &welcome=rhinomite
SarasotaHelpWanted.com	www.sarasotahelpwanted.com
St. Petersburg Times	www.sptimes.com
SHRM Jacksonville	www.shrmjax.org
SoFla.com	www.sofla.com
SouthFloridaHelpWanted.com	www.southfloridahelpwanted.com
SouthwestFloridaHelpWanted.com	www.southwestflorida helpwanted.com
SpaceCoastHelpWanted.com	www.spacecoast helpwanted.com
Sun-Sentinel Career Path	www.sun-sentinel.com/ Careerpath
TallahasseeHelpWanted.com	www.tallahassee helpwanted.com
Tampa Bay Employment	www.tampabaywired.com
Tampa Jobs.com	www.tampa-jobs.com
WestPalmBeachHelpWanted.com	www.westpalmbeach helpwanted.com

Georgia

The Albany Herald	www.albanyherald.net/ classbrowse.htm
AtlantaHelpWanted.com	www.atlantahelpwanted.com
Atlanta Human Resources Association	www.harb.net/ahra

Notes

Favorite sites, useful resources

Regional-USA (continued)

Georgia (continued)

Atlanta Job Resource Center	www.ajrc.com
Atlanta JobZone	www.atlantajobzone.com
Atlanta-Jobs	www.atlanta-jobs.com
Atlanta Journal and Constitution	www.ajcjobs.com
Augusta Chronicle	www.augustachronicle.com
AugustaHelpWanted.com	www.augustahelpwanted.com
ChattahoocheeHelpWanted.com	www.chattahoochee helpwanted.com
Emory University Rollins School of Public Health	www.sph.emory.edu/ studentservice
Georgia Academy of Family Physicians	www.fpjobsonline.org
Georgia Association of Personnel Services	www.jobconnection.com/ specialty
GeorgiaCareers.com	www.georgiacareers.com
Georgia Center for Nonprofits	www.gcn.org
Georgia Department of Human Resources	www.dhrjobs.com
Georgia Pharmacy Association	www.gpha.org
Georgia State University Career Services	www.gsu.edu/dept/admin/plc/ homepage4.html
Georgia Tech Career Services Office	www.career.gatech.edu
Job Net	www.westga.edu/~coop
Macon Telegraph	www.macon.com
MidGeorgiaHelpWanted.com	www.midgeorgia helpwanted.com
National Association of Securities Professionals (Atlanta) Current Openings	www.naspatlanta.com/ career.html
NW Georgia Careers	www.careerdepot.org
SavannahHelpWanted.com	www.savannah helpwanted.com
Savannah Morning News	www.savannahnow.com
SGAHelpWanted.com	www.sgahelpwanted.com
SHRM Atlanta	www.shrmatlanta.org
SoutheastGeorgiaHelpWanted.com	www.southeastgeorgia helpwanted.com
SouthwestGeorgiaHelpWanted.com	www.southwestgeorgia helpwanted.com
The Southeastern Employment Network	www.senetwork.com
SouthwestGeorgiaHelpWanted.com	www.southwestgeorgia helpwanted.com

Hawaii

HawaiiJobs.net	www.hawaiijobs.net
Hawaii Techies	www.hawaii.techies.com
Hawaii Tribune-Herald (Hilo)	www.hilohawaiitribune.com

Notes

Favorite sites, useful resources

Regional-USA (continued)

Hawaii (continued)

Honolulu Advertiser	www.honoluluadvertiser.com
HonoluluHelpWanted.com	www.honoluluhelpwanted.com
Honolulu Star-Bulletin	www.starbulletin.com
Jobs Hawaii	www.jobshawaii.com
JobsOnKauai.com	www.jobsonkauai.com
Maui.net	www.maui.net
Maui News	www.mauinews.com
Starbulletin	www.starbulletin.com
West Hawaii Today (Kailua)	www.westhawaiitoday.com

Idaho

BoiseHelpWanted.com	www.boisehelpwanted.com
Cedar Rapids Gazette	www.gazetteonline.com
The Daily Nonpareil (Council Bluffs)	www.nonpareilonline.com
Des Moines Register	www.dmregister.com
Idaho Department of Labor	www.labor.state.id.us/
IdahoJobs.com	www.idahojobs.com
NorthIdahoHelpWanted.com	www.northernidaho helpwanted.com
Quad City Times (Davenport)	www.qctimes.com
Sioux City Journal	www.trib.com/scjournal
SouthernIdahoHelpWanted.com	www.southernidaho helpwanted.com

Illinois

Accountant Jobs Chicago	www.accountantjobs chicago.com
Audit Jobs Chicago	www.auditjobschicago.com
BloomingtonHelpWanted.com	www.bloomington helpwanted.com
CapitalHelpWanted.com	www.capitalhelpwanted.com
CentralIllinoisHelpWanted.com	www.centralillinois helpwanted.com
Chicago AMA	http://chicagoama.org
ChicagoJobs.com	www.chicagojobs.com
ChicagoJobs.org	www.chicagojobs.org
Chicago Medical Society	www.cmsdocs.org
Chicago Software Newspaper	www.chisoft.com
Chicago Tribune	www.chicagotribune.com
Chicagoland's Virtual Job Resource	www.staffsolutions.com
Engineering Job Source	www.engineerjobs.com
FetchMeAJob.com	www.fetchmeajob.com
HelpWantedSpringfield.com	www.helpwantedspringfield.com
Herald & Review (Decatur)	www.herald-review.com

Notes

Favorite sites, useful resources

Regional-USA (continued)

Illinois (continued)

Human Resource Association of Greater Oak Brook	http://members.aol.com/hraob/main.htm
ILJobs.com	www.iljobs.com
IllianaHelpWanted.com	www.illianahelpwanted.com
IlliniHelpWanted.com	www.illinihelpwanted.com
Illinois Academy of Family Physicians	www.fpjobsonline.org
IllinoisCareers.com	www.illinoiscareers.com
Illinois CPA Society Career Center	www.icpas.org/icpas/career-services/carsrce.asp
IllinoisJobs.com	www.illinoisjobs.com
IllinoisJobs.net	www.illinoisjobs.net
Illinois Recruiters Association	www.illinoisrecruiters.org
Job Force Network	www.jobforce.net
Jobs in Chicago	www.jobsinchicago.com
Loyola College	www.loyola.edu/thecareercenter/index.html
The News-Gazette (Champaigne)	www.news-gazette.com
PeoriaHelpWanted.com	www.peoriahelpwanted.com
The Regional Technical Recruiter's Association	www.rtra.com
Register-News (Mount Vernon)	www.register-news.com
Sorkins Job Bank	www.sorkinsjobbank.com
The State Journal Register (Springfield)	www.sj-r.com
SuburbanChicagoHelpWanted.com	www.suburbanchicagohelpwanted.com
Tax Jobs Chicago	www.taxjobschicago.com
University of Chicago	www.uchicago.edu/alum/index.html

Indiana

BloomingtonHelpWanted.com	www.bloomingtonhelpwanted.com
CentralIndianaHelpWanted.com	www.centralindianahelpwanted.com
Engineering Job Source	www.engineerjobs.com
The Evansville Courier	http://ads.evansville.net/employment
FetchMeAJob.com	www.fetchmeajob.com
FortWayneHelpWanted.com	www.fortwaynehelpwanted.com
Indiana Engineering and Technical Opportunities	www.engineerjobs.com/in_jobs.html
The Herald-Times (Bloomington)	www.heraldtimejonline.com
IndianaJobs.com	www.indianajobs.com
IndianaHealthCareers.com	www.indianahealthcareers.com
IndianapolisHelpWanted.com	www.indianapolishelpwanted.com

Notes

Favorite sites, useful resources

Regional-USA (continued)

Indiana (continued)

Indianapolis Star News	www.indystar.com
Indy Mall	www.indymall.com/class-ad/ employmt.htm
LafayetteHelpWanted.com	www.lafayettehelpwanted.com
The News-Sentinel (Fort Wayne)	www.fortwayne.com
Online Jobs Indiana	www.indystar.com/classifieds
Purdue University Management Placement Office	www.mgmt.purdue.edu/ departments/gcs/
Post-Tribune (Gary)	www.post-trib.com
SouthBendHelpWanted.com	www.southbend helpwanted.com
South Bend Tribune	www.sbinfo.com
SouthIndianaHelpWanted.com	www.southernindianahelpwanted.com
TerreHauteHelpWanted.com	www.terrehaute helpwanted.com
TriStateHelpWanted.com	www.tristatehelpwanted.com

Iowa

CedarRapidsIowaCityHelpWanted.com	www.cedarrapidsiowacity helpwanted.com
CentralIowaHelpWanted.com	www.centraliowa helpwanted.com
Corridor Careers	www.corridorcareers.com
DesMoinesHelpWanted.com	www.desmoines helpwanted.com
DesMoines Register	www.dmregister.com/jobcity/ index.html
Drake University	www.drake.edu
DubuqueHelpWanted.com	www.dubuque helpwanted.com
Dubuque Iowa	www.dubuque-ia.com/jobs.cfm
EasternIowaHelpWanted.com	www.easterniowa helpwanted.com
FortDodgeHelpWanted.com	www.fortdodge helpwanted.com
Iowa Biotechnology Association	www.iowabiotech.org
Iowa Jobs	www.iowajobs.org
IowaJobs.net	www.iowajobs.net
NorthernIowaHelpWanted.com	www.northerniowa helpwanted.com
Our Dubuque	www.dubuque-ia.com/jobs.cfm
SiouxLandHelpWanted.com	www.siouxlandhelpwanted.com
SouthernIowaHelpWanted.com	www.southerniowa helpwanted.com

Notes

Favorite sites, useful resources

Regional-USA (continued)

Kansas

access Kansas	www.accesskansas.org
Daily Union (Junction City)	www.dailyu.com
Kansas City Kansan	www.kansascitykansan.com
Kansas JobLink	www.kansasjoblilnk.com
KansasJobs.net	www.kansasjobs.net
Salina Journal	www.saljournal.com
Sorkins Job Bank	www.sorkinsjobbank.com
The Topeka Capital Journal	www.cjonline.com
TopekaHelpWanted.com	www.topekahelpwanted.com
Wichita Eagle	www.kansas.com
WichitaHelpWanted.com	www.wichitahelpwanted.com

Kentucky

BluegrassHelpWanted.com	www.bluegrasshelpwanted.com
The Courier-Journal (Louisville)	www.courier-journal.com
The Daily News (Bowling Green)	www.bgdailynews.com
Grayson County News-Gazette (Leitchfield)	www.gcnewsgazette.com
HelpWantedLexington.com	www.helpwantedlexington.com
HuntingtonAshlandHelpWanted.com	www.huntingtonashland helpwanted.com
KentuckyJobs.com	www.kentuckyjobs.com
Lexington Herald Leader	www.kentucky.com
LouisvilleHelpWanted.com	www.louisvillehelpwanted.com
Louisville Internet Business Directory	www.beyondbis.com/lsvdir.html
Sentinel News (Shelbyville)	www.shelbyconnect.com

Louisiana

AcadianaHelpWanted.com	www.acadianahelpwanted.com
The Advocate (Baton Rouge)	www.advocate.com
BatonRougeHelpWanted.com	www.batonrouge helpwanted.com
CenLAHelpWanted.com	www.cenlahelpwanted.com
Info Louisiana	www.state.la.us
The Jackson Independent (Jonesboro)	www.jackson-ind.com
LouisianaJobs.com	www.louisianajobs.com
Med Job Louisiana	www.medjoblouisiana.com
MonroeHelpWanted.com	www.monroehelpwanted.com
NewOrleansHelpWanted.com	www.neworleans helpwanted.com
Orleans Parish Medical Society	www.opms.org
ShreveportHelpWanted.com	www.shreveport helpwanted.com
The Times (Shreveport)	www.shreveporttimes.com
The Times-Picayune (New Orleans)	www.nola.com

Notes

Favorite sites, useful resources

Regional-USA (continued)

Maine

Bangor Daily News	www.bangornews.com
Biotechnology Association of Maine	www.mainebiotech.org
CentralMaineHelpWanted.com	www.centralmaine helpwanted.com
EasternMaineHelpWanted.com	www.easternmaine helpwanted.com
⚑ Jobs in Maine	www.jobsinme.com
Kennebec Journal (Augusta)	www.kjonline.com
Lewiston Sun Journal	www.sunjournal.com
Maine-Job.com	www.maine-job.com
MaineJobs.net	www.mainejobs.net
Maine Street On-Line Classifieds Service	http://classifieds.maine.com
Portland Press Herald	www.portland.com
SouthernMaineHelpWanted.com	www.southernmaine helpwanted.com
The Times Record (Brunswick)	www.timesrecord.com

Maryland

BaltimoreHelpWanted.com	www.baltimorehelpwanted.com
Baltimore Sun	www.sunspot.net
The Capital (Annapolis)	www.hometownannapolis.com
Chesapeake Human Resource Association	www.chra.com
EasternShoreHelpWanted.com	www.easternshore helpwanted.com
FrederickHelpWanted.com	www.frederickhelpwanted.com
The Herald-Mail (Hagerstown)	www.herald-mail.com
Howard County Human Resources Society	www.hocohrs.org
Human Resource Association of the National Capital Area Job Bank Listing	http://hra-nca.org/job_list.asp
JobFetch.com	www.jobfetch.com
Maryland Association of CPAs Job Connect	www.macpa.org/services/ jobconnt/index.htm
MarylandJobs.com	www.marylandjobs.com
Maryland Times-Press (Ocean City)	www.marylandtimespress.com
MdBio, Inc. (Maryland Bioscience)	www.mdbio.org
Sailor	http://sailor.lib.md.us
The Star Democrat (Easton)	www.stardem.com
WashingtonJobs.com	www.washingtonjobs.com

Massachusetts

The Boston Globe	www.boston.com
Boston Hire	www.bostonhire.com
Boston Job Bank	www.bostonjobs.com

Notes

Favorite sites, useful resources

Regional-USA (continued)

Massachusetts (continued)

BostonJobs.com	www.bostonjobs.com
Boston JobZone	www.bostonjobzone.com
Boston Online Employment	www.boston-online.com/
BostonSearch.com	www.bostonsearch.com
BostonWorks.com	www.bostonworks.com
CapeAndIslandsHelpWanted.com	www.capeandislands helpwanted.com
The Eagle-Tribune (Lawrence)	www.eagletribune.com
HelpWantedBoston.com	www.helpwantedboston.com
JVS Career Moves	www.jvsjobs.org
Massachusetts Biotechnology Council	www.massbio.org
Massachusetts Environmental Education Society	www.massmees.org
Massachusetts Healthcare Human Resources Association	www.mhhra.org
MassachusettsJobs.com	www.massachusettsjobs.com
Personnel Management Association of Western New England	www.hrmawne.org
SpringfieldHelpWanted.com	www.springfieldhelpwanted.com
The Sun (Lowell)	www.lowellsun.com
The Salem News	www.salemnews.com
Town Online	http://townonline.com
Union-News & Sunday Republican (Springfield)	www.masslive.com
WesternMassWorks.com	www.westernmassworks.com
Worchester Polytechnic Institute	www.wpi.edu

Michigan

Ann Arbor News	www.annarbornews.com
Detriot Free Press	www.freep.com
Engineering Job Source	www.engineerjobs.com
FetchMeAJob.com	www.fetchmeajob.com
FlintHelpWanted.com	www.flinthelpwanted.com
Flint Journal	www.flintjournal.com
GrandRapidsHelpWanted.com	www.grandrapids helpwanted.com
Grand Rapids Press	www.gr-press.com
Human Resource Management Association of Mid Michigan Job Postings	http://hrmamm.com/jobs.asp
KalamazooHelpWanted.com	www.kalamazoohelpwanted.com
Lansing State Journal	www.lansingstatejournal.com
MichBIO	www.michbio.org
Michigan CareerSite	http://jobs.michigan.org
Michigan Job Hunter	www.michiganjobhunter.com
MichiganJobs.com	www.michiganjobs.com
Michigan-Online	www.michigan-online.com

Notes

Favorite sites, useful resources

Regional-USA (continued)

Michigan (continued)

Michigan Pharmacists Association	www.mipharm.com
Michigan Web	http://michiganweb.com/ empagency.html
MidMichiganHelpWanted.com	www.midmichiganhelp wanted.com
MotorCityHelpWanted.com	www.motorcityhelpwanted.com
MuskegonHelpWanted.com	www.muskegonhelpwanted.com
Oakland University	www2.oakland.edu/ careerservices
Pride Source	www.pridesource.com
SouthwestMichiganJobs.com	www.southwestmichigan jobs.com
UpperPeninsulaHelpWanted.com	www.upperpeninsula helpwanted.com

Midwest

jobsintheMidwest.com	www.jobsinthemidwest.com
MidWest Career Matrix	www.careermatrix.com

Minnesota

Duluth News-Tribune	www.duluthsuperior.com
Elk River Star News	www.erstarnews.com
The Journal (New Ulm)	www.oweb.com/NewUlm/ journal/home.html
HelpWantedMankato.com	www.helpwantedmankato.com
HelpWantedRochester.com	www.helpwantedrochester.com
Hennepin County Job Openings	www.co.hennepin.mn.us
MinJobs.com	www.minjobs.com
Minneapolis Jobs	www.minneapolis-jobs.com
Minneapolis Star Tribune	www.startribune.com
MinnesotaDiversity.com	www.minnesotadiversity.com
MinnesotaJobs.com	www.minnesotajobs.com
NorthlandHelpWanted.com	www.northlandhelpwanted.com
SouthernMinnesotaHelpWanted.com	www.southernminnesota helpwanted.com
StCloudHelpWanted.com	www.stcloudhelpwanted.com
Saint Paul Pioneer Press	www.twincities.com
TwinCitiesHelpWanted.com	www.twincitieshelpwanted.com

Mississippi

CentralMississippiHelpWanted.com	www.centralmississippi helpwanted.com
The Clarion Ledger (Jackson)	www.clarionledger.com

Notes

Favorite sites, useful resources

Regional-USA (continued)

Mississippi (continued)

GulfCoastHelpWanted.com	www.gulfcoast helpwanted.com
MeridianHelpWanted.com	www.meridianhelpwanted.com
Meridian Star	www.meridianstar.com
MississippiJobs.net	www.mississippijobs.net
The Natchez Democrat	www.natchezdemocrat.com
The Sun Herald (Biloxi)	www.sunherald.com
TupeloHelpWanted.com	www.tupelohelpwanted.com
The Vicksburg Post	www.vicksburgpost.com

Missouri

The Examiner (Independence)	www.examiner.net
Hannibal Courier-Post	www.hannibal.net
HeartlandJobs.com	www.heartlandjobs.com
Human Resource Management Association of Greater Kansas City	http://hrma-kc.org
Jefferson City News Tribune	www.newstribune.com
Joplin Globe	www.joplinglobe.com
JoplinHelpWanted.com	www.joplinhelpwanted.com
Kansas City.com	www.kansascity.com
KansasCityHelpWanted.com	www.kansascity helpwanted.com
Kansas City Jobs	www.kansascity-jobs.com
MidMissouriHelpWanted.com	www.midmissouri helpwanted.com
Missouri Academy of Family Physicians	www.fpjobsonline.org
Missouri Association of Personnel Services	www.moaps.com
MissouriJobs.com	www.missourijobs.com
Missouri Pharmacy Association	www.morx.com
Missouri Works	www.works.state.mo.us
Online Columbia	www.onlinecolumbia.com/ Jobsearch.asp
OzarksHelpWanted.com	www.ozarkshelpwanted.com
Springfield News-Leader	www.springfieldnews-leader.com
StLouisHelpWanted.com	www.stlouishelpwanted.com
St. Louis Jobs	http://st.louis.jobs.com
St. Louis Virtual Job Fair	www.stltechjobs.com
Sorkins Job Bank	www.sorkinsjobbank.com
SouthCentralMOHelpWanted.com	www.southcentralmo helpwanted.com

Montana

Billings Gazette	www.billingsgazette.com
BillingsHelpWanted.com	www.billingshelpwanted.com

Notes

Favorite sites, useful resources

Regional-USA (continued)

Montana (continued)

Bozeman Daily Chronicle	www.gomontana.com
Helena Independent Record	www.helenair.com
Missoulian	www.missoulian.com
MontanaHelpWanted.com	www.montanahelpwanted.com
Montana Job Service	http://jsd.dli.state.mt.us
MontanaJobs.com	www.montanajobs.com
The Montana Standard (Butte)	www.mtstandard.com
SouthwestMontanaHelpWanted.com	www.southwestmontana helpwanted.com
WesternMontanaHelpWanted.com	www.westernmontana helpwanted.com

Nebraska

Access Omaha	www.accessomaha.com/jobs/ jobs.html
Columbus Telegram	www.columbustelegram.com
CornhuskerHelpWanted.com	www.cornhusker helpwanted.com
Lincoln Journal Star	www.journalstar.com
NebraskaJobs.com	www.nebraskajobs.com
North Platte Telegraph	www.nptelegraph.com
OmahaHelpWanted.com	www.omahahelpwanted.com
Omaha World-Herald	www.omaha.com
Scotts Bluff Star-Herald	www.starherald.com

Nevada

Elko Daily Free Press	www.elkodaily.com
LasVegasHelpWanted.com	www.lasvegashelpwanted.com
Las Vegas Review-Journal	www.lvrj.com
Las Vegas Sun	www.lasvegassun.com
Nevada Appeal (Carson City)	www.nevadaappeal.com
NevadaJobs.com	www.nevadajobs.com
Nevada Mining	www.nevadamining.org
NVJobSearch.com	www.nvjobsearch.com
NVNurses.com	www.nvnurses.com
NVPublicJobs.com	www.nvpublicjobs.com
NVTeacherJobs.com	www.nvteacherjobs.com
NVMedicalJobs.com	www.nvmedicaljobs.com
NVAccountingJobs.com	www.nvaccountingjobs.com
NVTechnologyJobs.com	www.nvtechnologyjobs.com
RenoHelpWanted.com	www.renohelpwanted.com
Reno Gazette Journal	www.rgj.com
WorkReno	www.workreno.com

Notes

Favorite sites, useful resources

Regional-USA (continued)

New England

Independent Human Resource Consultants Association	www.ihrca.com/ Contract_Regular.asp
Jobfind.com	www.jobfind.com
JobsinNewEngland.com	www.jobsinnewengland.com
New England Job	www.newenglandjob.com
New England Careers	www.newenglandcareers.com
Northeast Human Resource Association	www.nehra.org
New England Higher Education Recruitment Consortium	www.faculty.harvard.edu/ 01/013.html
New England Journal of Medicine Career Center	www.nejmjobs.org
Opportunity NOCS	www.opnocs.org
SouthernNewEnglandHelpWanted.com	www.southernnewenglandhelp wanted.com
The Search Begins Online	www.todays-careers.com

New Hampshire

Across New Hampshire	www.across-nh.com
Concord Monitor	www.concordmonitor.com
JobsinNH.com	www.jobsinnh.com
Keene Sentinel	www.keenesentinel.com
NewHampshireHelpWanted.com	www.newhampshire helpwanted.com
NewHampshireJobs.net	www.newhampshirejobs.net
New Hampshire Legal Assistance	www.nhla.org
NH.com	www.nh.com
nhjobs.com	www.nhjobs.com
Portsmouth Herald	www.seacoastonline.com
The Telegraph (Nashua)	www.nashuatelegraph.com
The Union Leader (Manchester)	www.theunionleader.com

New Jersey

ACHelpWanted.com	www.achelpwanted.com
Atlantic City Jobs	www.acjobs.com
Asbury Park Press	www.app.com
Biotechnology Council of New Jersey	www.newjerseybiotech.org
CareerLocal.net	www.careerlocal.net
Courier-Post (Cherry Hill)	www.courierpostonline.com
Employment Channel	www.employ.com
In Jersey	www.injersey.com
Job Circle	www.jobcircle.com
JobNet	www.jobnet.com
MonmouthOceanHelpWanted.com	www.monmouthocaen helpwanted.com
The Montclair Times	www.montclairtimes.com

Notes

Favorite sites, useful resources

Regional-USA (continued)

New Jersey (continued)

NewJerseyHelpWanted.com	www.newjersey helpwanted.com
The New Jersey Higher Education Recruitment Consortium	www.njherc.com
New Jersey Human Resource Planning Group	www.njhrpg.org
NewJerseyJobs.com	www.newjerseyjobs.com
New Jersey Metro Employment Management Association	www.njmetroema.org
New Jersey Net Connections	www.netconnections.net/nj/ nj.html
New Jersey Online	www.nj.com
New Jersey Staffing Association	www.njsa.com
New Jersey Technical Recruiters Alliance	www.njtra.org
New Jersey Technology Council	www.njtc.org
New Media Association of New Jersey	www.nmanj.com
NJ Careers	www.njcareers.com
NJ Jobs	www.njjobs.com
NJPAHelpWanted.com	www.njpahelpwanted.com
NorthJerseyHelpWanted.com	www.northjersey helpwanted.com
Princeton Info	www.princetoninfo.com
The Star Ledger (Newark)	www.nj.com
The Trentonian	www.trentonian.com
Tri-StateJobs.com	www.tristatejobs.com

New Mexico

Albuquerque Journal	www.abqjournal.com
The Gallup Independent	www.gallupindependent.com
HelpWantedNewMexico.com	www.helpwanted newmexico.com
HighPlainsHelpWanted.com	www.highplainshelpwanted.com
Los Alamos Monitor	www.lamonitor.com
New Mexico High Tech Job Forum	www.nmtechjobs.com
NewMexicoJobs.net	www.newemexicojobs.net
Santa Fe New Mexican	www.sfnewmexican.com
The Silver City Daily Press	www.thedailypress.com

New York

IthacaCortlandHelpWanted.com	
411 NYC Jobs	www.411nycjobs.com
AdirondackHelpWanted.com	www.adirondack helpwanted.com
Albany Democrat Herald	www.dhonline.com
BigAppleHelpWanted.com	www.bigapplehelpwanted.com

Notes

Favorite sites, useful resources

Regional-USA (continued)

New York (continued)

BinghamtonHelpWanted.com	www.binghamton helpwanted.com
The Bookbinders Guild of New York Job Bank	www.bbgny.org/guild/jb.html
BuffaloHelpWanted.com	www.buffalohelpwanted.com
CapitalAreaHelpWanted.com	www.capitalarea helpwanted.com
CentralNewYorkHelpWanted.com	www.centralnewyork helpwanted.com
ColumbiaCountyJobs.com	www.columbiacountyjobs.com
ColumbiaGreeneHelpWanted.com	www.columbiagreene helpwanted.com
Cornell Career Services	http://student-jobs.ses. cornell.edu
daVinci Times	www.daVinciTimes.org
Employment Weekly	www.employment-weekly.com
FingerLakesHelpWanted.com	www.fingerlakes helpwanted.com
HelpWantedLongIsland.com	www.helpwanted longisland.com
HudsonValleyHelpWanted.com	www.hudsonvalley helpwanted.com
Human Resource Association of New York	www.nyshrm.org
IthacaHelpWanted.com	www.ithacahelpwanted.com
Ithaca Times	www.ithacatimes.com
Job Circle	www.jobcircle.com
Job Force NY	www.jobforceny.com
TheJobWire.com	www.thejobwire.com
LI Jobs	www.lijobs.com
LocalCareers.com	www.localcareers.com
National Association of Securities Professionals (New York) Underground Railroad	www.nasp-ny.org
The New York Biotechnology Association	www.nyba.org
New York Department of Labor	www.labor.state.ny.us
New York Foundation for the Arts	www.nyfa.org/opportunities. asp?type=Job&id=94&fid =6&sid=17
NewYorkJobs.com	www.newyorkjobs.com
New York New Media Association	www.nynma.com/jobs
New York Post	www.nypost.com
New York Society of Association Executives Career Center	www.nysaenet.org
New York Society of Security Analysts Career Resources	www.nyssa.org/jobs

Notes

Favorite sites, useful resources

Regional-USA (continued)

New York (continued)

New York State Academy of Family Physicians	www.fpjobsonline.org
New York State Society of CPAs	www.nysscpa.org/classified/ main.cfm
The New York Times	www.nytimes.com
New York's Preferred Jobs	www.nycityjobs.com
NYCareers.com	www.nycareers.com
NY Job Source	www.nyjobsource.com
NY Preferred Jobs	http://newyork.preferredjobs.com
NYC Job Bank	www.nycjobbank.com
NYPAHelpWanted.com	www.nypahelpwanted.com
OleanHelpWanted.com	www.oleanhelpwanted.com
Rensselier Polytechnic Institute Career Development Center	www.cdc.rpi.edu
RochesterHelpWanted.com	www.rochesterhelpwanted.com
Rochester, NY Careers	www.rochestercareers.com
SeawayHelpWanted.com	www.seawayhelpwanted.com
SiliconAlley.com	www.siliconalley.com
Silicon Alley Daily	www.siliconalleydaily.com
SyracuseHelpWanted.com	www.syracusehelpwanted.com
SyracuseJobs	http:syracuse.jobs-employment.net
Syracuse New Times	www.newtimes.com
Syracuse Online	www.syracuse.com
1000IslandsHelpWanted.com	www.1000islands helpwanted.com
Tri-StateJobs.com	www.tristatejobs.com
TwinTiersHelpWanted.com	www.twintiershelpwanted.com
USEmpleos.com	www.usempleos.com
WestchesterCountyJobs.com	www.westchestercountyjobs.com
Westchester Jobs	www.westchesterjobs.com
Western NY JOBS	www.wnyjobs.com

North Carolina

AshevilleHelpWanted.com	www.ashevillehelpwanted.com
Career Women	www.webcom.com/~nccareer
Carolina Computer Jobs	www.carolinacomputerjobs.com
CharlotteHelpWanted.com	www.charlottehelpwanted.com
Charlotte Observer	www.charlotte.com
Duke University Job Resources	http://career.studentaffairs. duke.edu
EastCarolinaHelpWanted.com	www.eastcarolina helpwanted.com
Employment Security Commission Home Page	www.neesc.com
FayettevilleHelpWanted.com	www.fayettevillehelpwanted.com

Notes

Favorite sites, useful resources

Regional-USA (continued)

North Carolina (continued)

Greensboro News-Record	www.news-record.com
Job Listing Form	www.charweb.org
News & Observer (Raleigh)	www.newsobserver.com
North Carolina Biotechnology Center	www.ncbiotech.org
North Carolina Genomics & Bioinformatics Consortium	www.ncgbc.org
North Carolina JobLink Career Center	www.joblink.state.nc.us
NorthCarolinaJobs.net	www.northcarolinajobs.net
The North Carolina Office of State Personnel	www.osp.state.nc.us
PiedmontHelpWanted.com	www.piedmonthelpwanted.com
TriangleHelpWanted.com	www.trianglehelpwanted.com
Welcome to North Carolina	www.ncgov.com
WilmingtonHelpWanted.com	www.wilmingtonhelpwanted.com
Wilmington Star	www.wilmingtonstar.com
Winston-Salem Journal	www.journalnow.com

North Dakota

BismarckMandanHelpWanted.com	www.bismarckmandan helpwanted.com
Bismarck Tribune	www.bismarcktribune.com
FargoJobs.com	www.fargojobs.com
Grand Forks Herald	www.grandforks.com
The Jamestown Sun	www.jamestownsun.com
Minot Daily News	www.minotdailynews.com
NorthDakotaJobs.com	www.northdakotajobs.com
NorthernPlainsHelpWanted.com	www.northernplainshelpwanted.com

Ohio

MidOhioHelpWanted.com	
CareerBoard	www.careerboard.com
Case Western Reserve University	www.cwru.edu
Cincinnati Enquirer	www.enquirer.com
Cincinnati/Jobs	http://careerfinder.cincinnati.com
Cleveland Careers	www.cleveland.com
ClevelandHelpWanted.com	www.clevelandhelpwanted.com
The Cleveland Nation	www.clnation.com
Columbus Dispatch	www.dispatch.com
ColumbusHelpWanted.com	www.columbushelpwanted.com
Dayton Daily News	www.daytondailynews.com
DaytonHelpWanted.com	www.daytonhelpwanted.com
FetchMeAJob.com	www.fetchmeajob.com
HelpWantedCincinnati.com	www.helpwantedcincinnati.com
LimalandHelpWanted.com	www.limalandhelpwanted.com

Notes

Favorite sites, useful resources

Regional-USA (continued)

Ohio (continued)

MahoningValleyHelpWanted.com	www.mahoningvalley helpwanted.com
MansfieldAreaHelpWanted.com	www.mansfieldarea helpwanted.com
Ohio Careers Resource Center	www.ohiocareers.com
Ohio Job Prospector	www.jobprospector.com
OhioJobs.com	www.ohiojobs.com
Ohio State Council	www.ohioshrm.org
SanduskyHelpWanted.com	www.sanduskyhelpwanted.com
SoutheasternOhioHelpWanted.com	www.southeasternohio helpwanted.com
Springfield News Sun	www.springfieldnewssun.com
ToledoHelpWanted.com	www.toledohelpwanted.com
TriStateJobMatch.com (Monster.com)	www.tristatejobmatch.com

Oklahoma

Altus Times	www.altustimes.com
Lawton Constitution	www.lawton-constitution.com
OKC - Cityhall.org	www.okc-cityhall.org
OklahomaCityHelpWanted.com	www.oklahomacity helpwanted.com
OklahomaJobs.com	www.oklahomajobs.com
Oklahoma State Medical Association	www.osmaonline.org
The Oklahoman (Oklahoma City)	www.newsok.com
Ponca City News	www.poncacitynews.com
Tulsa Area Human Resources Association	www.tahra.org
TulsaHelpWanted.com	www.tulsahelpwanted.com
Tulsa World	www.tulsaworld.com

Oregon

CentralOregonJobs.com	www.centraloregonjobs.com
Columbia-Willamette Compensation Group	www.cwcg.org
East Oregonian (Pendleton)	www.eonow.com
EugeneHelpWanted.com	www.eugenehelpwanted.com
Hiregate.com	www.hiregate.com
Oregon Bioscience Association	www.oregon-bioscience.com
Oregon Education Jobs	www.edjobs.net
Oregon Employment Department	www.emp.state.or.us
OregonJobs.com	www.oregonjobs.com
The Oregonian (Portland)	www.oregonian.com
PortlandHelpWanted.com	www.portlandhelpwanted.com
Portland Jobs	www.portland-jobs.com
The Portland Human Resource Management Assn	www.pdxhr.org
The Register-Guard (Eugene)	www.registerguard.com

Notes

Favorite sites, useful resources

Regional-USA (continued)

Oregon (contined)

SouthernOregonHelpWanted.com	www.southernoregon helpwanted.com
SouthernOregonJobs.com	www.southernoregonjobs.com
Springfield News	www.hometownnews.com
Statesman Journal (Salem)	www.statesmanjournal.com

Pennsylvania

Allegheny County Medical Society	www.acms.org
CentreCountyHelpWanted.com	www.centrecounty helpwanted.com
ClearfieldJeffersonHelpWanted.com	www.clearfieldjefferson helpwanted.com
Drexel University	www.drexel.edu/scdc
Erie Daily Times-News	www.goerie.com
ErieHelpWanted.com	www.eriehelpwanted.com
HarrisburgHelpWanted.com	www.harrisburghelpwanted.com
HelpWantedCentralPA.com	www.helpwantedcentralpa.com
HelpWantedTriState.com	www.helpwantedtristate.com
Job Circle	www.jobcircle.com
JobNet	www.jobnet.com
JohnstownHelpWanted.com	www.johnstownhelpwanted.com
KeystoneHelpWanted.com	www.keystonehelpwanted.com
LehighValleyHelpWanted.com	www.lehighvalley helpwanted.com
NEPAHelpWanted.com	www.nepahelpwanted.com
PAJobMatch.com	www.pajobmatch.com
Pennsylvania Academy of Family Physicians	www.fpjobsonline.org
PennsylvaniaJobs.com	www.pennsylvaniajobs.com
PennsylvaniaJobs.net	www.pennsylvaniajobs.net
PhiladelphiaHelpWanted.com	www.philadelphia helpwanted.com
The Philadelphia Inquirer	www.philly.com
Philadelphia-Jobs	http://philadelphia.jobs.com
Philly.com	www.philly.com
PhillyWorks	www.phillyworks.com
PittsburghHelpWanted.com	www.pittsburghhelpwanted.com
PittsburghJobs.com	www.pittsburghjobs.com
Pittsburgh Personnel Association	www.ppapitt.org
Pittsburg Post-Gazette	www.post-gazette.com
Scranton Times Tribune	www.scrantontimes.com
Three Rivers	http://trfn.clpgh.org
The Times Leader (Wilkes Barre)	www.timesleader.com
Tri-StateJobs.com	www.tristatejobs.com
WesternPAHelpWanted.com	www.westernpahelpwanted.com

Notes

Favorite sites, useful resources

Regional-USA (continued)

Pennsylvania (continued)
WilliamsportHelpWanted.com — www.williamsport helpwanted.com

Rhode Island
The Narragansett Times (Wakefield) — www.narragansetttimes.com
OceanStateHelpWanted.com — www.oceanstatehelpwanted.com
Networkri.org — www.networkri.org
The Pawtucket Times — www.pawtuckettimes.com
Providence Journal Bulletin — www.projo.com
Rhode Island Department of Labor and Training — www.det.state.ri.us
RhodeIsland Jobs.com — www.rhodeislandjobs.com
Sakonnet Times (Portsmouth) — www.eastbayri.com

South Carolina
Camden Chronicle Independent — www.chronicle-independent.com
Career Women — www.webcom.com/~nccareer
Carolina Computer Jobs — www.carolinacomputerjobs.com
Clemson University — www.clemson.edu
ColumbiaHelpWanted.com — www.columbiahelpwanted.com
Free Times (Columbia) — www.free-times.com
The Greenville News — www.greenvilleonline.com
HelpWantedCharleston.com — www.helpwantedcharleston.com
LowCountryHelpWanted.com — www.lowcountryhelpwanted.com
MyrtleBeachHelpWanted.com — www.myrtlebeach helpwanted.com
OrangeburgHelpWanted.com — www.orangeburghelpwanted.com
PeeDeeHelpWanted.com — www.peedeehelpwanted.com
The Post and Courier (Charleston) — www.charleston.net
SourthCarolinaJobs.net — www.southcarolinajobs.net
South Carolina State Jobs — www.state.sc.us/Jobs
SumterHelpWanted.com — www.sumterhelpwanted.com
The Sun Times (Myrtle Beach) — www.myrtlebeachonline.com
UpstateHelpWanted.com — www.upstatehelpwanted.com

South Dakota
Argus Leader (Sioux Falls) — www.argusleader.com
BlackHillsHelpWanted.com — www.blackhillshelpwanted.com
Brookings Daily Register — www.brookingsregister.com
The Capital Journal (Pierre) — www.capjournal.com
The Freeman Courier — www.freemansd.com
Huron Plainsman — www.plainsman.com
SiouxFallsHelpWanted.com — www.siouxfalls helpwanted.com
SouthDakotaJobs.com — www.southdakotajobs.com

Notes

Favorite sites, useful resources

Regional-USA (continued)

Southeast
MyGA.net	www.myga.net
Thinkjobs	www.thinkjobs.com

Tennessee
ChattanoogaHelpWanted.com	www.chattanooga helpwanted.com
Chattanooga Times Free Press	www.timesfreepress.com
ClarksvilleHelpWanted.com	www.clarksvillehelpwanted.com
CookevilleHelpWanted.com	www.cookevillehelpwanted.com
Daily Post-Athenian	www.dpa.xtn.net
GoodRover.com	www.goodrover.com
KnoxvilleHelpWanted.com	www.knoxvillehelpwanted.com
Knoxville News Sentinel	www.knoxnews.com
Memphis Flyer	www.memphisflyer
MemphisHelpWanted.com	www.memphishelpwanted.com
Middle Tennessee-SHRM Central	www.mtshrm.org
NashvilleHelpWanted.com	www.nashvillehelpwanted.com
MiddleTennesseeHelpWanted.com	www.middletennessee helpwanted.com
Nashvillejobslink.com	www.nashvillejobslink.com
TennesseeJobs.com	www.tennesseejobs.com
Tennessee Society of CPA's	www.tscpa.com
The Tennessean (Nashville)	www.onnashville.com
WestTennesseeHelpWanted.com	www.westtennessee helpwanted.com

Texas
Advocacy, Incorporated	www.advocacy.org/jobs.html
AmarilloHelpWanted.com	www.amarillohelpwanted.com
Austin American-Statesman	www.austin360.com
AustinHelpWanted.com	www.austinhelpwanted.com
Austin Jobs	www.austin-jobs.net
Austin@Work	www.catf-austin.org/title/ GreaterAustin@work
Austin Texas Jobs	www.search-beat.com/ austinjobs.htm
Austin-City Jobs	www.ci.Austin.tx.us
BrownwoodHelpWanted.com	www.brownwoodhelpwanted.com
CareersinHouston.com	
CoastalBendHelpWanted.com	www.coastalbend helpwanted.com
Dallas Human Resource Management Association	www.dallashr.org
Dallas Jobs	www.dallas-jobs.net
Dallas Morning News	www.dallasnews.com

Notes

Favorite sites, useful resources

Regional-USA (continued)

Texas (continued)

DFWHelpWanted.com	www.dfwhelpwanted.com
EastTexasHelpWanted.com	www.easttexashelpwanted.com
ElPasoHelpWanted.com	www.elpasohelpwanted.com
El Paso Times	www.elpasotimes.com
Harris County Medical Society	www.hcms.org
Houston Chronicle	www.chron.com
HoustonEmployment.com	www.houstonemployment.com
Houston Human Resource Management Association	www.hhrma.org/default.shtml
Houston Jobs	www.houston-jobs.net
Jobs in Higher Education Geographical Listings	http://volvo.gslis.utexas.edu/ ~acadres/jobs/index.html
LocalCareers.com	www.localcareers.com
LubbockHelpWanted.com	www.lubbockhelpwanted.com
Metroplex Association of Personnel Consultants	www.recruitingfirms:com
NACCB - Dallas - Ft. Worth Chapter	www.dfw-naccb.org
National Association of Hispanic Nurses Houston Chapter	www.nahnhouston.org
North Central Texas Workforce Development Board, Inc.	www.dfwjobs.com
San Antonio Express News	www.mysanantonio.com
SanAntonioHelpWanted.com	www.sanantonio helpwanted.com
SoutheastTexasHelpWanted.com	www.southeasttexas helpwanted.com
SouthTexasHelpWanted.com	www.southtexas helpwanted.com
StephenvilleHelpWanted.com	www.stephenville helpwanted.com
Texas Association of Staffing	www.texasstaffing.org
Texas Healthcare & Bioscience Institute	www.thbi.org
TxJobs.com	www.txjobs.com
TexasJobs.com	www.texasjobs.com
Texas Jobs & Employment Links	www.anancyweb.com/ texas_jobs.html
Texas Marketplace	www.texas-one.org
Texas Medical Association	www.texmed.org
Texas Workforce Commission	www.twc.state.tx.us
TexomaHelpWanted.com	www.texoma helpwanted.com
ValleyHelpWanted.com	www.valleyhelpwanted.com
Waco, TX Jobs	www.waco-jobs.com
WichitaFallsHelpWanted.com	www.wichitafalls helpwanted.com

Notes

Favorite sites, useful resources

Regional-USA (continued)

Texas (continued)
WorkAustin   www.workaustin.com
WT.Net   www.wt.net

Utah
The Daily Herald (Provo)   www.harktheherald.com
Herald Journal (Logan)   www.hjnews.com
SaltLakeCityHelpWanted.com   www.saltlakecity
                                                      helpwanted.com
Salt Lake Tribune   www.sltrib.com
SouthernUtahHelpWanted.com   www.southernutah
                                                      helpwanted.com
Standard-Examiner (Ogden)   www.standard.net
Utah Job Store   www.utahjobstore.com
UtahJobs.net   www.utahjobs.net
Utah Life Sciences Association   www.utahlifescience.com

Vermont
Addison County Independent (Middlebury)   www.addisonindependent.com
Burlington Free Press   www.burlingtonfreepress.com
Deerfield Valley News (West Dover)   www.dvalnews.com
NorthCountryHelpWanted.com   www.northcountry
                                                      helpwanted.com
Stowe Reporter   www.stowereporter.com
Valley News (White River Junction)   www.vnews.com
VermontJobs.net   www.vermontjobs.net

Virginia
BlueRidgeHelpWanted.com   www.blueridgehelpwanted.com
Career Pro   www.career-pro.com
CharlottesvilleHelpWanted.com   www.charlottesville
                                                      helpwanted.com
The Daily Progress (Charlottesville)   www.dailyprogress.com
Danville Register Bee   www.registerbee.com
HamptonRoadsHelpWanted.com   www.hamptonroads
                                                      helpwanted.com
HarrisonburgHelpWanted.com   www.harrisonburg
                                                      helpwanted.com
HighlandsHelpWanted.com   www.highlandshelpwanted.com
Human Resource Association
  of the National Capital Area Job Bank Listing   http://hra-nca.org/job_list.asp
JobFetch.com   www.jobfetch.com
LocalVirginiaJobs.com   www.localvirginiajobs.com
The News-Advance (Lynchburg)   www.newsadvance.com

Notes

Favorite sites, useful resources

Regional-USA (continued)

Virginia (continued)

North Virginia Job Openings	www.northern-viriginia.jobopenings.net
NRVHelpWanted.com	www.nrvhelpwanted.com
Pilot Online	www.pilotonline.com
RichmondHelpWanted.com	www.richmondhelpwanted.com
Richmond Preferred Jobs	http://richmond.preferredjobs.com
Richmond Times-Dispatch	www.timesdispatch.com
Roanoke.com	www.roanoke.com/index.html
ShenandoahValleyHelpWanted.com	www.shenandoahhelpwanted.com
TriCitiesHelpWanted.com	www.tricitieshelpwanted.com
University of Virginia Career Planning and Placement	www.virginia.edu/~career
Virginia Biotechnology Association	www.vabio.org
Virginia-Jobs	www.virginia-jobs.com
Virginia Working 925	www.working925.com
Virginian-Pilot (Norfolk)	www.pilotonline.com
WashingtonJobs.com	www.washingtonjobs.com
Washington and Lee University	http://www2.wlu.edu

Washington

The Columbian (Vancouver)	www.columbian.com
Communicators & Marketers Jobline (Seattle & Puget Sound)	http://cmjobline.org
LocalWashingtonJobs.com	www.localwashingtonjobs.com
Navigator Online	www.lwhra.org
The News Tribune (Tacoma)	www.tribnet.com
NorthwestWashingtronHelpWanted.com	www.northwestwashingtonhelpwanted.com
The Olympian (Olympia)	www.theolympian.com
PugetSoundHelpWanted.com	www.pugetsoundhelpwanted.com
SeattleJobs	www.seattle-jobs.com
Seattle Post-Intelligencer	www.seattlepi.nwsource.com
Seattle Times	www.seatimes.com/classified/Jobs
SoutheasternWashingtonHelpWanted.com	www.southeasternwashingtonhelpwanted.com
SpokaneHelpWanted.com	www.spokanehelpwanted.com
The Spokesman-Review (Spokane)	www.spokane.net
University of Washington	www.gspa.washington.edu
Washington Biotechnology & Biomedical Association	www.wabio.com

Notes

Favorite sites, useful resources

Regional-USA (continued)

Washington (continued)
Washington Workforce — www.wa.gov/esd/employment.html

WesternWashingtonHelpWanted.com — www.westernwashingtonhelpwanted.com

World Careers Network — www.wcnworld.com
YakimaHelpWanted.com — www.yakimahelpwanted.com

West Virginia
BluefieldHelpWanted.com — www.bluefieldhelpwanted.com
Charlestown Daily Mail — www.dailymail.com
CharlestonHepWanted.com — www.charlestonhelpwanted.com

Clarksburg Exponent Telegram — www.cpubco.com
The Dominion Post (Morgantown) — www.dominionpost.com
GreenBrierValleyHelpWanted.com — www.greenbriervalleyhelpwanted.com

HuntingtonAshlandHelpWanted.com — www.huntingtonashlandhelpwanted.com

OhioValleyHelpWanted.com — www.ohiovalleyhelpwanted.com

Times West Virginian (Fairmont) — www.timeswv.com
WestVaHelpWanted.com — www.westvahelpwanted.com
WestVirginiaJobs.com — www.westvirginiajobs.com
Wheeling News-Register — www.news-register.com

Wisconsin
CareerBoard.com — www.careerboard.com
ChippewaValleyHelpWanted.com — www.chippewavalleyhelpwanted.com

FetchMeAJob.com — www.fetchmeajob.com
Great Jobs WI — www.greatjobswi.com
Green Bay Press Gazette — www.greenbaypressgazette.com

HelpWantedMadison.com — www.helpwantedmadison.com
HelpWantedMilwaukee.com — www.helpwantedmilwaukee.com

HelpWantedWisconsin.com — www.helpwantedwisconsin.com
The Journal Times (Racine) — www.journaltimes.com
La Crosse Tribune — www.lacrossetribune.com
LocalCareers.com — www.localcareers.com
Milwaukee Jobs — www.employmentbureau.com
Milwaukee Journal Sentinel — www.jsonline.com
NEWHelpWanted.com — www.newhelpwanted.com
SouthValleyHelpWanted.com — www.southvalleyhelpwanted.com

Notes

Favorite sites, useful resources

Regional-USA (continued)

Wisconsin (continued)

University of Wisconsin-Madison School of Business Career Center	www.bus.wisc.edu/career/ default1.asp
Wisconsin.gov	www.wisconsin.gov
Wisconsin Academy of Family Physicians	www.fpjobsonline.org
Wisconsin Biotechnology Association	www.wisconsinbiotech.org
Wisconsin Department of Workforce Development	www.dwd.state.wi.us
Wisconsin Employment Connection	www.dwd.state.wi.us/dwe-wec/ default.htm
WisconsinJobs.com	www.wijobs.com
Wisconsin Medical Society	www.wisconsinmedical society.org
Wisconsin State Journal (Madison)	www.madison.com

Wyoming

Douglas Budget	www.douglas-budget.com
The Wyoming Job Bank	http://wyjobs.state.wy.us
WyomingHelpWanted.com	www.helpwanted.com
WyomingJobs.com	www.wyomingjobs.com
Wyoming News.com	www.wyomingnews.com
Wyoming Tribune-Eagle	www.wyomingnews.com

Religion

Catho Online [Brazil]	www.catho.com.br
ChristiaNet	www.christianet.com
Christian Help	www.christianhelp.org
Crosswalk.com	www.crosswalk.com
Gospel Communications Network	www.gospelcom.net
Jewish Vocational Service Career Moves	www.jvsjobs.org
Ministry Connect	http://ministryconnect.org
MinistryJobs.com	www.ministryjobs.com
MinistrySearch.com	www.ministrysearch.com

Retail

AllRetailJobs.com	www.allretailjobs.com
Be The 1	www.bethe1.com
RetailChoice.com [United Kingdom]	www.retailchoice.com
⚏ EmploymentGuide.com	www.employmentguide.com
Grocer Jobs [United Kingdom]	www.grocerjobs.co.uk
iHireRetail.com	www.ihireretail.com
In Retail [United Kingdom]	www.inretail.co.uk
Jobs Retail	www.nowjob.com

Notes

Favorite sites, useful resources

Retail (continued)

MyRetailJobs.net	www.myretailjobs.net
RetailHomepage.co.uk [United Kingdom]	www.retailhomepage.co.uk
Retail Job Net	www.retailjobs.com
RetailJobs.ca [Canada]	www.retailjobs.ca
RetailResume.com	www.retailresume.com
Retailer News Online	www.retailernews.com
RetailingJobs.com	www.retailingjobs.com
TriStateJobMatch.com (Monster.com)	www.tristatejobmatch.com

-S-

Sales and Marketing

Sales & Marketing-General

⊠ CareerJournal.com	www.careerjournal.com
Career Marketplace.com	www.careermarketplace.com
iHireSalesPeople.com	www.ihiresalespeople.com
Just Sales and Marketing [United Kingdom]	www.justsalesandmarketing.net
TheLadders.com	www.theladders.com
NationJob Network: Marketing and Sales Job Page	www.nationjob.com/marketing
Sales & Marketing Executives International Career Center	www.smei.org/ classified.cfm
Simply Sales and Marketing [United Kingdom]	www.simplysalesandmarketing. co.uk

Sales-Specific

ACareerinSales.com	www.acareerinsales.com
CareerinSales.com	www.careerinsales.com
Jobs4Sales.com	www.jobs4sales.com
MySalesCareer.net	www.mysalescareer.net
National Association of Sales Professionals Career Center	www.nasp.com
SalesAnimals.com	www.salesanimals.com
Sales Classifieds	www.salesclassifieds.com
SalesEngineer.com	www.SalesEngineer.com
SalesJob.com	www.salesjob.com
SalesProJobs.com	www.salesprojobs.com
SalesRep.ca [Canada]	www.salesrep.ca
Sales Trax	www.salestrax.com
SalesWise.co.uk [United Kingdom]	www.saleswise.co.uk
SellingJobs.com/BrandingJobs.com	www.sellingjobs.com
Tigerjobs.com, Inc.	www.tigerjobs.com
Top Sales Positions	www.topsalespositions.com

Notes

Favorite sites, useful resources

Sales and Marketing (continued)

Marketing-Specific

American Marketing Association Career Center	www.marketingpower.com/live/ content.php?Item_ID=966
iHireMarketing.com	www.ihiremarketing.com
Jobs In Marketing [United Kingdom]	www.jobs-in-marketing.co.uk
MarketingHire.com	www.marketinghire.com
⇲ MarketingJobs.com	www.marketingjobs.com
Marketing Online	www.marketing.haynet.com
Marketing Sherpa	www.marketingsherpa.com
MyMarketingJobs.net	www.mymarketingjobs.net
Promotion Marketing Association Job Bank	www.pmalink.org/resources/ careers.asp

Industry-Specific

Advertising Age's Online Job Bank	http://adage.com
Aeroindustryjobs	www.aeroindustryjobs.com
AllRetailJobs.com	www.allretailjobs.com
American Association of Pharmaceutical Sales Professionals	www.pharmaceuticalsales.org
Autojobs.com, Inc.	www.autojobs.com
BrokerHunter.com	www.brokerhunter.com
CallCenterCareers.com	www.callcentercareers.com
CallCenterJobs.com	www.callcenterjobs.com
CRN	www.channelweb.com/sections/ careers
Direct Marketing Association	www.the-dma.org/jobbank
DirectMarketingCareers.com	www.directmarketingcareers.com
DMjobs.co.uk [United Kingdom]	www.dmjobs.co.uk
GxPJobs.com [United Kingdom]	www.gxpjobs.com
iHireRetail.com	www.ihireretail.com
Industry Sales Pros	www.industrysalespros.com
InfoPresseJobs.ca [Canada]	www.infopressejobs.ca
In Retail [United Kingdom]	www.inretail.co.uk
Job.com Retail JobNet	www.job.com
Just Tech Sales Jobs	www.justtechsalesjobs.com
Medical Marketing Association	www.mmanet.org
MedicalSalesJobs.com	www.medicalsalesjobs.com
Motorstaff.com	www.motorstaff.com
National Association of Pharmaceutical Sales Representatives	www.napsronline.org
National Field Selling Association	www.nfsa.com
OnlineMarketingJobs.com [UnitedKingdom]	www.onlinemarketingjobs.com
NewHomeSalesJobs.com	www.newhomesalesjobs.com
Pharmaceuticalrepjobs.com	www.pharmaceuticalrepjobs.com
Retail-Recruiter	www.retail-recruiter.com

Notes

Favorite sites, useful resources

Sales and Marketing (continued)

Industry-Specific (continued)

RetailingJobs.com	www.retailingjobs.com
Software & IT Sales Employment Review	www.salesrecruits.com
Television Bureau of Advertising	www.tvb.org/jobcenter/index.html

Science/Scientists

Academic Physician & Scientist	www.acphysci.com
AIP Physics Career Bulletin Board	www.aip.org
American Agricultural Economic Association Employment Service	www.aaea.org/classifieds
American Association for the Advancement of Science	www.aaas.org
American Association of Brewing Chemists	www.asbcnet.org/SERVICES/career.htm
American Association of Cereal Chemists	www.aaccnet.org/membership/careerplacement.asp
American Association of Pharmaceutical Scientists	www.aaps.org
American Chemical Society cen-chemjobs.org	www.cen-chemjobs.org
American Institute of Biological Sciences	www.aibs.org
American Institute of Physics Career Services	www.aip.org/careersvc
American Meteorological Society Employment Announcements	www.ametsoc.org
American Psychological Society	www.psychologicalscience.org
American Society of Agronomy	www.asa-cssa-sssa.org/career
American Society of Animal Science	www.fass.org/job.asp
American Society for Cell Biology	www.ascb.org
American Society for Clinical Laboratory Science	www.ascls.org
American Society for Clinical Pathology	www.ascp.org
American Society of Clinical Pharmacology and Therapeutics	www.ascpt.org
American Society for Microbiology	www.asm.org
American Society for Gravitational and Space Biology	www.indstate.edu/asgsb/index.html
American Society of Horticultural Science HortOpportunities	www.ashs.org/careers.html
American Society of Plant Biologists	www.aspb.org
American Water Works Association Career Center (Water Jobs)	www.awwa.org
Association for Applied Human Pharmacology [Germany]	www.agah-web.de
Bay Area Bioscience Center	www.bayareabioscience.org

Notes

Favorite sites, useful resources

Science/Scientists (continued)

Bermuda Biological Station for
  Research, Inc. — www.bbsr.edu
BioCareers.co.za [South Africa] — www.biocareers.co.za
Biofind — www.biofind.com
BioSource Technical Service — www.biosource-tech.com
Bio Research Online — www.bioresearchonline.com
BioSpace Career Center — www.biospace.com/b2/
  job_index.cfm
Biotechnology Calendar, Inc. — www.biotech-calendar.com
Bioview — www.bioview.com
Board of Physics and Astronomy — www.nas.edu/bpa
C & I Job Database — http://ci.mond.org
California Agricultural Technical
  Institute ATI-Net — www.atinet.org/jobs.asp
California Separation Science Society — www.casss.org
Cell Press Online — www.cellpress.com
Cen-ChemJobs.org — www.cen-chemjobs.org
Center for Biological Computing — http://papa.indstate.edu
Chemistry & Industry — http://chemistry.mond.org
Citysearch.com-Biotech — www.biofind.com
Controlled Release Society — www.controlledrelease.org
Earth Works — http://ourworld.compuserve.
  com/homepages/eworks
Easyline.co.uk [United Kingdom] — www.easyline.co.uk
Environmental Careers World — www.environmental-jobs.com
Environmental Careers Bulletin Online — www.eceajobs.com
Environmental Jobs & Careers — www.ejobs.org
Environmental Careers Organization — www.eco.org
FASEB Career Resources — http://ns2.faseb.org/careerweb
GeoWebServices-RocketHire — www.geowebservices.com
GIS Jobs Clearinghouse — www.gjc.org
GxPJobs.com [United Kingdom] — www.gxpjobs.com
History of Science Society — www.hssonline.org
HUM-MOLGEN
  [Germany] — www.informatik.uni-rostock.ed/
  HUM-MOLGEN/anno/
  position.html
iHireChemists.com — www.ihirechemists.com
Institute of Clinical Research
  [United Kingdom] — www.instituteofclinical
  research.org
Institute of Physics — www.iop.org
International Society for Molecular
  Plant-Microbe Interactions — www.ismpinet.org/career
The Internet Pilot to Physics — http://physicsweb.org/TIPTOP
Jobs.ac.uk [United Kingdom] — www.jobs.ac.uk
Jobscience Network — www.jobscience.com

Notes

Favorite sites, useful resources

Science/Scientists (continued)

LaboratoryNetwork.com	www.laboratorynetwork.com
The London Biology Network [United Kingdom]	www.biolondon.co.uk
Meteorological Employment Journal	www.swiftsite.com/mejjobs
MeteorologyJobs	www.meteorologyjobs.com
National Organization for Professional Advancement of Black Chemists and Chemical Engineers University of Michigan Chapter	www.engin.umich.edu/soc/ nobcche
National Weather Association Job Corner	www.nwas.org/jobs.html
Naturejobs	www.nature.com/naturejobs
New Scientist	www.newscientist.com
NukeWorker.com	www.nukeworker.com
Oceanography Society	www.tos.org
Ohio State University: College of Food, Agricultural and Environmental Sciences	http://cfaes.osu.edu/career
Optics.org	http://optics.org/home.ssi
Organic Chemistry Jobs Worldwide [Belgium]	www.organicworldwide.net/jobs/ jobs.html
Physics Today Online	www.aip.org
Plant Pathology Online APSnet	www.scisoc.org
Plasma Gate [Israel]	http://plasma-gate.weizmann.ac.il
Poly Sort	www.polysort.com
Royal Society of Chemistsry	http:chemistry.rsc.org
RPh on the Go	www.rphonthego.com
RPhrecruiter.com	www.rphrecruiter.com
Sci Central	www.scicentral.com
Science Careers	www.sciencecareers.org
Sciencejobs.com	www.sciencejobs.com
Science Online	www.scienceonline.org
Science Professional Network	http://recruit.sciencemag.org
ScientistWorld.com [United Kingdom]	www.scientistworld.com
Scijobs.org	http://scijobs.org
Society of Mexican American Engineers and Scientists	www.maes-natl.org
Space Jobs	www.spacejobs.com
SPIE Web-International Society for Optical Engineering	www.spieworks.com
Student Conservation Association	www.thesca.org
Texas A&M Poultry Science Department	http://gallus.tamu.edu/ careerops.htm
Texas Healthcare & Bioscience Institute	www.thbi.org
Utah Life Sciences Association	www.utahlifescience.com
Weed Science Society of America WeedJobs: Positions in Weed Science	www.wssa.net/weedjobs

Notes

Favorite sites, useful resources

Search Engines-Employment

GetTheJob	www.getthejob.com
Google Base	http://base.google.com
Indeed	www.indeed.com
JobAhoy [United Kingdom]	www.jobahoy.com
JobCentral.com	www.jobcentral.com
Jobster	www.jobster.com
Oodle.com	www.oodle.com
SimplyHired	www.simplyhired.com
Zudora.com	www.zudora.com

Search Firms/Staffing Agencies/Recruiters

Accounting Position	www.taftsearch.com
AD&A Software Jobs Home Page	www.softwarejobs.com
Adecco	www.adecco.com
All Advantage	www.alladvantage.com
Alpha Systems	www.jobbs.com
American Staffing Association	www.staffingtoday.net
Amos & Associates	www.netpath.net/amos/ linkstonf.htm
Aquent Partners	http://cbt.aquentpartners.com
Aron Printz & Associates	http://mindlink.net/vci/apahp.htm
The Beardsley Group	www.beardsleygroup.com
Best Internet Recruiter	www.bestrecruit.com
J. Boragine & Associates	www.jboragine.com
Buck Systems Inc.	www.bisinc.com
The Caradyne Group	www.pcsjobs.com/jobs.htm
Career Image Associates	www.career-image.com
Career Quest International	www.careerquest.com
Champion Personnel System	www.championjobs.com
Chancellor & Chancellor's	www.chancellor.com
Comforce	www.comforce.com
Corporate Staffing Center, Inc.	www.corporate-staffing.com
Creative Focus	www.focusstaff.com
Cross Staffing Services	www.snelling.com/cross
Daley Consulting & Search/Daley Technical Search	www.dpsearch.com
Darwin Partners	www.seek-consulting.com
Datalake-IT.com	www.datalake-IT.com
Dawson & Dawson Consultants, Inc.	www.dawson-dawson.com
EPCglobal.com	www.epcglobal.com
ePlaced	www.eplaced.com
Erickson & Associates, Inc.	www.nursesearch.com
Executive Placement Services	www.execplacement.com
Experience on Demand	www.experienceondemand.com
Fogarty and Associates, Inc.	www.fogarty.com

Notes

Favorite sites, useful resources

Search Firms/Staffing Agencies/Recruiters (continued)

Gables	www.gablessearch.com
Global Careers	www.globalcareers.com
Go Partnership Limited	www.gogogo.org
Hamilton, Jones & Koller [Australia]	www.hjk.com.au
Headhunters 4u	www.headhunters4u.com
Healthcare Recruiters	www.hcrphx.com
HealtheHire, Inc.	www.healthehire.com
The HEC Group	http://hec-group.com
Hire Quality	www.hire-quality.com
Home Page of Malachy	www.execpc.com/~maltoal
HR Connections	www.hrconnections.com
Humanys.com	www.humanys.com
The Hunting Group's Career Network	www.hgllc.com
Hyman & Associates	www.teamhyman.com
Ian Martin Limited	www.iml.com
Insurance National Search, Inc.	www.insurancerecruiters.com
Insurance Overload Systems	www.insuranceoverload.com
Inter-City Personnel Associates	www.ipaservices.com
Laser Computer Recruitment [United Kingdom]	www.laserrec.co.uk
Life Work, Inc.'s Military Recruiting Group	www.lifeworkinc.com
The Little Group	www.littlegroup.com
Manpower	www.manpower.com
MarketPro	www.marketproinc.com
McGregor Boyall [United Kingdom]	www.mcgregor_boyall.co.uk
Medical Sales Associates	www.msajobs.com
Metroplex Association of Personnel Consultants	www.recruitingfirms.com
Mindsource Software	www.mindsrc.com
National Banking Network	www.banking-financialjobs.com
1ExecutiveStreet.com	www.1executivestreet.com
On-Campus Resources, Inc.	www.on-campus.com
1To1Jobs	www.1to1jobs.com
Pacific Coast Recruiting	www.pacificsearch.com
Pemberton & Associates	www.biddeford.com/pemberton
People Connect Staffing	www.peopleconnectstaffing.com
Power Brokers	www.powerbrokersllc.com
Premier Staffing, Inc.	www.premier-staff.com
PressTemps	www.presstemps.com
Price Jamieson	www.pricejam.com/index/le4.html
Priority Search.com	www.prioritysearch.com
Pro Match of Silicon Valley	www.promatch.org
Pro Med National Staffing	www.promedjobs.com
ProQwest, Inc.	www.proqwest.com
Provident Search Group	www.dpjobs.com
RAI	www.raijobs.com
Recruit PLC [United Kingdom]	www.newdawn.co.uk/recruit

Notes

Favorite sites, useful resources

Search Firms/Staffing Agencies/Recruiters (continued)

Recruiter Networks	www.recruiternetworks.com
Recruiters for Christ	www.edmondspersonnel.com
RecruitingOptions	www.recruitingoptions.net
RGA	www.rga-joblink.com/docs/ home.html
Robert Half	www.roberthalf.com
Rollins Search Group	www.rollinssearch.com
Romac International	www.romacintl.com
Sanford Rose Associates	www.sanfordrose.com
Self Opportunity	www.selfopportunity.com
Silverman McGovern Staffing	www.SilvermanMcGovern.com
SnagAJob	www.snagajob.com
Solomon Page Executive Search	www.spges.com
Sonasearch	www.sonasearch.com/who.htm
Spherion Corporation	www.spherion.com
Stanley, Barber & Associates	www.stanleyb.com
Student Search System, Inc.	www.studentsearch.com
TechNix Inc. [Canada]	www.technix.ca
TKO International	www.tkointl.com
TMP Worldwide eResourcing	http://na.eresourcing.tmp.com/
Van Zoelen Recruitment [United Kingdom]	www.vz-recruitment.nl/uk/ indexuk.htm
Volt Information Sciences	www.volt.com
Winter, Wyman & Co.	www.winterwyman.com
The Virtual Coach	www.virtual-coach.com
H. L. Yoh Company	www.hlyoh.com
Amy Zimmerman & Associates, Inc.	www.weemployyou.net

Security/Building & Business

iHireSecurity.com	www.ihiresecurity.com
Insecure.org	www.seclists.org
RehiredBadge.com	www.rehiredbadge.com
SecurityFocus.com	www.securityfocus.com
SecurityJobs.net	www.securityjobs.com
SecurityJobsToday.com	www.securityjobstoday.com
Transportation Security Administration	www.tsa.gov

Senior Workers/Mature Workers/"Retired" Workers

AARP	www.aarp.org/careers
BoomerCareer.com	www.boomercareer.com
Careersat50	www.careersat50.monster.com
50Connect.co.uk [United Kingdom]	www.50connect.co.uk
GeezerJobs.com	www.geezerjobs.com

Notes

Favorite sites, useful resources

Senior Workers/Mature Workers/"Retired" Workers (continued)

RetiredBrains   www.retiredbrains.com
TheRetiredWorker.com   www.theretiredworker.com
RetirementJobs.com   www.retirementjobs.com
SeniorHelpWanted.com   www.seniorhelpwanted.com
SeniorJobBank.com   www.seniorjobbank.com
Seniors4Hire.org   www.seniors4hire.org
SeniorsforJobs.com   www.seniorsforjobs.com

Social Service/Human Service

ExOffenderReentry.com   www.exoffenderreentry.com
Georgia Department of Human Resources www.dhrjobs.com
HSCareers.com   www.hscareers.com
HSPeople.com   www.hspeople.com
iHireSocialServices.com   www.ihiresocialservices.com
National Association of Social Workers www.socialworkers.org/
  Joblink   joblinks/default.asp
The New Social Worker's Online Career Center www.socialworker.com/
                                        career.htm
SocialService.com   www.socialservice.com
SocialWorkJobBank.com   www.socialworkjobbank.com
Social Work & Social Services Jobs   http://128.252.132.4/jobs
Tripod   www.tripod.com
Worklife Solutions   www.worklifesolutions.com

Statistical

American Statistical Association
  Statistics Career Center   www.amstat.org/careers
Bio Staticianjobs.com   www.biostaticianjobs.com
Math-Jobs.com   www.math-jobs.com
MathJobs.org   www.mathjobs.org
Phds.org   www.phds.org
San Francisco Bay Area
  American Statistical Association   www.sfasa.org/joblist.html
StatisticsJobs.com   www.statisticsjobs.com
Statistics Jobs Announcements   www.stat.ufl.edu/vlib/jobs.html
Statistics Jobs in Austral;ia & New Zealand www.statsci.org/jobs/

-T-

Telecommunications

Active Wireless   www.activewireless.com
Anywhere You Go   www.anywhereyougo.com

Notes

Favorite sites, useful resources

Telecommunications (continued)

BroadbandCareers.com	www.broadbandcareers.com
Cellular-News.com	www.cellular-news.com
Get the Phone	http://getthephone.com/ Jobpostings.html
Hire Top Talent	www.hiretoptalent.com
MobileWirelessJobs.com	www.mobilewirelessjobs.com
MyTelecommunicationsJobs.net	www.mytelecommunicationsjobs .net
New England Telecom	www.n-e-t-a.org
Porta Jobs	www.portajobs.com
RF Job Network	www.rfjn.com
Society of Satellite Professionals International Career Center	www.sspi.broadbandcareers.com /Default.asp
Telco Rock	www.telcorock.com
TelecomCareers.net	http://telecomcareers.net
Telecom Jobs	www.telecom-jobs.net
Telecom Jobsite	www.telecomjobsite.com
Telecom Engineer	www.telecomengineer.com
Telecommunication Industry Association Online	www.tiaonline.org
Telepeople	www.telepeople.com
Teletron	www.telecomcareers.com
Utility Jobs Online	www.utilityjobsonline.com
WirelessCoyote.com	www.wirelesscoyote.com
WirelessResumes.com	www.wirelessresumes.com
Workaholics4Hire.com	www.workaholics4hire.com
Wow-Com	www.wow-com.com

Telecommuting

GenerationMom.com	www.generationmom.com
MommysPlace.net	www.mommysplace.net
Telecommuting Jobs	www.tjobs.com
TeleworkRecruiting.com	www.teleworkrecruiting.com
VirtualAssistants.com	www.virtualassistants.com

Trade Organizations

American Industrial Hygiene Association	www.aiha.org
Biotechnology Industry Organization	www.bio.com
Building Industry Exchange	www.building.org
Drilling Research Institute	www.drillers.com
Drug Information Association Employment Opportunities	www.diahome.org/docs/Jobs/ Jobs_index.cfm
Equipment Leasing Association	www.elaonline.com
Financial Executives Institute Career Center	www.fei.org/careers

Notes

Favorite sites, useful resources

Trade Organizations (continued)

GamesIndustry.biz — www.gamesindustry.biz
Institute of Food Science & Technology — www.ifst.org
Institute of Real Estate Management
Jobs Bulletin — www.irem.org/sec1ins.cfm?sec=iremfirst&con=iremjobs-intro.cfm&par=

International Association of
Conference Centers Online — www.iacconline.com
International Association of Employment Web Sites — www.employmentwebsites.org
International Map Trade Association — www.maptrade.org
Media Communications Association International
Job Hotline — www.mca-i.org
National Association of Colleges &
Employers (NACE) — www.nacelink.com
National Association for Printing
Leadership — www.napl.org
National Contract Management Association — www.ncmajobcontrolcenter.com
National Federation of Paralegal
Associations Career Center — www.paralegals.org/display common.cfm?an=20
National Field Selling Association — www.nfsa.com
National Fire Prevention Association
Online Career Center — www.nfpa.org/catalog/home/CareerCenter/index.asp
National Weather Association — www.nwas.org
Petroleum Services Association
of Canada Employment — www.psac.ca
Risk & Insurance Management Society
Careers — www.rims.org/Template.cfm?Section=JobBank1&Template=/Jobbank/SearchJobForm.cfm

Securities Industry Association
Career Resource Center — www.sia.com/career
Sheet Metal and Air Conditioning
Contractor's Association — www.smacna.org
Society of Automotive Engineers Job Board — www.sae.org/careers/recrutad.htm

Society of Risk Analysis Opportunities — www.sra.org/opptys.php
SteelontheNet.com — www.steelonthenet.com
Technical Association of the Pulp & Paper
Industry Jobline — www.tappi.org/index.asp?ip=-1&ch=14&rc=-1
Telecommunication Industry Association
Online — www.tiaonline.org

Training

American Society for Law Enforcement Training — www.aslet.org
American Society for
Training & Development Job Bank — http://jobs.astd.org

Notes

WEDDLE's Books I Want to Order

Training (continued)

Instructional Systems Technology Jobs	http://education.indiana.edu/ist/students/jobs/joblink.html
International Society for Performance Improvement Job Bank	www.ispi.org
OD Network	www.odnetwork.org
San Francisco State University Instructional Technologies	www.itec.sfsu.edu
TCM's HR Careers	www.tcm.com/hr-careers
TrainingConsortium.com	www.trainingconsortium.com
Training Forum	www.trainingforum.com
Trainingjob.com	www.trainingjob.com
The Training Net	www.trainingnet.com
The Training SuperSite	www.trainingmag.com

Transportation

The Airline Employment Assistance Corps	www.avjobs.com
All-Trucking-Jobs.com	www.all-trucking-jobs.com
AutomotiveCareerCenter.com	www.automotivecareercenter.com
Aviation Employee Placement Service	www.aeps.com
Careers in Gear	www.careersingear.com
Find a Pilot	www.findapilot.com
FindaTruckingJob.com	www.findatruckingjob.com
International Seafarers Exchange JobXchange	www.jobxchange.com
Jobs4Trucking.com	www.jobs4trucking.com
◪ JobsinLogistics.com	www.jobsinlogistics.com
JobsinTrucks.com	www.jobsintrucks.com
Just Rail [United Kingdom]	www.justrail.net
Layover.com	www.layover.com
The Mechanic	www.the-mechanic.com/jobs.html
MyTransportationJobs.net	www.mytransportationjobs.net
National Parking Association	http://careers.npapark.org
NewRoadTechs.com	www.newroadtechs.com
RailJobSearch.com [United Kingdom]	www.railjobsearch.com
TransportationJobStore.com	www.transportationjobstore.com
TruckDriver.com	www.truckdriver.com
TruckerJobSearch.com	www.truckerjobsearch.com
Truck Net	www.truck.net
TruckingJobs	www.truckingjobs.com
TruckinJobs	www.truckinjobs.com

Notes

WEDDLE's Books I Want to Order

-V-

Volunteer Positions

Do-It [United Kingdom]	www.do-it.org.uk
GetaLife.org.uk [United Kingdom]	www.getalife.org.uk
GlobalCrossroad.com	www.globalcrossroad.com
⚑ Monster.com	http://volunteer.monster.com
Volunteer Match	www.volunteermatch.org
VSO Worldwide Vacancies [United Kingdom]	http://database.vso.org.uk/jobsearch.asp

-Y-

Young Adult/Teen Positions

CanadaParttime.com	www.canadaparttime.com
CoolWorks.com	www.coolworks.com
GrooveJob.com	www.groovejob.com
InternsWanted	www.campusinternships.com
TheJobBox.com	www.thejobbox.com
JobDoggy.com	www.jobdoggy.com
MySpace	http://careers.myspace.com
Part-Time Jobs	www.gotajob.com
SnagaJob.com	www.snagajob.com
StudentJobs.gov	www.studentjobs.gov
Summerjobs.com	www.summerjobs.com
Teens4Hire	www.teens4hire.org

Notes

WEDDLE's Books I Want to Order